THE SUMMONING OF TIME

John 2 and 20

Mystery, Majesty and Mathematics in John's Gospel #2

ANNE HAMILTON

The Summoning of Time—John 2 and 20:
Mystery, Majesty and Mathematics in John's Gospel #2

© Anne Hamilton 2024
Published by Armour Books
P. O. Box 492, Corinda QLD 4075 Australia

Cover & Interior Design and Typeset by Beckon Creative

Cover image composite: Lucky Girl Creative © 2020, Cottage Arts © 2019,
  Forever Artisan 6 © 2023 courtesy of Forever.com;
  Alamy GALILEE: CANA, c1895. /Men resting in a field before the village of
  Cana in Galilee. Photochrome, c1895.
Part 1: Creative Fabrica | Micon Designs lightning,
  Etsy | Honeypress Creative Co. pocket watch
Part 2: Etsy |Raccoon Girl Design Studio bokeh
Part 3: Creative Fabrica | VYC Store stucco, ShDigitalShop rings;
  DesignBundles wallpaper
Part 5: Unsplash | Johnny Briggs 'A close up of a wheel';
  Lightstock | Pearl 'Resurrection of Jesus'
Part 6: Unsplash | Lennon Caranzo chalice; Lexi Laginess 'A dark tunnel with a
small window in it', Alena Torgonskaya napkin
Page 206: Deposit Photos | Alexxich 'Rameses Ii'
Part 7: PickPik
Part 8: Blessing Printing
Part 9: Lightstock | JesusPixs 'Jesus Christ with outstretched arms. He is Risen.' ;
  Adobe Stock | New Africa 'Jesus Christ on hills at sunset, back view';
  DepositPhotos | grandfailure 'Man with a lantern standing in front
  of the big goden clockwork'
All other artwork: Beckon Creative

ISBN: 978-1-925380-75-0

 A catalogue record for this book is available from the National Library of Australia

All rights reserved. No part of this publication may be reproduced, stored in, or introduced into a retrieval system, or transmitted, in any form, or by any means (electronic, mechanical, photocopying, recording or otherwise) without the prior written permission of the publisher.

Note: Australian spelling and grammar conventions are used throughout this book.

The Summoning of Time

Anne Hamilton

Unless otherwise noted, Scripture quotations are taken from The Holy Bible, Berean Study Bible, BSB Copyright ©2016 by Bible Hub Used by Permission. All Rights Reserved Worldwide.

Scripture quotations marked AMP are taken from the Amplified Version of the Bible Copyright © 2015 by The Lockman Foundation, La Habra, CA 90631. All rights reserved. www.lockman.org

Scripture quotations marked BLB are taken from the The Blue Letter Bible. Used by permission. blueletterbible.org

Scripture quotations marked BSB are taken from the The Holy Bible, Berean Study Bible, BSB Copyright ©2016 by Bible Hub Used by Permission. All Rights Reserved Worldwide.

Scripture quotations marked CEV are from the Contemporary English Version Copyright © 1991, 1992, 1995 by American Bible Society. Used by Permission.

Scripture quotations marked CSB are taken The Christian Standard Bible. Copyright © 2017 by Holman Bible Publishers. Used by permission. Christian Standard Bible®, and CSB® are federally registered trademarks of Holman Bible Publishers, all rights reserved.

Scripture quotations marked ESV are taken from the ESV® Bible (The Holy Bible, English Standard Version®), copyright © 2001 by Crossway, a publishing ministry of Good News Publishers. Used by permission. All rights reserved.

Scripture quotations marked GNT are from the Good News Translation in Today's English Version—Second Edition Copyright © 1992 by American Bible Society. Used by Permission.

Scripture quotations marked ISV are taken from the Holy Bible: International Standard Version®. Copyright © 1996-forever by The ISV Foundation. ALL RIGHTS RESERVED INTERNATIONALLY. Used by permission.

Scripture quotations marked NASB are taken from the New American Standard Bible®, Copyright © 1960, 1962, 1963, 1968, 1971, 1972, 1973, 1975, 1977, 1995 by The Lockman Foundation. Used by permission. (www.Lockman.org)

Scripture quotations designated NET are from the NET Bible® copyright ©1996-2016 by Biblical Studies Press, L.L.C. http://netbible.com Scripture quoted by permission. All rights reserved.

Scripture quotations marked NLT are taken from the Holy Bible, New Living Translation, copyright 1996, 2004. Used by permission of Tyndale House Publishers, Inc., Wheaton, Illinois 60189. All rights reserved.

Scripture quotations marked NIV are taken from the Holy Bible, New International Version®, NIV®. Copyright © 1973, 1978, 1984, 2011 by Biblica, Inc.™ Used by permission of Zondervan. All rights reserved worldwide. www.zondervan.com The "NIV" and "New International Version" are trademarks registered in the United States Patent and Trademark Office by Biblica, Inc.™.

Scripture quotations marked NKJV are taken from the New King James Version. Copyright © 1982 by Thomas Nelson, Inc. Used by permission. All rights reserved.

Table of Contents

Introduction	11
Preface	15

Part 1 — 18
1.1	Pots and Porcelain	21
1.2	Chiasmus and Chronology	24
1.3	Chiasmus and Chainlink	27
1.4	Numbers and Numerics	29
1.5	Identity and Anonymity	32
1.6	Son of Thunder	34

Part 2 — 38
2.1	Investigating Time	41
2.2	The End of the Age	42
2.3	The End of the Era	45
2.4	The End of Empires	47
2.5	From Eternity Into Time	49
2.6	Times and Calendars	53
2.7	Appointed Times	57
2.8	The Atonement Clock	61
2.9	Relativistic Time	68
2.10	Watches and Watchers	71
2.11	The Dates	74
2.12	Joyous Water-drawing	77

Part 3 — 82

- 3.1 On The Way to Cana — 85
- 3.2 Goddesses of Canaan — 88
- 3.3 The Spirit of Cana — 91
- 3.4 The Clue of 'Cana' — 95
- 3.5 The Lifting Up of the Third Day — 98
- 3.6 Detour into Design — 101
- 3.7 Behold the New Messiah — 104
- 3.8 Reeds and Wicks — 106
- 3.9 Bridal Scent — 109
- 3.10 Mountains of Spices — 111
- 3.11 Lightning and the Mountain Stag — 114

Part 4 — 118

- 4.1 Houston, we have a problem — 121
- 4.2 Wedding Perfume — 123
- 4.3 The Messiah's Marriage — 126
- 4.4 The War Against All — 129
- 4.5 The Rulers of This Age — 132
- 4.6 The Image of God — 134
- 4.7 The Sons of Zeus — 137
- 4.8 'Where is the Lord?' — 140

Part 5 — 146

- 5.1 'Woman' — 149
- 5.2 Dreams — 152
- 5.3 Quoting Genesis — 155
- 5.4 Boundaries — 157
- 5.5 Appointments — 161
- 5.6 Risk — 163

Part 6 — 166

- 6.1 Fine, Fine Wine — 169
- 6.2 The Unknown Hour — 172
- 6.3 Time and Body — 175
- 6.4 Threshold Sacrifice — 178
- 6.5 Neither the Time, nor the Number — 180
- 6.6 The Turn of the Age — 183
- 6.7 Threefold Time — 186
- 6.8 Anat and Kairos — 189
- 6.9 Anat and Athaliah — 191

6.10	Anat and Joseph	194
6.11	Joseph the Dispossessor	197
6.12	Dispossess and Repossess	201
6.13	Back in Egypt	204
6.14	Time the Dispossessor	209
6.15	Anat and Deborah	214
6.16	The Folded Cloth	218
6.17	Royal Raiment	222
6.18	The Tablemaster and the Cupbearer	226
6.19	Cupbearers Amongst the Gods	229

PART 7 — 234

7.1	Belief in the Resurrection	237
7.2	Home	242
7.3	Time Shift	244
7.4	Archimedes	247
7.5	The Weight of Glory	253
7.6	Cherubim	256
7.7	Seraphim	260
7.8	Leviathan and Anat	263

PART 8 — 272

8.1	Zealous and Jealous	275
8.2	Prophet, Priest and King	279
8.3	The Road to Emmaus	283
8.4	The War Messiah	287
8.5	The Third Day Reprised	290
8.6	Forty-six Years	294

PART 9 — 298

9.1	Signs and Epiphany	301
9.2	Time and Takedown	305
9.3	Almost Final Thoughts	307
9.4	Final Thoughts	312

MAPS	Galilee	90
	Judea	236

DEDICATION

to my dad

who would have loved the electrical engineering aspects
of John 2

and to my mum

who would have loved the historical healing aspects of John 20

Thanks:

Anneli	Iain	Lucy
Beck	Janice	Mary
Ben	Jess	Michael
Coco	Joy	Quang
Donna	Julie	Richard
Fay	Kevin	Sean

Introduction

When I first conceived the idea of a small *booklet* on John's gospel that would feature its mirror symmetry, I thought any treatment would be very short. It would touch on broad themes and occasionally delve into finer detail. However, as soon as I started to examine his work systematically, I realised how profoundly I'd underestimated John's artistry.

Still, I never expected the mosaic of ideas in the gospel to be so complex or to range so widely through the Hebrew Scriptures, Greek mathematics, philosophy and science, or the epic sagas of pagan deities—some of whom I'd never heard of previously.

In the first book in this series, I examined the passing of Elijah's mantle. Although John moves on to describe the wedding at Cana, he isn't entirely finished with Elijah. Nevertheless, he introduces a new mantle and weaves its history into his majestic lyric of praise to Jesus. That mantle—actually more of a coat-of-many-colours—also has to pass, like Elijah's, through the hands of Jesus before being gifted further. And once again, be prepared for a big surprise about the recipient's identity.

John stitches together an intricate tapestry linking his second chapter to his second-last chapter, as well as each of those chapters to the ones adjacent to them. That tapestry is embroidered on a canvas of poetry and mathematics.

However the grace-filled beauty of his work is that the gospel can be understood without consciously recognising any element of the embedded design or any of the subtle allusions. Still, there are philosophic, mythic and scientific threads we can track if we can catch a first glimpse of them in the poetry or mathematics and begin to watch for them thereafter.

My intention is more devotional than academic. Nevertheless I plan to track two overarching themes:

- the war against what CS Lewis described as 'principalities and powers and depraved hypersomatic beings at great heights'[1]
- the healing of history, the repair of the past, the undoing of wounds lodged in the landscape

Jesus didn't wait until after the resurrection to begin His work of restoration. Nor did He wait until the Cross to declare war on the enemies of God and of mankind.

His epiphany—the first public revelation of His power and the manifestation of His glory—was at Cana in Galilee. It was, apparently, an electrifying experience: both figuratively and literally. And it's only as we dive deep into the poetry we can see that, at some level, John knew that this first 'sign' of Jesus was connected to lightning.

Before we look at the individual threads making up the tapestry, let's turn the canvas over to view its flipside. It's not as messy as we might expect. By looking at the back itself—the poetic

---

1   CS Lewis, *Perelandra: Voyage to Venus*, Pan 1983

structure and the mathematical underlay—we can appreciate more than the artist's skill. We can sense His yieldedness to the Holy Spirit in shaping this epic poem to praise and glorify the Saviour of the World.

Anne Hamilton

Seventeen Mile Rocks, Australia
October, 2023

PREFACE

THE ELIJAH TAPESTRY, THE PREVIOUS VOLUME of this series, focuses on the first and last chapter of John's gospel and shows how ideas and thematic elements are matched and mirrored. Like this volume, it looks front and back at John's first-century literary masterwork to bring to light a design based on a poetic form known as 'chiasmus'. This structure is defined as 'the arrangement of repeated, parallel, or contrasted words or phrases in two pairs, the second of which reverses the order of the first.'[2]

A simple example is: do not *live to eat* but *eat to live*.

Chiastic patterning was particularly favoured by the Hebrew prophets. Ultimately John's intensive deployment of the technique shows that his gospel was composed as an epic poem, rich with allusion and subtle imagery.

Along with many glittering gems lying on the surface, there are deep treasures to be unearthed in John's testimony. Most of us are content with gathering what is plainly visible, but if we dig a little, we not only find a hidden hoard tucked away but a detailed map of clues that John has kindly provided.

Many people wonder why can't he speak plainly. Why aren't his clues transparent and obvious, his explanations clear and

---

[2] *The American Heritage® Dictionary of the English Language*, 5th Edition.

concise, his communication unmistakeable and unambiguous? I've encountered believers who become angry when they realise the hidden depths are, in fact, *hidden*—almost secretive—and thus so easy to miss.

But why should John be different to Jesus? Why shouldn't he take as his role model the oblique sayings and veiled parables of his Lord? Why shouldn't there be experiences of the Word that, as the reader's relationship to Jesus grows, can be appreciated afresh—sometimes at a greater height, sometimes at a greater depth?[3]

The Elijah Tapestry brings to the surface a pattern involving Elijah in John's first and last chapters. It's hard to miss the references at the start, since John the Baptiser is asked a direct question about Elijah. However, it's very easy to miss those allusions in the final chapter—and perilously easy to miss John's forthright statement: *I am not like Elijah. Jesus did not proclaim me deathless. Nor did I receive Elijah's mantle. That, as I have indicated, was given to another.*

In addition to the surface story of Peter's restoration, John also includes a sub-surface account of his commissioning to complete an unfinished task originally given to Elijah.

As we move into the second chapter of John's gospel—where the wedding feast at Cana and the cleansing of the Temple are described—the surprises continue. Echoes of past wounds reverberate through the miracles of Jesus as He brings deep healing to history.

---

3   John Sandford comments on this use of symbolism by Jesus: 'The Eastern principle of speaking indirectly is founded upon this principle, that each man retains best what he has discovered for himself. So God often prefers to speak indirectly. We may prefer to be like Thomas, who directly put his fingers in Jesus' side, but Jesus pronounced us more blessed who have believed not seeing directly.' John and Paula Sandford, *The Elijah Task*, Victory House 1977

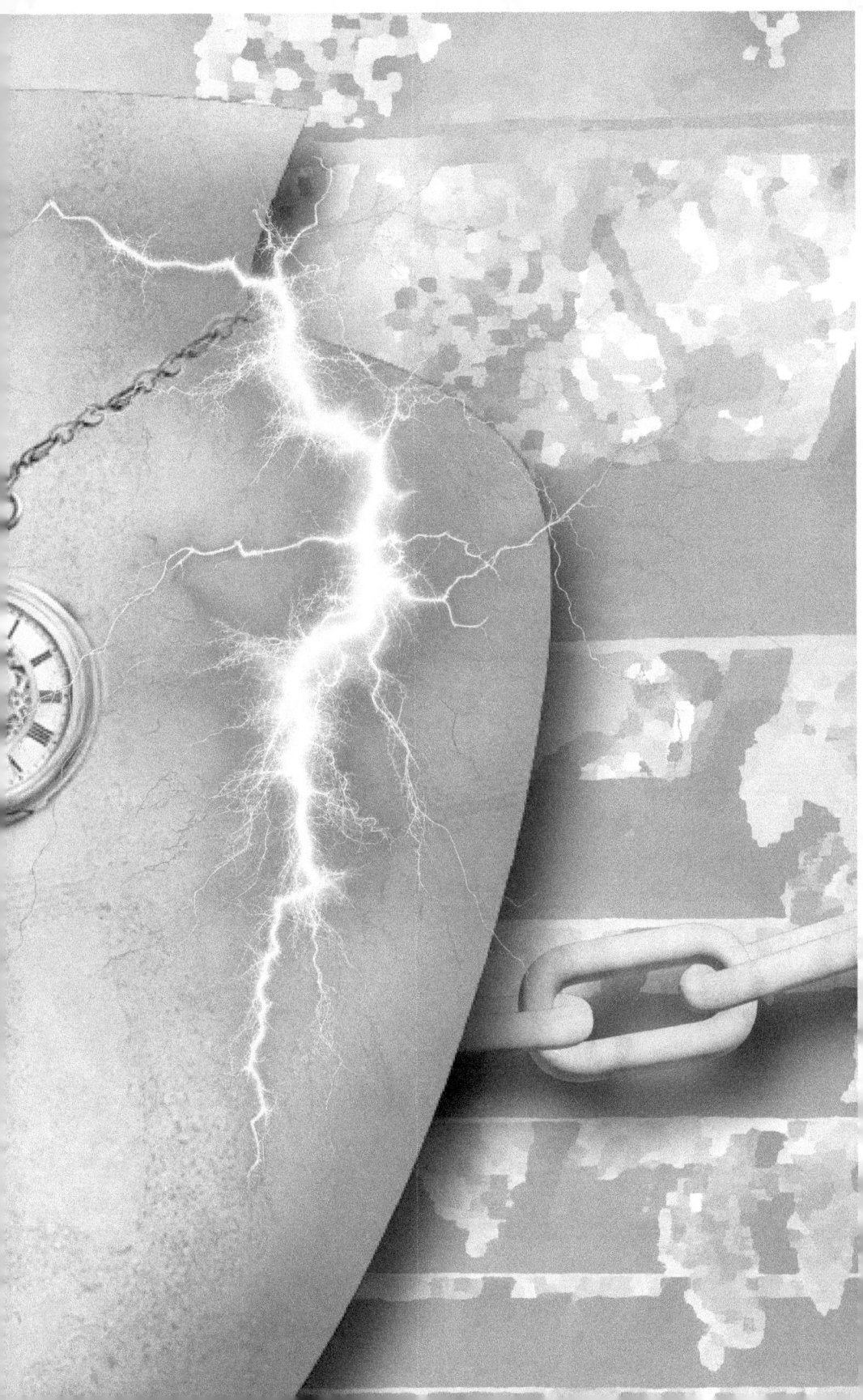

1.1 Pots and Porcelain

My father was a quiet achiever. At his funeral my mother was approached by a professor of electrical engineering who was baffled by what he considered a critical omission in the eulogies. He commented that our family seemed completely unaware my father had a worldwide reputation for excellence and efficiency in the generation of electricity. The professor was right—we had no idea! Engineers from around the globe, he revealed, regularly visited my dad on inspection tours.

So to honour my dad I'm beginning this commentary with an electrical engineering story—simply because he'd have appreciated it.

Gene Eby was an electrical engineer who worked on the Hoover Dam project in the 1930s.[4] A massive concrete arch-gravity dam, one of its purposes was to provide hydroelectric power to be carried across country by mega-voltage high-tension wires. Suitable bushings—ceramic insulators capable of withstanding the passage of multi-millions of volts—were needed to ensure safe transmission. However, despite years of experimentation by a dedicated team that included engineers, mechanics, test operators, chemists and porcelain specialists, they'd encountered only frustration and failure at every turn. Every bushing they tried exploded.

---

4   Richard Eby recounts these events in the life of his father, Gene, in *Caught Up Into Paradise*, Fleming H Revell Company 1984

Finally, exhausted, Gene was ready to give up, all but convinced there was no solution to the problem. But before he did, he turned the matter over to God and asked Him to either show the team an answer or to give them the peace to quit.

When he awoke the next morning, his eyes lighted on his Bible, open at the second chapter of John. The story of Cana was one he knew well. But God had a fresh insight. His voice was quite clear that day: 'Know ye not that I have spoken through My Word? Did I not use 6 pots? Big ones? Was it not My power that changed the water?'

Gene suddenly realised that millions of volts would be involved in the transformation of water into wine. When Jesus spoke, it must have been like bombs going off inside the stone pots. Yet they'd withstood the unleashing of a staggering amount of power. Gene realised that there had to be an answer to the bushing problem. The team just hadn't found it.

A month later, crisis point had been reached. A communique came from the President asking for the scheduling of an immediate conference. Huge transformers were on their way, ready to be installed. However, if the bushing problem couldn't be solved, the dam would be useless as a power source.

Gene decided to talk to his top porcelain man. Cermak had just been on a month's holiday to Europe—he'd been through France, Italy, Greece and Egypt. There he'd visited King Tutankhamun's newly opened tomb and had managed to bribe a guard to palm a small souvenir. He encouraged Gene to embark on a similar tour and then commented he'd heard about the intense pressure being exerted by the President.

Gene was disappointed. Still no breakthrough. But that night, as he worried away at the problem, sure God would not let him down, he pondered: 'Pottery... man-made... ancient... near

East… water jug.' And then, like a lightning bolt, a possibility hit him. At 4 a.m., he phoned Cermak, apologised, and asked what the souvenir he'd picked up in King Tutankhamun's tomb was.

Cermak was suddenly concerned Gene might be about to get him into trouble over a 'measley piece of pottery'—probably, he surmised, a piece of a water jug for one of King Tut's feasts. But Gene only wanted the sample analysed—and more than that, he wanted a priority testing of a bushing made to its specified composition.

A fortnight later, they went to the lightning lab to order the testers to fire up every available condenser the transformers could handle. The resulting arc of electricity shook the entire building but 'King Tut's bushing' took it all in its stride.

The bushing was made of steatite—often called soapstone. It's a common metamorphic rock that's easy to carve, doesn't absorb water and doesn't react with wine. And it can also handle the millions of volts generated in a water-wine transformation.[5] Soapstone is undoubtedly the best possible candidate for the composition of the six stone pots at the wedding feast of Cana.

---

5   A tonne of grapes makes around 650 litres of wine. This is approximately the total capacity of those six stone pots Jesus used. It also takes 2618 gigajoules (2,618,000,000,000 or 2.618 trillion joules) of energy to convert a tonne of grapes to wine.

1.2 Chiasmus and Chronology

Before examining any of the individual threadlines in the gospel, let's look first at its design. Chiasmus[6] is a literary device frequently embedded in the historical narratives, as well as the prophecies, letters and story-telling of Scripture. The Greek letter, chi, shaped like an X, inspired the name, 'chiasmus', since the parallelism used in this poetic feature was seen as 'crossing over', just as X does.

It's a very ancient technique using mirror symmetry for effect. An early literary instance of chiasmus occurs in the book of Genesis, where the account of Noah and the flood is arranged in this fashion.[7]

(A) Seven days waiting to enter Ark (7:4)
    (B) Second mention of seven days waiting (7:10)
        (C) 40 days (7:13,17)
            (D) 150 days (7:24)
(X) God remembers Noah (8:1)
            (D') 150 days (8:3)
        (C') 40 days (8:6)
    (B') Seven days waiting for dove (8:10)
(A') Second seven days waiting for dove (8:12)

---

6   Also called 'chiasm', for short.
7   Todd D. Moore, 'Pericope and Chiasm', nas.org/blogs/article/ask_a_scholar_pericope_and_chiasm (accessed 1 November 2022)

John arranged his gospel in a similar fashion—his three mentions of the Logos at the beginning parallel his three references to writing at the end; his report of the three questions posed to John the Baptist counterpoint his account of the three questions posed to Simon, son of Jonah, at the end; his count of five disciples following Jesus to Galilee at the start match his count of five groups of disciples setting out after Jesus to Galilee in the final chapter.[8]

As we move on to examine the second chapter, this chiastic structure remains prominent. There are two episodes in this section—two pericopes, or set of verses, that each form a coherent unit. They are the wedding at Cana and the emptying of the Temple. These are chiastically and thematically linked to the emptying of the tomb and the meeting of Jesus with Mary Magdalene in the garden.

Now the chiasmus in the account of Noah and the flood happens to be in chronological order. However, that's not always the case.

Sometimes, a narrative is broken up by the insertion of an episode that fits in with the chiastic structure but not the time sequence. This occurs in John's second chapter. The account of Jesus clearing out the Temple courts of the money-changers and stall-holders is out of order. John subtly signals this by suddenly dispensing with the time-stamps that mark his account to that point. There's no longer any reference to 'the next day' or 'three days later'.

Since a major theme of the miracle at Cana involves the disruption of ordinary time, John basically continues that same idea by following it with the eviction of the traders from the Temple— an incident that occurred in the week before the crucifixion. In order to flow through the natural time sequence of events in the

---

8   Anne Hamilton, *The Elijah Tapestry: John 1 and 21*, Armour Books 2023

resurrection story *as well as* keep the chiasm intact, John was constrained to introduce the Temple-cleansing story early in his gospel, not later.

Chiasmus, it seems, always trumped chronology.

1.3 Chiasmus and Chainlink

THE DESIGN OF THE FOURTH GOSPEL is not a simple clear-cut mirror reflection. The beginning and end aren't always *perfectly* symmetrical. There are certainly laser-sharp moments when clear and unequivocal parallels emerge, but there are also flows of thematic elements into small eddies—and, at these points, it would be more accurate to say that there are corresponding swirls rather than exact line-ups.

The chapters, of course, don't coincide perfectly. It's impossible to match the first and last chapter exactly or the second and second-last.

Chapter numbering is thought to have been first introduced by Stephen Langton in the twelfth century. The sub-division of chapters into verses did not occur until the sixteenth century. By that time, well over a millennium and a half after the gospel was written, it was unclear where John had intended particular scenes to end. Sometimes the line of demarcation between pericopes is quite fuzzy. It would be very surprising if this weren't the case. To regiment the episodes into perfectly parallel formations would result in an unnatural literary style that would detract from the story. It shouldn't matter at what level readers approach the gospel; it should make sense whether they notice the chiastic patterns, the linking chains and the numerical underlay—or *not*.

The eddies and the fuzziness might make analysis difficult for the likes of Maarten Menken[9] who has investigated the arithmetic patterns of this gospel and found it necessary to restrict his study to those sections that are clearly and obviously defined—but, for the rest of us, they simply aid readability.

Now the chapter divisions aren't arbitrary. However they weren't set up with John's parallelisms in mind. Thus, chiastic scenes run across chapter borders. *The Elijah Tapestry* consequently examines John 20:17–21:25 as a parallel for the first chapter. This volume, *The Summoning of Time*, despite the official sub-title, actually looks at the second chapter's alignment with John 19:28–20:18;30. I want to crib just a little out of the third last chapter because there's such an important name clue embedded in its last few verses.

John designed his structure so the scene at the front informs the one at the rear and is, in turn, informed by it. Likewise, adjacent scenes have their own interplay, reinforcing and illuminating each other. The movement between one scene and the next through to its chiastic partner and back again creates a swell of interconnected literary artistry.

---

[9] Maarten JJ Menken, *Numerical Literary Techniques in John: The Fourth Evangelist's Use of Numbers of Words and Syllables*, Brill 1985

1.4 Numbers and Numerics

Throughout the ancient world, both east and west, high class literary texts were fusions of words and numbers.[10] A mathematical underlay provided additional texture for the theme, augmented the verbal meaning and, at least in the classical world, allowed authors to design their works according to a canon of stylised, approved forms.

Although chiasmus, the Hebrew poetic structure, dominates John's arrangement, he didn't ignore Greek literary ideals. However, instead of adhering to its model outlines, he did so as an iconoclast—a deliberate wrecker of form.

Several numbers are significantly featured in his opening and closing chapters. They're generally overlooked today because word-number fusions aren't taught in modern curricula.[11] However, for the Greek literati schooled in these techniques from childhood, the word, syllable and sentence counts would have stood out like blazing torches.

---

10 See, for example, the analysis of Ed Condren, Robert Stevick, Joan Helm, Eleanor Bulatkin, Donna Crawford, Maren Sofie Røstvig, David Howlett, J. Smit Sibinga, MJJ Menken, George Duckworth, Thomas Elwood Hart, Thomas Hill, Charles Thomas and A. Kent Hieatt. These scholars cover a wide spectrum from the poets of classical antiquity through the gospel writers to the early Renaissance.

11 Although I use this technique in a very limited way—simply keeping to a particular word count in any particular section—I trust you actually won't notice its deployment in this book all that often. There are three reasons I write like this: first, because I simply love the idea of a word-number fusion; second, because the gospel and epistle writers did so; and, third, because someone once unwisely criticised numerical literary style with the scornful arithmophobic remark: 'No one would ever do that.' And thinking to myself, 'But I would,' I decided to give it a go. I've been doing it ever since.

17 was a natural favourite for John. It often turns up in other gospels as well as epistles, so it's no surprise to discover his first sentence is 17 words long. In fact, given its widespread use in the early Christian world, it would have been remarkable if he'd omitted it. 17 is the number *par excellence* for asserting opposition to Gnostic Pythagoreanism within any text.

Maarten Menken, in analysing the numerical-literary structure of the first chapter, has shown there are seven different summations of 17 words, either uttered by Jesus or in the combined dialogue between the Baptiser and his disciples, together totalling 136 words. This multiple of 17 (8x17) also occurs in the syllable count from John's final words in the opening chapter, 'Look, the Lamb of God!' to the end of the account of the wedding feast. In the sequence, all the speakers other than Jesus[12] and His mother utter 136 syllables and, if we include Mary who also speaks 17 syllables, the total count is 153.

153 is the seventeenth triangular number—called the 'measure of the fish' since the time of Archimedes. It appears prominently in John's last chapter. As it happens, Archimedes is also subtly referenced towards the end of the second chapter—causing me to realise I'd missed a significant allusion to his work in John's very last line. But more on that later.

Another aspect of 153 that recurs in the second chapter is the notion of inheritance and possession—as unearthed in *The Elijah Tapestry*—and going back to God's promise to Joshua:

> *I have given you every place on which the sole of your foot treads, just as I promised to Moses.*
>
> Joshua 1:3[AMP]

---

[12] Jesus Himself speaks 183 words, the same number as the days in half a year (or between equinoxes). That might seem coincidental. However, there are so many references to time in the second chapter it seems unlikely to me—particularly since, as we shall see, 365 also appears.

The triangular number, 496—a number designated 'perfect' since ancient times—is embedded in the first and last chapters. There are 496 syllables at the beginning and 496 words at the end. This lovely underlay reinforces John's message that the Word is, was, and will always remain, *perfect.*

Of course, the usual suspects are present: the 'sacred numbers' 3 and 7. There are seven mentions of *light*,[13] hinting at the seven-branched menorah with its flower-cups of flame. There are three questions posed to John the Baptiser, and three to Simon bar Jonah.

Most importantly and obviously of all, there's a number—or rather, more accurately, a *ratio*—the Greeks called the LOGOS. Our translators invariably render it as 'Word'. That *ratio* is embedded three times in the opening verse of Genesis and is God's signature across all creation.[14]

---

13   The last of those references is actually *enlighten*—which, happily, in both English and Greek contains *light.*

14   The ratio also appears, as once again Maarten Menken has shown in *Numerical Literary Techniques in John: The Fourth Evangelist's Use of Numbers of Words and Syllables*, in the proportion of the syllables uttered by John the Baptiser to those uttered by Jesus. 731:1185 = 0.617, a very fine approximation to the *logos* or golden ratio.

1.5 Identity and Anonymity

A SIGNIFICANT DESIGN ELEMENT IN JOHN'S gospel involves naming. At first sight, there's no connection between the wedding at Cana and its chiastic partner: the meeting between Jesus and the Magdalene in the garden outside His tomb. Apart, of course, from the fact both scenes focus on a major interaction between Jesus and someone named Mary.

Yet one of the two Marys is not identified—the reader needs to be aware that Jesus' mother is named Mary to recognise the match. This patterning continues the approach John used in his first and last chapters: a clear identification contrasted with virtual anonymity.

In the first chapter John the Baptiser is in the foreground, but in the last, John the apostle backgrounded his identity so much that some scholars question if he is indeed *the disciple Jesus loved*. Likewise, in the first chapter, Elijah is mentioned up front. However, at the end, the passing of his mantle is revealed only through the subtlest of clues. In the first chapter, Nathanael has a snippet scene of his own and, while he is mentioned in passing in the final chapter amongst the group of disciples heading for Galilee, he plays no prominent role. It's only if the reader is aware that doubting Nathanael is also Bartholomew, *son of Tolmai*, that the mirror match-up with doubting Thomas, whose name is also related to Tolmai, becomes apparent.

Open identification contrasted with deliberate, almost impenetrable namelessness certainly helps us discern various clues, but not always to grasp their meaning. Anonymity becomes particularly problematic because naming throughout the ancient world was a royal grant of destiny and inheritance.[15]

When Jesus spoke to Nathanael in the gospel scene that gives him his fifteen minutes of fame, He constantly addressed him with references to the patriarch Jacob. It's only when we match Nathanael to Thomas—so often and redundantly dubbed 'the twin'—that we can draw out the careful allusions to Jacob's twin, Esau, during Thomas' absence while Jesus is bestowing the birthright of the Holy Spirit on His assembled disciples.

This stylistic device—recognition by name versus hidden identity—doesn't stop at the end of the first chapter, though it does undergo a flip. To begin with, there's identification in the front of the gospel and anonymity towards the end. Then anonymity is featured at the front and identification at the back. Mary the mother of Jesus is not named at the wedding, but Mary the Magdalene is identified at the end.

Because of this sustained literary artistry, we cannot be sure the unnamed individuals with speaking roles are *not* identified. For example, does the mention of Joseph of Arimathea suggest the unnamed tablemaster at the wedding was Joseph, the foster-father of Jesus? It's too hard to tell. But whether absent or present, Joseph casts a long shadow over the story because the haunting presence of his namesake—the dreamer who famously became a ruler in Egypt—shapes events in both practical and symbolic ways.

---

15   In *Hunting for the Tree of Life: A Spiritual Journey in the Garden Traditions*, Maria Theresa de Donato and Anneli Sinkko point out that the recognition scene with naming and counter-naming manifests who Jesus is, and who Mary is. The last royal acts of naming take place in the garden of crucifixion and the tomb: the giving of Mary as mother to John and of John as son to Mary, as well as the naming of the Magdalene outside the tomb.

1.6 SON OF THUNDER

ALTHOUGH THE FOURTH GOSPEL IS ANONYMOUS, it's traditionally been credited to the apostle John.[16] In *The Elijah Tapestry*, I set out the reasons for believing this conventional belief is accurate. There I pointed out that the conclusion of the gospel makes some very subtle but forthright statements about the writer.

He is *not* like Elijah—nor did he inherit Elijah's mantle. It's a mistake, John tells his readers, to believe Jesus said he would be like Elijah and never die. What Jesus had said, he relates, was very ambiguous. Peter had asked what would happen to John:

> 'Lord, what about him?'
>
> Jesus answered, 'If I want him to remain alive until I return, what is that to you? You must follow Me.'
>
> John 21:21–22^{NIV}

In addition to highlighting the precise words of Jesus and indicating there is no explicit promise of deathlessness in them, John points out that Peter was given Elijah's legacy. It was Peter who was tasked with completing Elijah's unfinished work, along with Elisha's and Jonah's.

---

16   Richard Bauckham makes a strong case for the 'beloved disciple' being John the Elder, rather than John the Apostle.

Still, John's denials undoubtedly rang somewhat hollow in the minds of the early Christian community. Hadn't he testified that his namesake, John the Baptiser, had told inquirers that he wasn't the Elijah-who-is-to-come either? And obviously the Baptiser was wrong—because Jesus, no less, had claimed he was the forerunner to the Messiah.

In addition, it's easy to see why any Christian community would have seen John the apostle as someone fitting the 'Elijah mould'. This, after all, was the disciple who had wanted to call down fire from heaven to punish some Samaritans who had disrespected Jesus. That response would have reminded them of Elijah's reaction when King Ahaziah sent out troops to haul him in. The first squadron of fifty, plus their leader, were killed when the prophet called down fire from heaven. So was the second squadron. The leader of the third squadron[17] approached Elijah on his knees to plead for his own life and that of his men.[18]

This last major interaction between Elijah and Ahab's family recalls the fire descending from heaven during the confrontation with the prophets of Baal and Asherah on Mount Carmel. It also foreshadowed Elijah's imminent ascension in a whirlwind accompanied by a chariot of fire. Furthermore this firefall occurred on a hill somewhere in Samaria.

James and John, in wanting punish a Samaritan village, were simply following Elijah's example.

> *He sent messengers ahead of Him, who went and entered a village of the Samaritans, to make preparations for Him. But the people did not receive Him, because His face was set toward Jerusalem. And when His disciples James and John*

---

17 Note he is the 153rd man of the troops sent to bring in Elijah.
18 2 Kings 1:9-1

saw it, they said, 'Lord, do You want us to tell fire to come down from heaven and consume them?' But He turned and rebuked them. And they went on to another village.

Luke 9:52–56[ESV]

Jesus doesn't ever say Elijah was wrong. But He most definitely implies it.[19]

Although we tend to approve the behaviour of many faith heroes simply because Scripture is non-judgmental, it's unwise to assume lack of criticism equals divine endorsement. God's commentary is found in the restrained actions and subtle reprovals of Jesus.

Now the incident near the Samaritan village is our only clue about the nickname *'sons of thunder'*, revealed by Mark:

These are the twelve He appointed: Simon (to whom He gave the name Peter), James son of Zebedee and his brother John (to them He gave the name Boanerges, which means 'sons of thunder'), Andrew, Philip, Bartholomew, Matthew, Thomas, James son of Alphaeus, Thaddaeus, Simon the Zealot and Judas Iscariot, who betrayed him.

Mark 3:16–18[NIV]

The gospels don't actually reveal what incident precipitated the nickname. Even if it had been given earlier, the proposal of James and John to call fire from heaven on the Samaritans would surely reinforce it.

---

19   Jesus doesn't ever say Ezra and Nehemiah did the wrong thing either when they compelled the men who'd married foreign women to divorce their wives and send away their families. But the entire incident with the woman at the well in Samaria revolves around the choice they *should* have presented to the men and women, but didn't. And that choice was simply: Yes or no? Will you be like Ruth and Rahab, Zipporah and Bithiah, and covenant with us that Yahweh will be your God as well as that of your husband?

Now I believe John confirms his identity as a son of thunder by chiastically matching the unnamed *'other disciple, the one whom Jesus loved'*[20] in the story of the running apostles with the narrative of the lightning in the pots.

Yet how is it possible for anyone in the first century to know about such electrical discharges? Surely only by the mysterious illumination and inspiration of the Holy Spirit.

---

20   John 20:2[BSB]

On the third day a wedding took place at Cana in Galilee. Jesus' mother was there and Jesus and His disciples had also been invited to the wedding.

John 2:1-2

John 20:1

Early on the first day of the week, while it was still dark, Mary Magdalene went to the tomb and saw that the stone had been removed from the entrance.

2.1 Investigating Time

Ultimately, the miracle of the transformation of water into wine is about *time*. But time in this instance is such an exquisitely cut diamond: there are so many facets to it that it becomes difficult to define it adequately. There's the time dilation that compresses the months that grapes normally take to mature into hours, perhaps minutes. There are the pointers to the ending of one age and the start of another. There are the echoes of bygone eras, as well as the setting of calendars—some human in origin, some divine. There's the ringing in of a New Year, a Jubilee, a change of seasons, the start of a long-prophesied countdown to a date with destiny. There's ordinary time, appointed time and, wonder beyond wonders, *relativistic* time. There's also a connection between time and identity.

All of this—and, to cap it off, a possible exact date when it comes to pass.

2.2 The End of the Age

The age of the dinosaurs ended with a bang. An unexpected visitor from space plunged into the Gulf of Mexico, liquefied the top layer of the earth's crust, tossed molten rocksplatter into the high reaches of the atmosphere, changed the climate irrevocably across the entire planet and brought about the extinction of many species of mega-fauna. If the visitor were a comet and not simply an asteroid, there would have been a considerable water dump as ice and rock plummeted down through the atmosphere and then vaporised on impact.

The saga of Noah describes the end of an age in similar terms. The sudden obliteration of the world in the cataclysm of a global flood changes everything from the lifespan of the survivors to the structure of the atmosphere. His turbulent story belies his name, *rest*.

Noah was the leader of a family who lived through an unimaginable trauma. The world as he knew it was simply swept away. It may have been corrupt beyond measure but that does not mean his grief would necessarily be less. His diligence and faith in preparing for the catastrophe may have been vindicated but the old society that may have, at long last, applauded his unrelenting hard work was entirely gone.

All that was left was a remnant of humanity, as well as birds and beasts, who had been brought safely through the waters in a divinely designed ark. God's grace had saved an untainted group of eight people.[21] God's grace had also destroyed a whole world of tribes and clans, families and communities, that had been irremediably contaminated by angelic interference—both physically, intellectually and culturally. God truly left it until the very last moment to salvage what He could and ensure His long-term plan of redemption for humanity could proceed to fruition.

And so came a new beginning. Echoes of the original beginning resound through the narrative. The waters of chaos give way to God's order—this is true both for the primeval sea and for the flood deluge. In the first instance, the Spirit of God 'moved' on the face of the waters and, in the second, the ark 'walked' on the face of the waters.

Noah's father Lamech may have known Adam, the steward and regent of Eden. After all, Lamech was born fifty-six years *before* Adam died. If there was any hope that death would claim Adam but bypass his descendants—except for accident or violence—it would have waned as Adam's son, Seth, became frail and elderly. Seth had just a few years left when Noah was born. The knowledge of mortality and the ravages of time on humanity obviously weighed heavily on Lamech. He harked back to the events of Eden when he spoke over his newborn, *'May this one comfort us*

---

21 By 'untainted', I mean human beings with DNA that was not contaminated by a bloodline that involved the nephilim, the giants who had been fathered by fallen angels. During the conquest of Canaan by the Israelites, God gave instruction for some people groups to be left alone and others to be entirely exterminated. The distinguishing feature of those in the second group was the practice of human sacrifice, particularly that of children, but also descent from giant clans. Apparently the issue was that the redemption won by Jesus was intended for solely humanity (see, for example 1 Peter 1:12 and Ephesians 3:10) and not for any hybrid entity.

in the labour and toil of our hands caused by the ground that the Lord has cursed.'[22]

Noah had the opportunity to be the new Adam, the one who imaged God for the age of the renewed earth. He was blameless in his generation.[23] The parallels with Adam are highlighted to us when it's revealed that Noah tended a vineyard, where he lay around naked and not ashamed.

Yet there are also parallels with God, indicating Noah was called to be His image-bearer. After finishing His task of creation, God rested.[24] After finishing his task of preservation, Noah rested. God organised a garden just as Noah organised a vineyard.

And then, just as in Eden, a curse is uttered. God merely made life difficult for humanity with thorns and thistles, sweat on the brow, pain in child-bearing and authority vested in the husband.[25] Noah upped the ante considerably: his curse was one of dispossession, slavery and oppression. It divided brother against brother, setting in place a hierarchy of nations—even before there were nations.

It is no coincidence that Jesus made new wine at Cana, just as Noah made new wine in his vineyard. Nor is it coincidence that both events are part of the inauguration of a new age. Finally, in Jesus of Nazareth, Lamech's hope was fulfilled:

> *May this one comfort us in the labour and toil of our hands caused by the ground that the Lord has cursed.*

---

22 Genesis 5:29[BSB]

23 Genesis 6:9

24 He rested in the sense that He finished His work of creation, though this did not mean He stopped maintaining and sustaining what He had created.

25 Death was not a result of the curse God spoke; death was the result of making the choice to eat the fruit of the forbidden tree.

2.3 The End of the Era

So much of the wedding feast at Cana involves notions of time. John carefully records the passing of the days leading up to the celebration: one by one by one by three. He matches the third day with the third day of the resurrection. He notes that Jesus commented that His time was not yet come. He describes a miracle that is, from a scientific standpoint, one of time dilation—after all, there's nothing particularly extra-ordinary about water turning into wine. However it's normally a process that, in a grapevine, takes five months plus whatever extra is needed for ageing.

Most subtle of all time references are John's allusions to the first dawnlight limning the horizon of a new Day. The promised age of the Messiah has arrived. His herald has appeared and now He himself has, after a triad of spiritual trials, come forth from the wilderness.

Peter describes our salvation as being guarded so it can be revealed at the end of the age.[26] The prophets had searched carefully, trying to determine the timing of this salvation, as well as its setting—a mystery that even angels long to investigate.[27] There's a sense in

---

26   1 Peter 1:5

27   1 Peter 1:10–12

which the ages of Scripture are divided into the time before the redemption of Christ and the era afterwards. For many believers today, 'redemption' is code for the Cross and Resurrection.

However, it's my view that John's retelling of the Cana story shows us that redemption began then and there, if not before. Jesus' first sign involved buying back the past—mending the wounds of history. John matches two gardens—Eden and Noah's vineyard—in the chiastic parallel he set up. Yet it isn't as simple a focus as gardens. In the meeting between Jesus and the Magdalene outside the tomb there are Scriptural references that go far beyond Eden. And in the pericope of the wedding at Cana, there are allusions to the end of other eras besides the one that culminated in the Flood.

So, rather than look at 'ages', especially since many theologians would consider the minimal division into *before and after redemption* as too rough and simplistic, let's pinpoint instead eras or epochs that ended in disaster. One particular disaster I want to highlight later in this study is the widespread famine that led to Jacob's family migrating to Egypt. Without Joseph's foresight and his elevation to a high position in Egypt, there would have been little, if any, preparation for the impending catastrophe. Few—in any nation—would have survived. His father, his brothers and their dependents would have all perished.

This event heralded the end of an era in the sense that, although a global disaster was averted, the Hebrews lived in Egypt for many centuries thereafter. Moreover, if we look closely at Joseph's story, we can see several links back to the days when Noah planted his vineyard. The most significant of these are *dispossession and slavery*.

2.4 THE END OF EMPIRES

FORTY YEARS AGO, THE IDEA THAT the age of dinosaurs ended with a bang was laughable. The very suggestion that a cosmic impact might have been responsible for their abrupt demise in the geological record was met with hysterical, falling-on-the-floor derision. I know, because I've long held to catastrophism rather than uniformitarianism and, on the rare occasion in those days that someone managed to winkle my views about megafauna die-off out of me, that's precisely the response I met. At the present point in time, I hold to a consensus position, but that's not because I've changed.

Science moves slowly when it comes to nudging aside established orthodoxy, theology even more so. Many commentators deny any possibility of global catastrophe and frame their belief about the Scriptural record in that light. Yet dendrochronological evidence—the history of the world's weather as recorded in tree rings—has moved much of the scientific community beyond such naïvety.

The last brink-of-extinction event was in the sixth century across the years 536–540 AD. It had everything anyone would expect of 'end times'—climate collapse, several years without a summer, devastating crop failure, famine, starvation, depopulation—and that was even before the plague hit. An atmospheric dust veil totally obscured the moon and stars, and caused the sun to appear for just a few hours a day in a weak, blue haze. This wasn't a local calamity—it was on a worldwide scale.

This breakdown of civilisation ushered in the Dark Ages. The remains of the Roman Empire disintegrated, but it was far from the only collapse. In Britain, it was said to be possible to walk across the entire country without meeting a single person. In China, 80% of the population allegedly died in a single year, and the reigning Emperor lost the 'mandate of heaven'. All across the globe, kingdoms toppled as what appeared to be an endless winter took hold.[28]

How did such a monumental event escape the notice of historians for so long? Simple: history was dismissed as legend. The prevailing wisdom until the end of the twentieth century was that catastrophes never happen on a scale described in the records. Only when dendrochronologists—tree-ring specialists—started asking probing questions did historians begin to re-evaluate the stories they'd classified as 'myth'. The scientists believed, rightly as it turned out, that no contemporary chronicler would fail to record several years without summer.

Curiously the motif of wine and dispossession recurs as the door opens to the Dark Ages. In Italy, during these 'years of the blue sun', water became so contaminated that people filled their water storage vats with wine. Those vats were centuries old, and lined with lead. Water doesn't react with lead, but wine does.

Lead poisoning results in anemia, nerve disorders, memory loss, inability to concentrate, erratic mood swings, difficulty processing information, lowered intelligence, behavioural problems and infertility.[29] In short, a dispossession—in the main—of mental faculties.

---

28 See, for example, Mike Baillie, *Exodus to Arthur: Catastrophic Encounters with Comets*, Batsford, 1999.

29 arstechnica.com/science/2021/07/did-lead-poisoning-cause-downfall-of-roman-empire-the-jury-is-still-out/ (accessed 20 December 2022)

2.5 From Eternity Into Time

'In the beginning was the Word...'

THE PHRASE *'IN THE BEGINNING'* IMPLIES TIME, the start of a stopwatch, the calibration of a clock. Yet as John opens his gospel, he takes us into a realm beyond time, to an arena that is prior to any epoch beginning or ending. His vision of the eternal Word in the deep and misty prelude to the ages transitions all the way through to a definite day in a specific historical moment.

Following a mathematically 'perfect' hymn of praise to the life-giving light-bringing LOGOS, John brings us down to earth with a sudden thud from that rarefied atmosphere that hinted at ideal and abstract geometric forms. He transports us to a particular day, and to make sure we are properly grounded in time, he takes us in a particular place where a particular man was baptising.

His first chapter unfolds a series of events, separated into three distinct time intervals:

- The next day (John 1:29)
- The next day (John 1:35)
- The next day (John 1:43)

As his second chapter begins, John informs us of another time marker:

- On the third day (John 2:1)

Some commentators suggest this is simply 'Tuesday', the third day of the Hebrew week. However, by the time John was writing, the phrase 'the third day' would have been inescapably evocative of the day of resurrection.

So I believe it's a simple count of three, designed to complement the 'first day of the week' mentioned in the first verse of the second-last chapter. This chiastic positioning of John 2:1 and 20:1 sets up a parallel between the 'first day of the week' and the 'third day'—simultaneously pointing to the third day after Jesus' death and the wedding at Cana.

John wants to signify, right from the outset, that while the symbolism of *the third day* naturally points to resurrection, it's also indicative of marriage and betrothal. The other gospel writers have not made this connection and John wants to make it explicit. The resurrection and the marriage of the Lamb are indissoluble, inextricable, inseparable.

Now assuming the reference to 'the third day' at the start of the second chapter is indeed a counting instruction and not just Tuesday, a lot more information is encoded in the text than initially appears. By adding the three mentions of 'the next day' to 'the third day', it's six days in total since John the Baptiser was confronted by some priests sent from Jerusalem to investigate who he claimed to be. This is significant, because we can now date the wedding feast at Cana with precision. Perhaps we can even discover the year.

John the Baptiser was questioned on Yom Kippur, the Day of Atonement. Six days after Yom Kippur[30] brings us to the beginning of the week-long Feast of Tabernacles. The Hebrew name for this celebration is *Sukkot*.[31] God had mandated the feast and commanded that it be observed by the building of 'sukkot'—temporary shelters roofed with palm fronds or green-boughed foliage. These rough booths need to be constructed beforehand because the festival itself is a time of rest and refreshment. People eat and sleep in their sukkot,[32] but no work is done—and even today in the twenty-first century the holiday atmosphere is retained for the first two days of the feast by observant Jews.

The booth's roof lattice of leaves symbolises God's overshadowing protection during the forty years in the wilderness. Appointed by Him as a week of rest, Sukkot also serves as a period to reflect on and appreciate God's provision and nurture. The Feast of Tabernacles links in very naturally to the tabernacling of God with men that John spoke of in his opening chapter.[33]

It's also called the Festival of Ingathering, Harvest Festival, or Festival of Booths and occurs during the first month of the civil calendar. This corresponds to the seventh month of the sacred calendar. On the tenth of the month is the fast of Yom Kippur, the last day in the forty-day period of Teshuvah, *repentance*. Jesus had spent those forty days in the wilderness, been tempted on Yom Kippur and then returned to the site where John was baptising at Bethany-beyond-the-Jordan the next day.

---

30 The Hebrew word, 'kippur', is related to *atonement, covering, mercy-seat, pitch, snow, palm frond, palm of the hand, sole of the foot*, and most significantly of all, *cornerstone*. The name that Jesus gives Simon at Caesarea Philippi on the Day of Atonement is Cephas, usually translated *rock* but more accurately being *cornerstone*.

31 According to Jeremy Chance Springfield, 'sukkot' basically means *thin coverings* and so a *lattice roof* or a *leafy bower* can be used as a symbol of a divine *cloud*. (See randomgroovybiblefacts.com/the_cloudy_tabernacle.html, accessed 10 March 2023)

32 The word 'sukkot', *shelters* or *tabernacles* is the plural form of 'sukkah', *shelter* or *tabernacle*.

33 John 1:14 says that the Word made His dwelling among us. *Dwelling* in the original Greek is *tabernacle*.

By the time the Feast of Tabernacles was in full swing, on the fifteenth of the month, Jesus was in Cana with five disciples in tow. His mother was there. It's unclear whether his foster-father Joseph was present but his brothers and sisters were in attendance.[34] Their presence, along with the inclusion of Jesus' newly acquired followers, suggests a family gathering. The marriage of one of Jesus' sisters is probable and would explain His mother's concern.

---

34   Once again, John has built an aura of anonymity around himself and the family of Jesus. He didn't ever explicitly name the mother of Jesus as 'Mary' anywhere in his gospel; it's unclear whether Joseph the foster-father of Jesus appears or not, and none of the brothers or sisters of Jesus are named either. From Mark 6:3 and Matthew 13:55, we are able to know these names—James, Joseph, Jude, Simon—and to realise there must have been at least two sisters but, for some reason, John is completely consistent in keeping these names out of sight.

2.6 Times and Calendars

THE TIMING OF THE WEDDING IS profoundly significant, particularly when the curse of Noah is taken into account. It's not simply that the miracle of Jesus indicates He has used it as the setting for the beginning of a new age, He's reset a calendar as well.

Of course calendar reform automatically inaugurates a new era. About 76 years before the wedding at Cana, Julius Caesar had issued an edict changing the old Roman republican dating system to a new model. The old civil system had drifted about three months off the solar year and many far-flung provinces were confused about the date, so the intent of Caesar's decree was to bring about a permanent alignment of the seasons with the movement of the sun and make dating across the republic completely consistent. One lasting result we have inherited of Caesar's establishment of the New Year on 1 January is that September, meaning *seventh month*, became the ninth month; October, *eighth month*, became the tenth; November, *ninth month*, became the eleventh; and December, *tenth month*, became the twelfth and last.

This dating system was named the Julian calendar. It remained dominant across Europe until the sixteenth century when our present calendar, the Gregorian system, was slowly phased in. Back in the first century, however, the calendar the Romans used was the one authorised by Julius Caesar.

Now two years after his assassination, Gaius Julius Caesar had been deified—he'd been proclaimed divine. A temple was built on the site of his cremation and a life-size wax statue with twenty-three stab wounds was erected in the Forum. His adopted son and successor, his grandnephew Octavian, who eventually took the name Augustus, was proclaimed 'son of the divine'.

These were proclamations Jesus did not leave unanswered. Just as He met the challenges of the principalities and powers with definitive signs of His authority over them, He tackled the question of the divinity of the Caesars with a set of miracles. John doesn't record any of these, but he didn't need to. Matthew's gospel had already detailed them with unmistakable clarity.

After Jesus finished the Sermon on the Mount and returned to Capernaum, a centurion came to Him to ask for healing for his servant. The soldier made the incredibly faith-filled assertion that Jesus didn't actually need to tend to the servant Himself, all He needed to do was to order the healing to take place. That's how authority works in the legions and that, so the centurion implied, is how he believed it should work spiritually. Just give the command, just say the word, thereby proclaiming Your authority over illness and disease, and it will be obeyed. Jesus commended the centurion for his astounding faith and healed his servant.[35]

Jesus then went on to heal Peter's mother-in-law, a crowd seeking deliverance from demons, and another crowd with a range of illnesses. It was very late by the time the disciples managed to sneak Jesus away and get Him onto a boat. Exhausted, Jesus fell asleep. A wild storm sprang up. He was woken by the panicking disciples and simply calmed the tumult—demonstrating a level of authority that can be objectively compared with Julius Caesar.[36]

---

35 Matthew 8:1–13
36 Matthew 8:14–27

The centurion's words about authority are reinforced in this episode. An oft-repeated famous story in contemporary literature about Caesar recounted an incident that occurred during a storm. The captain of the boat Caesar was on was about to turn around, when Caesar delivered a speech of impassioned encouragement to the struggling rowers. However, their best efforts were futile. The boat was eventually turned back by the rage of the elements.

These two stories—about the authority of Jesus far exceeding that of Caesar—climax in the third episode in Matthew's story cycle.[37] The lords of the legions, the emperors of Rome, are simply out of their league compared to Jesus. In the aftermath of the storm, the disciples' boat was blown down to the region of the Gadarenes. It was there Jesus healed the man possessed by multitudes of demons, simply by casting out 'Legion'.

Matthew's presentation is quite comprehensive. Nevertheless, it does miss the *time* angle. John's focus on the authority of Jesus in relation to the Caesars emphasises the setting of the calendar. In this, Jesus is a contrast to Rome, while also reflecting the work and activity of His Father.

> 'Whatever the Father does, that the Son does likewise.'
>
> John 5:19^{ESV}

And indeed, God had been the architect of calendar reform. Way back, just prior to the very first Passover celebration, He declared to Moses and Aaron:

> 'From now on, this month will be the first month of the year for you.'
>
> Exodus 12:2^{NLT}

---

37 See: *Like Wildflowers, Suddenly: Jesus and the Healing of History #01*, Armour Books 2019

Jesus, however, demonstrates considerable reluctance about this recalibration of time.

> *My hour has not yet come.*
>
> John 2:4^{NASB}

Perhaps this is simply stating He was not yet ready to disclose Himself in an 'epiphany'. This Greek word, often associated with the visit of the magi to Bethlehem, actually means *a manifestation of a divinity amongst humanity*. John, somewhat surprisingly, never records his own reaction to the transcendent beauty and majesty of the Transfiguration—it is possible that, even decades later, words simply failed him. Yet the epiphany at Cana—and he uses a related word to describe the revelation of glory there—may be the substitute he's chosen. He may have thought it better to recount a public revelation rather than a private one.

Yet I wonder if there is more to the hesitation of Jesus. Perhaps He was articulating the quandary He found Himself in. To start a new era at that time was, in fact, to reinstate the oldest calendar of all—the one from the days of Noah. The civil New Year of the Hebrew people occurred fourteen days before Sukkot, while the sacred New Year—the one God had commanded—began fourteen days before Passover. Strictly speaking, Jesus was either a little late, or way too early.

On the other hand, the timing was impeccable for the Canaanite New Year and a sign involving new wine.

2.7 Appointed Times

Dispossession is a major theme of John's second chapter. The first pericope deals with the curse of dispossession on the Canaanites. The second examines the struggle by the guardian cherub[38] who once enjoyed God's favour in Eden to retrieve the status he'd been dispossessed of—for dispossessing others. So, on the one hand, people are to be returned to their inheritance, but the satan is to be resisted unto death.

The second major theme, as we've seen, is time and its facets: ages, epochs and eras, calendar and date alignments. Yet there's so much more: 'appointed' times as well as relativistic time. When it dawned on me that turning-water-to-wine isn't a big deal but the time taken to do it was stupendously compressed, I was aghast to realise I'd never noticed the time dilation before. I was disappointed in myself—shocked to realise that I'd spiritualised the essences of time featured in the Cana event to such a degree that I'd missed the obvious.

Of course, in retrospect, relativistic time has to be there. It's intrinsic to the nature of time in our world. But more on that later. For the moment, let's focus on 'appointed times'.

---

38 This guardian cherub was also the prince (or principality) behind the King of Tyre. It is no coincidence that we find allusions to Jezebel, the daughter of the king of Tyre, in the chiasmus.

There are two ways of looking at *appointed times* and they are culturally quite distinct. They are also, in many senses, mutually exclusive. The Hebrew way of viewing *appointed time* looks to a feast or a fast ordained by God, a 'mo'ed'. The Greek way looks at an opportune moment that must be seized instantly or forever lost: a 'kairos'.

The Hebrew sense is of a God-appointed communal assembly; the Greek sense is of a fortuitous and fleeting chance to be grasped by an individual.

The symphonic movement of John's gospel opens in deep heaven with eternal verities, with sevenfold light and motes of life and grace, then moves into ordinary time. Sweeping down into the Hebrew calendar, it informs us in the first two chapters alone of significant events occurring at three appointed times: first on the Day of Atonement, then at the Feast of Tabernacles, then at Passover. It begins by landing on a specific date—the Day of Atonement when John the Baptiser is quizzed about his identity[39]—and then step by step, marking out the days, it takes us to the Feast of Tabernacles.

On that appointed day, John the apostle hasn't brought us to Jerusalem or Rome. His setting is not a world stage. Nor is the event he's describing a global disaster or even a local tragedy. He's taken us to a quiet backwater in Galilee and given us a glimpse of a wedding that's right at a tipping point. The wine has run out; the hospitality of the host is about to be impeached. Shame and humiliation to last a lifetime are soon to be heaped on the bridegroom and his family. It's not something they'd ever be able to live down. Every time a wedding occurred in Cana thereafter,

---

39 As noted in *The Elijah Tapestry*, questions of naming and identity are a feature of Yom Kippur. This is in keeping with the association of the day with God's name. It is the only day on which the name of God was spoken, and then only by the high priest in the Holy of Holies. At all other times, the euphemism HaShem, The Name, was used. Yom Kippur is 'The Day of God's Name'.

the occasion when the guests were dishonoured by an inadequate supply of wine would be remembered. And let's face it: the wine supply problem wasn't exactly secret—if it had been, the disciples wouldn't have had any reason to believe in Jesus or realise He had revealed His glory.

Yet, the potential for shame, disgrace and ignominy is there. It's not on the same scale as the shame experienced by Noah, but it's another echo of that landmark moment in the transition between ages.

But now—*now* Jesus transforms such thresholds entirely. Prior to His intervention, the beginning of a new age was marked by a seismic rift from the one preceding. Rebuilding, remaking and even new calendars were the order of the day. Yet this era—the age of the Redeemer—begins with the joy and merry-making of a provincial wedding. It was so ordinary, so domestic, so unremarkable we don't even know the names of the newlyweds. Yet the bride was probably one of his sisters.

The bridegroom was probably a manual worker. The very fact Sukkot was chosen for the wedding celebration suggests it was difficult for him to get time off. So he'd taken advantage of one of the appointed festivals, a time when work was forbidden anyway, to collect his bride from her village[40] and bring her home to his father's house for the ceremony and feast.

Sukkot is not the only 'appointed time' in the Hebrew calendar. At Mount Sinai, God ordained the observance of seven feasts or fasts. They are grouped together:

---

40 Nazareth was only about six kilometres (four miles) from Cana. Incidentally, foreshadowing events in the third chapter of John's gospel, it was a similar distance from Cana to a village called Rumeh where a wealthy family of Pharisees from Jerusalem had estates. Prominent in this family was a man who would become famous in Christianity and a legend amongst first century Jews, Buni ben Gurion, nicknamed Nicodemus.

- Passover, Unleavened Bread, First Fruits
- Pentecost
- Trumpets, Day of Atonement, Sukkot

When God changed the calendar, He designated Pesach—Passover—to begin on the fourteenth day of the first month, as the sun set, on the evening of a full moon. The following evening was the beginning of the feast of Unleavened Bread and the day after that was First Fruits.

Fifty days after Passover was Shavuot, also called Pentecost or the Feast of Weeks. On the first day of the seventh month—corresponding to the first day of the civil calendar—is Rosh Hashanah, the Feast of Trumpets. The sacred New Year is fourteen days before Passover but the civil New Year occurs seven months later. Ten days after the Feast of Trumpets comes Yom Kippur, the Day of Atonement, and six days after that is Tabernacles.[41]

Of these, the most joyful is Tabernacles. In fact, when God appointed this feast, He *commanded* the people to be joyful and restful. He insisted on it. That might seem like a tall order: how can we, in this bent and broken world, be joyful when the wine runs out? Or worse? Because, let's face it, a paucity of wine is a miniscule disaster in the cosmic scheme of things.

Wonderfully, God gives us a discipline to draw joy into our lives. It's thankfulness. As we daily practice thankfulness to Him, joy begins to permeate our lives and that elusive rest we seek actually comes looking for us.

---

41 These dates are calculated by an inclusive count of days. This is different from our modern system of exclusive counting where we omit the first day in any calculation. So, if today we were to say, 'Seven days from now,' we would start the count by designating tomorrow as Day 1, and the day after tomorrow as Day 2 and so on. However, the ancient system was to count today as Day 1, tomorrow as Day 2, the day after tomorrow as Day 3 and so on.

2.8 The Atonement Clock

John begins his account at Bethany-beyond-the-Jordan on Yom Kippur, the Day of Atonement. It's neither the civil New Year, nor the sacred New Year. Out in the wilderness, although John's record doesn't mention it, Jesus is enduring three tests. Perhaps 'out in the wilderness' gives a precise impression that's not entirely accurate, since Jesus was also taken to the topmost point of the Temple and to a high mountain during those temptations.

Christian Gedge's analysis[42] of the Hebrew calendar provides a beautifully simple possibility regarding John's choice of starting point in time. First, Gedge notes that the present calendar as used by twenty-first century Jews follows the metonic cycle of 19 years, with the number of months in any particular year varying according to a complex system. Passover was a significant consideration in determining the dates in this lunar-solar combination: it had to fall after the northern spring equinox and once the barley harvest had ripened.

The only real simplicity is that the calendar repeats every 19 years. However, Gedge demonstrates that, pre-dating the metonic system

---

42 EC Gedge, *The Atonement Clock*, academia.edu/12760428/The_Atonement_Clock and also EC Gedge, *The Date of Artaxerxes Decrees*, academia.edu/37887708/Date_of_Artaxerxes_Decrees (accessed 10 January 2023)

by over a millennium—and going way back to the Exodus—is a much simpler system that can be deduced from the information given in Scripture. In the three-and-a-half years from the Day of Atonement until the first day of the sacred year when a *'time, times, and half a time'* are fulfilled there are invariably either 1260 days or 1290 days.[43]

> *The woman was given the two wings of a great eagle, so that she might fly to the place prepared for her in the wilderness, where she would be taken care of for a time, times and half a time, out of the serpent's reach.*
>
> Revelation 12:14[NIV]

> *The woman fled into the wilderness to a place prepared for her by God, where she might be taken care of for 1,260 days.*
>
> Revelation 12:6[NIV]

These verses echo the prophecy of Daniel:

> *And from the time the daily sacrifice is abolished and the abomination of desolation set up, there will be 1,290 days.*
>
> Daniel 12:11[BSB]

Gedge comments that this statement seems unfinished. There will be 1290 days *'from the time the daily sacrifice is abolished'*— until when? He remarks that contemporary readers would have been aware of the calendar markers running from the Day of Atonement to 'New Year's Day' three-and-a-half years later and so would have understood Daniel's meaning immediately.

---

[43] With regard to the option of 1260 or 1290 days, sometimes an extra month of 30 days would have to be factored into the three-and-a-half years, in order to position Passover in the season of spring, rather than late winter. The Firstfruits festival, just after Passover, obviously needed an offering of early grain from the barley harvest. This would not be possible if Passover occurred too early.

Let me note in passing that, by the same calendar reckoning, there are either 1260 days or 1290 days from the end of the feast of Tabernacles to the first day of Passover three-and-a-half years later. This tells us that the timespan of the ministry of Jesus almost exactly followed the pattern of *'time, times and half a time'* mentioned in both Daniel and Revelation. John draws our attention to the time span between Sukkot one year and Passover three-and-a-half years later by going straight from the account of the wedding to the last week of Jesus' life: to the incident where He drove the money-changers out of the Temple.

So, this begs the question: Was Jesus' remark, *'My time is not yet come,'* an implicit cry of: 'Don't ruin the countdown!'? In other words, 'If I start now, the prophesied number of days to the Atonement will be ever so slightly out.'

But He did indeed start early. And, in many respects, it's supremely important that He did so. Otherwise prophecy becomes a tool of fatalism. When prophecy is viewed as an inflexible, predetermined, inevitable, unalterable unfolding of events, then it's in its death throes. Prophecy is the living word, capable of supple and subtle changes to accommodate various freewill choices—and is always a call to draw closer to God.[44] It will be fulfilled but often not in the way we expect. And frequently, we have to pray it in.

Daniel did not regard Jeremiah's prophecy that the desolation of Jerusalem would last for seventy years as such a foregone conclusion that it was just a matter of waiting for the appointed day. He fasted, he prayed, he donned sackcloth, he put on ashes,

---

44 So what does the revised countdown of days in the life of Jesus now point to? I'd suggest, as John hints, that it points to His cleansing of the Temple. That, as we shall see, is still indicative—through the chiasmus—of the overcoming of Death in the tomb. Therefore it still fits within the prophetic framework while accommodating the small, subtle changes made by the freewill choice of Jesus to prioritise relationship with His family and friends over the constraints of the most literal interpretation of prophecy.

he acknowledged the breaking of the Law, confessing his own sin and that of the people. He asked the Lord for forgiveness. He petitioned heaven with great intensity.[45]

Prophecy is made for man, not man for prophecy. Just as Sukkot is made for man, not man for Sukkot. Let's face it, by turning water into wine, Jesus worked during Sukkot—during a time God had designated for rest. He was already establishing the principle that He would later articulate explicitly:

> 'The Sabbath was made for man, not man for the Sabbath.'
>
> Mark 2:27[NIV]

The Sabbath, the Feast of Tabernacles, Passover, the Day of Atonement—all of these are divinely appointed times. In fact, the chiastic stories—Cana and the encounter in the garden outside the tomb—are set during two of the 'mo'edim' ordained by God. A 'mo'ed' is a *divinely appointed time for assembly*. Some celebrations, such as Hanukkah[46] and Purim,[47] looked back on momentous historic turning points. However, they were human commemorations. The 'mo'edim' were instigated by God Himself.

The wedding at Cana happened during Sukkot, F*east of Tabernacles*, also called *Booths*. It occurred during first month of the civil calendar,[48] starting on the fifteenth day and lasting for seven days.

The meeting between Jesus and the Magdalene in the garden took place on the Day of Firstfruits. This time of celebration was set down for the sixteenth day of the first month of the sacred

---

45   Daniel 9:1–19
46   The Festival of Lights or Feast of Dedication.
47   Purim means 'lots' as in *lottery*.
48   This corresponded to the seventh month of the sacred calendar.

calendar. Passover begins two days before the Feast of Firstfruits, on the fourteenth of the month.[49]

The firstfruits offering was barley. Fifty days later, a further grain offering—wheat—was made at Shavuot, the *Feast of Weeks* or *Pentecost*, another of the 'mo'edim' designated by God.

Now, while the Jewish people did not have a festival peculiarly dedicated to a wine offering, their predecessors in the land, the Canaanites, did. One of their cultic celebrations was Ra'shu Yeni, *first wine*. It was observed from the thirteenth to the twenty-first day of the twelfth month of the Canaanite year and marked the beginning of the grape harvest for making wine.[50] While the king made sacrifices to nearly thirty deities, the people beseeched divine favour by building temporary booths of cut branches on the temple roof.

This week-long celebration, Ra'shu Yeni,[51] is remarkably like the 'mo'ed', Sukkot. During the Feast of Tabernacles, the Israelites built temporary shelters with open roofs covered with cut branches of palms or leafy boughs. They lived in these booths for seven days in memory of God's protection for their ancestors during the years of the wilderness wanderings.

The Canaanite new wine festival was thus very similar to Sukkot, both in its ritual requirement of booth-building, as well as in its week-long duration. It also occurred at a very similar time of

---

49 This corresponded to the seventh month of the civil calendar, thus reversing the pattern of timing for Sukkot.

50 Adam J Howell, *The Neighbors of Bronze Age Israel: A Descriptive Study of Canaanite Religion*, academia.edu/16504061/The_Neighbors_of_Bronze_Age_Israel_A_Descriptive_Study_of_Canaanite_Religion (accessed 30 November 2022).

51 Similar to Sukkot which began on the fifteenth day of the month of Tishrei, the first month of the Hebrew civil calendar, the Canaanite festival of new wine began on the fourteenth day of the month of Rišyn, likewise their first month, and this would correspond to the time Noah harvested his grapes.

year, the beginning of the grape harvest in the northern autumn. Moreover, it was thought to involve a sacred marriage ritual involving the king in order to promote fertility in the land.

John records that Jesus later proclaimed Himself 'the True Vine'. That very phrase presupposes there are other claimants for the title: counterfeits and imitators. When Jesus performs the miracle at Cana, He not only has the Greek divinity of wine, Dionysius, in His sights but also those thirty Canaanite godlings.

The whole of this three-and-a-half year cycle is bookended not only by New Year celebrations but by New Era considerations.

Furthermore, as Gedge points out, in 26 AD, a Jubilee year would have come around—by his reckoning the 30th since the Exodus.[52] He also makes several valid observations about the likelihood the Jubilee year overlapped the 49th and 50th years[53] and was announced on the Day of Atonement, half way through the 49th year.[54] That Day of Atonement is precisely where John opens his gospel: with the questioning of the Baptiser. Jesus appears the following day, emerging from the desert after fending off the temptations of the satan.

---

52   His charts indicate it is 1470 years since the Exodus, that is 210 Sabbath-Years since that time and 30 Jubilees. Not all of these were celebrated, but he points out Scriptures indicating that some Jubilees were.

53   He suggests that the Sabbath-Years began on 1 Nisan, the first day of the sacred year, and in the forty-ninth year, the Jubilee began 7 months later on 1 Tishrei, the first day of the civil calendar.

54   He suggests it actually began on the first day of the *civil* year but that the announcement was delayed until the 10th of the month when all the people would be gathered for the solemn rites of the Day of Atonement. His argument for the overlapping of a half year in both the 49th and 50th years includes both calendric and agricultural considerations: the Sabbaths would get out of alignment with the Jubilees otherwise; the people would starve if no planting occurred in the 49th or 50th years, since it would be harvest in the 51st year before there was another full crop. The harvest would effectively have to last three years, not two.

John begins his account on the very day the Jubilee should have been announced[55] back in Jerusalem.[56] And Jesus was there, on the pinnacle of the Temple, listening to the suggestion, 'Throw Yourself down,' while He should have been hearing the high priest's proclamation of freedom for slaves and a return of inheritance to all who had lost it.

It's not obvious at first sight, but these are the very issues He's about to tackle, head-on, at Cana.

---

55   Leviticus 25:9 sets the time for the announcement of the Jubilee: it is to be on the tenth day of the seventh month, that is, on Yom Kippur, the Day of Atonement.

56   One of the very few places that I would dispute Gedge's superb analysis involves the start date of the ministry of Jesus. It is my contention that Jesus was baptised on the first day of the month of Elul. Driven out into the desert, He then fulfilled the Jewish custom of prayer and fasting for the forty days of Teshuvah, *repentance*. These forty days commemorate the time Moses was atop Mount Sinai receiving the second set of tablets for the commandments. During this period the people repented of the sin of worshipping the golden calf. Teshuvah runs from Elul into the month of Tishrei and finishes on Yom Kippur, the Day of Atonement. It therefore passes over the civil New Year to culminate ten days later. To me, Jesus was following a very ancient pattern and observing both the feasts, fasts and traditions of the people of Israel. He faced the enemy of our souls on the day the Jubilee should have been announced and returned to Bethany-beyond-the-Jordan to where John was baptising the following day.

2.9 Relativistic Time

Long before Einstein developed the theory of relativity, with its attendant conclusions that we perceive time differently depending on our speed of travel, Scripture overtly spoke of time as being relative, not fixed.

> *A thousand years in Your sight are like a day that has just gone by, or like a watch in the night.*
>
> Psalm 90:4[NIV]

> *Beloved, do not let this one thing escape your notice: With the Lord a day is like a thousand years, and a thousand years are like a day.*
>
> 2 Peter 3:8[BSB]

Now, the great thing about these statements is that they entirely bypass Einstein's formula and simply give us the transformation factor. Most likely that isn't a particularly exciting item of information for you, but personally I think it's exceptionally cool. That's because, by knowing the factor and plugging it into Einstein's equation, we can calculate the travelling speed of heaven! Come on, admit it, it never occurred to you to wonder if heaven was moving, let alone what speed it had.

Yet relativistic time has practical implications for our understanding of Scripture. Eden, after all, was in the east, an ambiguous word that means not just a *direction* but that points to a *prior time*, or even perhaps in context *'before time'*. Can there be a time before the beginning of time? Perhaps it's simply trying to express the idea that we can't apply our current mode of thinking to that situation. Indeed if, to use scientific terminology, Eden were in the same 'frame of reference' as heaven, then as Adam experienced a year, between 365,000 years and 2.2 million years would have gone by on earth.[57] The variation depends on whether it's a 'day' or a 'watch in the night' that we use as our baseline. The plain fact is we don't know how long Adam was in Eden before the serpent created doubt about what God said.

Now I have to admit that Peter really complicates the matter with his coda *'...and a thousand years are like a day.'* Just when we think we can understand the rules for time in the heavenly realm, there's an inversion that tells us our best equations are seriously inadequate and only part of the story.

Now I haven't found a better explanation of time dilation than the one at *Brainstorming box*. Since I can't do better, I'm just going to quote it. It concerns the fastest ball ever bowled in cricketing history to date, and an imaginary mosquito. Shoaib Akhtar was the bowler. The year was 2003. The ball's speed was 161.3 km/hr.

> 'Now, imagine that a mosquito wearing a miniature timer is sitting pretty on a cricket ball lying on the field. This timer is perfectly in sync with the watch strapped to the umpire's wrist... Shaoib Akhtar is about to bowl the fastest ball. He picks up the ball (with the mosquito on it) from the field, makes his long run, and releases it. As soon as the ball is released, both the mosquito and

---

57 This isn't difficult mathematics. Grab your calculator. (I'm going to round off to 365 days for a year because I'm only looking for a ballpark figure.) 1 day in heaven = 1000 years on earth. So 1 year in heaven = 1000 x 365 years on earth = 365,000 years on earth.

the umpire start their respective timers. Let us assume that the England batsman (who had gracefully played the ball) doesn't play it but leaves it to run its course. Even the wicketkeeper leaves the ball and it manages to travel at the same speed of 161.3 kmph for around 490 yards (0.448 kilometres).

At that very moment, the umpire records the time to be 1 second, but the mosquito finds that the time on its watch hasn't even crossed half a second; in fact, the creature would record a time of around *0.449 seconds!* Thus, essentially, the mosquito would have travelled over half a second into the future after the ball stops! This shows that the time is dilated for the stationary umpire in comparison with the fast-moving mosquito.'[58]

Now, time dilation is what I suspect happened for the wedding guests with respect to the water in the stone pots. Obviously the pots aren't speeding anywhere but their contents are being subjected to millions of volts of electricity. Do differing levels of electromagnetism result in time dilation, just as different speeds do?

I'd love to be able to answer that question definitively. However, there is no consensus on this point. Some scientists hypothesise it isn't possible; yet others suggest it simply *must* be an automatic inclusion within our present theories of light and electromagnetism. And if it is, then we have clues towards a neat explanation concerning what process Jesus was using.

I'm not trying to explain away His miracle—far from it. I simply want to show it is in accord with God's hidden laws of creation, not in violation of them.

---

58   brainstormingbox.org/time-dilation-how-time-behaves-explained/ (accessed 10 January 2023)

2.10 Watches and Watchers

A 'watch', a timepiece for the wrist, was first devised with military applications in mind. The word comes from the practice of 'keeping watch'—a task that combines *looking* and *time*. Soldiers on watch were expected to observe, monitor, guard and protect the encampment for a specific period, staying awake and alert, while spotting anything out-of-the-ordinary and differentiating friend from foe without mistake.

Here John weaves two of his great themes together: that of appointed time and of identity. Once again, we find echoes of Eden:

> *Then the Lord God took the man and placed him in the Garden of Eden to cultivate and keep it...*
>
> *And out of the ground the Lord God formed every beast of the field and every bird of the air, and He brought them to the man to see what he would name each one. And whatever the man called each living creature, that was its name. The man gave names to all the livestock, to the birds of the air, and to every beast of the field. But for Adam no suitable helper was found.*
>
> Genesis 2:15;19–20^{BSB}

God appointed Adam as the keeper of Eden—the Hebrew word, 'shomer', also means *watcher* and *preserver, protector* and *guardian*. In the Genesis account, we are told that God instructed Adam there were restrictions placed on him as a keeper and that He then commented it was not good for man to be alone. Then He brought the animals to Adam to name.

God's first gift to mankind, apart from life itself, is the right and privilege of naming. Adam's first act as a watcher and keeper was to name the creatures he was given to steward. This is a natural part of the role of the keeper since *name*, 'shem', is part of the word 'shomer', *watcher, guardian, preserver.*

Naming, identifying, prophesying both the identity and destiny of those yet-unnamed—all these are tasks we are called to fulfil as stewards of creation. So, perhaps with its focus on both time and identity, John's gospel directs a question to us as readers: 'Can you name the unnamed in the story? Are you a true "shomer"?'

In Hebrew, other words for *watchers* referred to fallen angels—those cosmic entities who had come to earth, mated with human women and also taught forbidden arts and sciences. Their actions had led to the ravaging of the world—and then to the cleansing flood of Noah that backgrounds John's story of the wedding.

Jesus was a true shomer. At Cana, He began His campaign against these unholy Watchers.

In fact, the very name 'Cana', *reeds*, evokes the first whisper of salvation in the ancient myths of Mesopotamia. In those legends, the creator-engineer godling, Enki, sent sages called Apkallu up from the primeval abyss to civilise humanity. The Apkallu were demi-gods, part-fish, part-human, sometimes part-bird. Originally considered wise and benevolent by the Sumerians, they were seen as malignant by the Hebrews[59] since the enlightenment they offered enabled the creation of weapons for warfare, cosmetics for seduction and potions for poisoning.

---

59 The people of Mesopotamia were not consistent in their views of the Apkallu over time, and gradually these demi-gods came to be considered by some as wicked and demonic. So it wasn't simply a case of the Hebrews reacting to the beliefs of their neighbours. There was already a movement in that direction.

In the Mesopotamian flood story, the king of the gods decides to eliminate humanity. He convenes a Council and extracts a promise from the assembled divinities that none of them will warn the people of the world about the coming catastrophe. Enki, despite his oath, decides to save mankind. In a subterfuge, instead of informing anyone directly, he whispers instructions to a wall of reeds. Atrahasis, who happens to be on the other side of these reeds, hears directions to build an enormous boat. By doing so, he saves his family and many other living creatures from the seven-day deluge. After the flood, he sends out a swallow, a raven and a dove to find if the waters have receded. When his boat finally lands, Atrahasis—the Noah-figure of this account—offers a sacrifice.

Royal inscriptions from Sumerian palaces mention 'the reeds of Enki', showing how significant reeds were culturally. Cana, through its name and the actions of Jesus there, draws in this extra-biblical account of the Flood. But it also links—through the allusions to Noah, to baptism and rebirth—themes flowing from John's first chapter and through into his third.

Peter wraps up the matter of Noah, salvation, baptism and the Watchers, whom he calls *'the spirits in prison'* in one succinct summary:

> *He [Jesus] went and preached to the spirits in prison, after they were disobedient long ago when God patiently waited in the days of Noah as an ark was being constructed. In the ark a few… were delivered through water. And this prefigured baptism, which now saves you… through the resurrection of Jesus Christ.*
>
> 1 Peter 3:19–21^{NET}

At Cana, Jesus gave an unambiguous sign He had come to save the world in an even more comprehensive way than Noah ever did.

2.11 THE DATES

1 September, 26 AD	—	Jesus is baptised
30 September, 26 AD	—	Jubilee year commences
9 October, 26 AD	—	Jesus is tempted, Jubilee year should be announced
18 October 26 AD	—	The first miracle at Cana, the fifth day of Sukkot

TO CONCLUDE THAT THESE ARE THE most probable dates for these events, I have used Gedge's calculations for the Jubilee year and Beattie's information for the corresponding festival dates.[60] I have decided on the fifth day of Sukkot as the time of the miracle by noting that, for the prophecy of Daniel to correspond to the cleansing of the Temple four days before the Passover instead of to the Passover itself, then the miracle must have occurred four days before *the day after* the Feast of Tabernacles had ended.

I know many people will object to taking such latitude with prophecy and will protest it should be exact, that four days

---

[60] See: cgsf.org/dbeattie/calendar/?roman=26 (accessed 25 January 2023)

difference is too much and it's not possible to justify the difference by pointing to a chiastic parallel.[61] However, quite apart from the fact this reduces prophecy to rock hard determinism where freewill is an illusion, it also ignores the repeated testimony of Scripture that God values relationship with us so much that He repeatedly responds to human pleas. So many prophets negotiate with God, asking Him to alter a decree—and He does!

Amos, for example, negotiated with Him about the fate of Israel (Amos 7); Ezekiel negotiated about the kind of dung he could use for cooking fuel (Ezekiel 4); Abimelech negotiated over his death sentence (Genesis 20); so did Hezekiah (2 Kings 20); Moses negotiated over God's proposal to abandon the idolatrous Israelites and start over (Exodus 32); Habakkuk negotiated about the apparent lack of a divine answer to his complaint (Habakkuk 1); the Syro-Phoenician woman negotiated for her daughter, wanting just the crumbs that fell from the Master's table (Matthew 15) and Simon Peter negotiated Jesus down from 'agápē', *sacrificial love*, to 'phileo', *friendship* (John 21).

An earthly king might fear to lose his authority or might worry he'd be seen as weak or vacillating if he changes his mind. But God is authority; He doesn't need to worry about anyone's perception of Him. When God 'changes His mind', it's not about making a mistake. It's about valuing His relationship with us so very much more than He values His own dignity.

---

61   It would be easy to get this idea from, for example, the analytic and interpretative work of Jonathan Cahn where precise dates are so important. However, Cahn is not looking at prophecy per se but at templates for disaster. The dark spirits of this world, unable to create, have counterfeited biblical patterns in the outworking of their plans. They do not have the ability to successfully modify prophecy as a living word, but can only use it in a concrete, fatalistic and legalistic sense. God, on the other hand, is able to fulfil His word in subtle and unexpected ways, even accounting for all the freewill choices of humanity with their endless potential for the derailment of the word.

So, to accede to His mother's request just because she made one, simply meant that the prophecy of Daniel had to be fulfilled another way. And, as we shall see, it was.

Now in addition to all the assumptions I've made in calculating these dates, I've also supposed that, while the time for Jesus had not yet come, it was close at hand. Had He not invoked the principle that rest is made for man, not man for rest—which applies to both the Sabbath and Sukkot—then He would have demonstrated much greater reluctance to perform the miracle until Sukkot was over. But by then it would have been too late to avert the shame and humiliation that the bridegroom's family would have had to endure.

Finally, the natural implication of this set of dates for the start of Jesus' ministry is that 30 AD is the year of Jesus' death. Passover in that year was 5 April.

2.12 Joyous Water Drawing

IN THE THREE-AND-HALF YEARS of Jesus' ministry, Sukkot would have occurred four times. From the information and clues scattered throughout the gospels, we know what Jesus was doing during at least three of those festivals. First, He was at Cana. Last, He was on the Mount of Transfiguration. On one of the other two occasions—probably the third—He was in Jerusalem. And if I had to guess about His whereabouts on the other occasion, I'd suggest He was possibly in Samaria, talking to a woman who was about to draw water from a well.

The reason I suggest this is because the other three times all have something to do with drawing water. And while that might be quite obvious at Cana, it's not so for the other two occasions.

Now there were many rituals and sacrifices performed at the Temple during the Feast of Tabernacles. One of them was a tradition of water libation called the 'Joyous Water-Drawing Ceremony'. During this ritual a priest went with a golden pitcher to the Pool of Siloam, filled it and then took it through the Water Gate into the Temple where it was poured over the altar with wine from a bowl. This ceremony was accompanied by joyful shouts and blasts on the shofar.

John tells us that Jesus, on the last and greatest day of the Feast of Tabernacles—the day called the 'Hoshana Rabbah', *Great Salvation*—Jesus stood up and cried out:

> *If anyone thirsts, let him come to Me and drink. The one believing in Me, as the Scripture has said: 'Out of his belly will flow rivers of living water.' Now He said this concerning the Spirit, whom those having believed in Him were about to receive; for the Spirit was not yet given, because Jesus was not yet glorified.*
>
> John 7:37–39[BLB]

On this final day, no doubt as the Joyous Water-Drawing Ceremony was being enacted, Jesus proclaimed Himself as the Living Water, just as He did to the Samaritan woman. Prior to that moment at Jacob's Well, at the very beginning of His ministry, He directed the servants at Cana to pour water and then draw it. In a miracle, in a supernatural Joyous Water-Drawing Ceremony, water did more than mix with wine—it *became* wine.

The wedding at Cana is a precursor, a springboard, for John's hop-skip to the Samaritan woman where he introduces the theme of the Living Water before jumping to the words of Jesus concerning Himself as that same Living Water. This foreshadows the Holy Spirit as Living Water, and also as New Wine.[62]

On the last Sukkot before His death, Jesus took three of His disciples up the Mount of Transfiguration. Now it might not be obvious what that event has to do with any water-drawing ceremony, or the coming of the Holy Spirit. But of course it is connected.

The trek up the mountain took place six days after Yom Kippur, the day Simon confessed Jesus as the Christ. On the Day of Atonement, a scapegoat was chosen by lot, then driven out into

---

62   Acts 2:13 and Ephesians 5:18

the wilderness, sending away the sins of the nation to the goat-demon Azazel. Often the scapegoat was led to a cliff and pushed off, so it could never return and bring back its burden of sin.

Many commentators are extremely dubious that this could ever have been commanded by God. The thought that the sins would be sent away to a goat-demon is too bizarre. However, when we consider the actions of Jesus, I don't believe there can be any doubt that's exactly what was intended.

Jesus was in the wilderness, at Caesarea Philippi, visiting the 'Gates of Hell'—a cave in a cliff face within the temple precinct to the rustic goat-god, Pan. To drop by a pagan shrine is unusual in itself, but to go to a place dedicated to a goat-idol on the Day of Atonement simply isn't a coincidence. Jesus was imaging Himself as the scapegoat. In addition, He was right in the territory of Azazel: Caesarea Philippi was in the shadow of Mount Hermon, the place where—so the stories in the Book of Enoch and the Book of Jubilees detailed—a cohort of angels descended. In an episode of mutual cursing, they agreed to seek mates amongst human women.

On the top of Mount Hermon, there is a bowl carved into the rock which, according to the nineteenth century description of the summit, would have had to have been approached by a spiral path after entering a temple complex.[63] Derek Gilbert, drawing on the work of archaeologist Charles Clermont-Ganneau, points out that the usual translation in the Book of Jubilees is that the angels descended 'in the days of Jared,' the great-great-great grandson of Adam—however, a much more accurate translation of these words may well be 'in the days of the *yarid*.' Instead of Jared being a person, it is a 'yarid', a water libation ceremony. Also called hydrophory, this rite was practised throughout the ancient

---

63 It is not presently possible to go to the top of Mount Hermon. It is a restricted zone. A United Nations peace-keeping installation is there.

world, and 'consisted chiefly in drawing water, which was borne in procession and thrown into a sacred tank.'[64]

The fallen angels fathered the nephilim, who in turn fathered the gibborim, the mighty men of the era before the Flood. These giants were drowned in the Flood, but their spirits survived and, in the first century, were understood to have become demons. Thus there is a distinct difference between the fallen angels, the so-called Watchers, and their children—those human-angelic hybrids who are constantly seeking to be re-embodied in flesh.

Everything in the story of the Watchers suggests that they were originally throne guardians in heaven—high-ranking angelic equerries who knew enough of God's plan for the redemption of the human race to try to foil it at every turn. Their particular target seems to be the work of the Holy Spirit, since their demon-children counterfeit the indwelling of the Spirit through possession; and the process they used to mate with human women seems to be an attempt to imitate the overshadowing of Mary by the Holy Spirit.[65]

It is therefore no wonder, in the context of a water-drawing ceremony during Sukkot, that Jesus starts to set matters right and to allude to the Holy Spirit as the giver of Living Water.

It is also no wonder that Jesus—even at Cana, even in His first miracle, even in the subtlest of ways and faintest of references—begins to indicate His ultimate target: the principalities alleged to have their house of assembly on Mount Hermon, along with the king of the Canaanite pantheon who was said to have his palace further to the north.

---

64   Edward Lipiński, *El's Abode: Mythological Traditions related to Mount Hermon and to the Mountains of Armenia*, Orientalis Lovaniensa Periodica II, 1971.

65   See: Anne Hamilton, *Dealing with Belial: Spirit of Armies and Abuse*, Armour Books 2022

Nisan

First Day	Second Day	Third Day	Fourth
2	3	4	5
9	10	11	12
16 JOHN 20:1 NIV	17	18	19
23	24	25	26
30			

> Early on the first day of the week while it was still dark, Mary Magdalene went to the tomb and saw that the stone had been removed from the entrance.

Tishrei

Day	Fifth Day	Sixth Day	Sabbath Day
			1
6		7	8
	SPICES		
13	14		15 JOHN 2:1-2 NIV
20			
27			

On the third day a wedding took place at Cana in Galilee. Jesus' mother was there and Jesus and His disciples had also been invited to the wedding.

Part 3

3.1 On the Way to Cana

BACK IN JOHN 1:43 IT'S MENTIONED THAT, on the third day after the questioning of John the Baptiser, Jesus set out for Galilee. Since the Baptiser was initially at Bethany-beyond-the-Jordan, Jesus left from there.

In the days of Elijah, this was the brook Cherith—the prophet's first hiding place while Ahab was scouring the countryside for him. When the stream dried up, Elijah moved north. Similarly, in a later century, John the Baptiser moved from Bethany-beyond-the-Jordan to Aenon, near Salim. The Baptiser didn't move far—it's most likely he simply went to the junction of the brook with the Jordan river and crossed to the opposite bank.[66]

Jesus is likely to have taken a similar route as He travelled to Galilee with five new disciples in tow. They'd have crossed the Jordan, then headed north. A few hours later it's likely they stopped for

---

66   There are several candidates for Aenon near Salim, the most likely in my view being the one on the opposite bank of the river to Bethany-beyond-the-Jordan and just a few kilometres downstream. This would equate 'Salim' with 'Salumias' at the junction of the Jezreel and Jordan valleys. However, despite my pragmatic belief in this as the most practical solution, my belief that Jesus always healed history suggests to me that 'Salim' might be 'Sulam', the name for the city once called Shunem where a dead boy was raised by the prophet Elijah. I will make a small case for this possibility in the next volume in this series, *The Lustral Waters*.

food and provisions in Scythopolis. This city was situated at the junction of the Jezreel Valley and the great rift that forms the watercourse for the Jordan as it flows towards the lowest point on the earth's surface, the Dead Sea. Scythopolis itself was about 120 metres below sea level. During the time of Jesus, it was the capital of the Decapolis and the only one of the ten cities on the western side of the Jordan river.

Scythopolis had a patchwork history. Originally known as Beit She'an, it was variously occupied by the Egyptians, Philistines, Greeks and Romans. Back at the very end of Saul's reign, it was the Philistine outpost where his body and those of his sons were exposed on the wall after their final defeat.

Beit She'an was re-founded more than half a millennium later by the Ptolemies, the Greek rulers of Egypt. The Ptolemies claimed descent from both the heroic demi-god Herakles and the wine-god Dionysius. They settled Scythian mercenaries there in the third century before Christ and associated the city with Dionysius. They alleged it was his birthplace and claimed he had buried his nursemaid Nysa there, and that he'd then set up residence with his Scythian personal guard. Sometimes it was called Scythopolis-Nysa, to honour her and emphasise the connection.

A large temple was built during this time period and, while archaeologists have been unable to identify the deity worshipped there, it was probably Dionysius or, if not, Herakles. The city lasted over a thousand years until it was levelled in an earthquake. Consequently, that temple to one of the city's spiritual patrons would have been a prominent feature as Jesus and His disciples walked its streets.

In the centuries before Beit She'an was occupied by the Scythians, it was an important Canaanite and Egyptian outpost. There were naturally shrines and sanctuaries to their deities. After

Saul's defeat in battle, his armour was placed in the temple of the Ashtoreths,[67] while his head was displayed in the precinct of Dagon.[68] It's therefore clear at least two major worship centres existed at that time as well.

---

67 1 Samuel 31:10. The parallel passage in 1 Chronicles 10 says the armour was placed in the temple of their gods, but this is not inconsistent with saying 'the Ashtoreths', since this simply specifies which particular deity.

68 1 Chronicles 10:10

3.2 Goddesses of Canaan

DURING THE ERA WHEN THE PHARAOHS ruled most of Canaan, Beit She'an was a major Egyptian outpost. Ashtoreth was then understood to be the same as a war goddess called Anat. Originally a cult favourite of the Canaanites, Anat came to be adopted as the special patron of Rameses II who named his daughter and dog after her.

To begin with, the Canaanites focussed their worship on Asherah, the fertility goddess, the 'mistress of serpents' and 'mother of the gods'. However, around 1400 BC, her worship declined steeply and she was supplanted by her daughter, the warrior Anat, who was apt to work off her frustrations in sudden orgies of completely barbaric violence and blood-letting.

This change in allegiance by the Canaanites was probably a natural response to the threat posed by the Israelites coming in from the desert and then settling in their midst: instead of a primary focus on agriculture and the fertility of the land, they began to worship a warrior-protector. Anat had a savage, untamed tear-things-apart character not dissimilar to the 'maenads', *raving ones*, who were the female attendants of Dionysius. She threatened to beat up her father if he didn't give Baal a palace. Tellingly, her mother, Asherah,[69] was afraid of her.

---

69   Known as 'Athirat' in the Baal Cycle. It was only later she was called Asherah, the name by which she is so well-known in Scripture. Her title, 'mother of gods', was at some point given over to Anat.

The Israelites, on the other hand, tended to adopt Asherah worship whenever they abandoned Yahweh. They also sacrificed to one of Asherah's sons, the storm-god Baal-Hadad, whom they called Rimmon. Anat, however, was apparently side-lined.

Asherah is mentioned dozens of times in Scripture, but there are very few mentions of Anat. Dedications to her are largely confined to placenames—Anatoth,[70] Jeremiah's hometown; and Beth Anat, perhaps not coincidentally near Cana. One of the judges of Israel, Shamgar, was the 'son of Anat', but whether that is a man, woman, town or title[71] is unknown. Joseph's wife, Asenath, is sometimes thought to be named after Anat[72] and it's my personal belief that Zaphenath-Paneah, the title Pharaoh bestowed on Joseph, also encodes the name.

Now curiously 'anat' from 'anah', along with 'she'an' as in Beit She'an, may both be related to *appointed time*.[73] In Egyptian mythology, Anat is associated with the antler-crowned gatekeeper of the underworld, the stag deity Resheph. And not surprisingly, Beit She'an is known to have been a centre of Resheph worship. It was a thorough-going pagan metropolis.

We'd have to suspect its sights and sounds and smells lingered on in the minds of the disciples as they travelled on to Nathanael's hometown of Cana. Dionysius, Herakles, Dagon, Anat, Resheph— were any of these pagan divinities the topic of conversation on the

---

70   By the time of Jesus, Anathoth was apparently renamed Bethany—famous as the hometown of Lazarus, Martha and Mary.

71   It's thought that 'son of Anat' might have been a coveted title bestowed on a victorious young warrior.

72   Her name is variously interpreted as *belonging to Anat*, or *holy to Anat* or *belonging to Neith* (the Egyptian counterpart of Anat), or *harm* or *evils* or *thorn bush*.

73   One of the possible derivations of 'she'an' is 'shanah', *year* or *change*, as in Rosh Hashanah, the Hebrew phrase for New Year's Day.

first day of their journey, the third day after Yom Kippur, as they passed through Scythopolis on their way north?

It seems likely, at the very least, that wine-mad Dionysius—the wildling nature-god of grapes, vineyards, revelry, frenzy, ecstacy and mutilation who was said to be able to grant his favourites the ability to make wine from anything—was on their minds. And if the other spiritual potentates had escaped their notice, we can be sure of one thing: they certainly hadn't been overlooked by Jesus.

Because John is about to describe a targeted take-down of every last one of them.

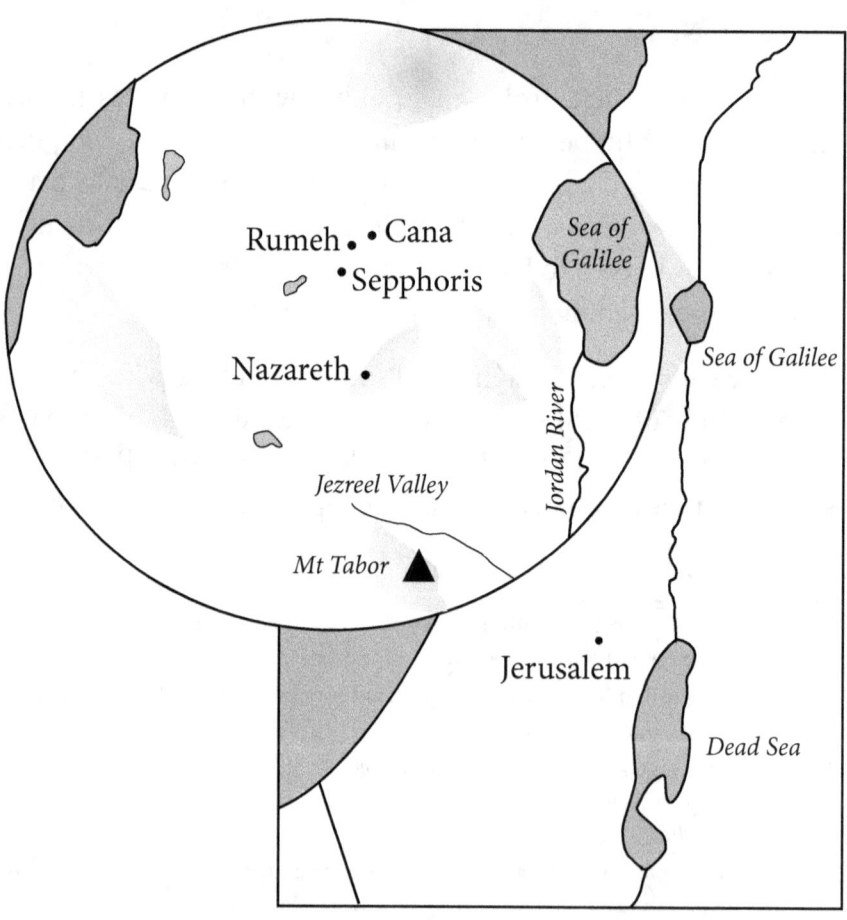

3.3 The Spirit of Cana

THE ONLY TIME CANA IS EVER MENTIONED in Scripture is in John's gospel. In the first century it was close to Sepphoris—at that time the capital of Galilee. Both were situated in the Beit Netofa Valley, below the Nazareth Ridge. Cana, incidentally, was just a few kilometres north of the town of Rumeh where the family of a very prominent and wealthy Pharisee, Nicodemus, had extensive estates.[74]

We don't know Cana's backstory nor do we have any clues about what happened there in earlier times. We have no insight into any interplay between the actions of Jesus and the town's past.

The Romans had a phrase, 'genius loci', *spirit of a place*. It recognised that every locality has its own unique qualities, not only in terms of the physical landscape but also in the way people perceived its surrounding atmosphere.[75] Roman architects were expected to be sensitive to the presence and territorial rights of a local deity.

---

[74] During the Jewish Revolt, Josephus, commander of the Jewish forces in Galilee, made Cana his strategic headquarters for a time *(The Life of Flavius Josephus)*. Its prime location, overlooking Sepphoris—the capital of Galilee during the Roman era—and the cities of the Beit Netofa Valley, made it an ideal location. Also, Jewish tradition describes the priestly family of Eliashib, mentioned in 1 Chronicles 24:19 as one of the 24 orders of *Cohanim* or priest, as coming from Cana. (See: biblicalarchaeology.org/daily/people-cultures-in-the-bible/jesus-historical-jesus/mark-and-john-a-wedding-at-cana-whose-and-where/ (accessed 25 November 2022)

[75] 'Genius Loci', oxfordreference.com/view/10.1093/oi/authority.20110803095847893 (accessed 2 November 2022)

It's easy to dismiss this idea as primitive. The concept of spirits presiding over a tract of land may seem archaic and naïve. Note however that, when large areas were involved, Paul called them *'principalities'*—spiritual governors of cities, regions or nations. Jesus often went into combat against them—and we can observe their distinctive, individual nature by the different ways He tackled them when He ventured into their terrain.

Placenames are extremely important in the gospels. Whenever a specific location is recorded and we can delve into its history, we find that Jesus isn't healing a random person. He healed people who perfectly represented the town's history.

It's no coincidence He met a five-times married woman by Jacob's well, once we know what has happened there in the past. It's no coincidence He raised a widow's son from the dead at Nain, once we realise it's close to long-disappeared Shunem. It's no coincidence Jesus travelled from Bethany-beyond-the-Jordan to Bethany near Jerusalem to raise Lazarus from the dead.

Each of these stories—and many more—have profound historical resonances that demonstrate Jesus was not healing just anyone, but focusing on people who in some way represented the past ruptures and unhealed wounds of their place of residence.

I call it 'the healing of history', though many people refer to it as 'healing the land'.[76]

So, although we know absolutely nothing about Cana's historical background prior to the first century, some of those incredibly unusual clues we've already unearthed point us to an event that occurred in the general vicinity about a millennium and a half

---

76 My understanding of the 'healing of history' is an extension of recapitulation theory (as expressed by Justin Martyr and Irenaeus) in combination with the healing of the land.

previously. Now you might have thought that all the electrical activity in the stone pots, all those bolts of *lightning*, was just incidental. Not actually a hint to that historical event way back in the past. But it is. Moreover, the goddess Anat is specifically mentioned in relation to that event.

The incident in question is the destruction of the Canaanite army by the forces of Barak and Deborah. Barak's name means *lightning*, and Deborah was the one and only female judge of Israel in the period prior to the kings. But not just any female. She's actually been compared to the war goddess, Anat. Moreover, she mentioned Anat in her victory song, while naming the judge Shamgar. While this might seem like a casual reference to his parentage—Shamgar ben Anath—it is more likely a deliberate pointer to the shrine of Anat said to have been on Mount Tabor.[77]

Perhaps John in his gospel copied the technique Deborah used: making an allusion through a person's name to point to a spirit without specifying it. Nathanael could be considered to have Anat encoded in his name, when we consider that the Egyptian equivalent of Anat was the goddess Neith. Anat was the dispossessor par excellence, yet Nathanael under the fig tree is symbolic of a return of inheritance in the Messianic age.

Now Deborah and Barak were opposed by a mighty army from Hazor in Upper Galilee. They strategically stationed their battalions on the slopes of Mount Tabor, a round hill not far from the ridge where Nazareth is perched. Mount Tabor is situated on the Jezreel Plain in the next valley over from Cana. Aided by a flooded river and by the stars of 'appointed time', Deborah and Barak's farmer-troops routed the chariots, horses and forces under the command of the Canaanite general Sisera.[78]

---

77 anistor.gr/english/enback/p011.htm (accessed 6 October 2023)
78 He was, apparently, a worshipper of Anat. See: section 6.15.

Now, before we delve into these connections with Deborah, it's worthwhile taking a look at the most significant aspect of Cana. That, undoubtedly, is its name. There are several possibilities and one of the most commonly cited is 'qaneh', *reed*. Reeds symbolise thresholds; they mark the dangerous liminal space between land and water.

Reeds are, of course, important in the history of Israel. Consider Moses who, as a baby, was placed in a basket amongst the reeds of the Nile. Or think of the departure of the Israelites from Egypt as Moses led them through the waters of the Red Sea or Reed Sea.

Yet there's another significant nuance of *reeds* that should not be overlooked. One of the Hebrew words for *reeds* also means *brothers*.

Just what does *brothers* evoke for us as we meditate on the long history of Israel? Cain and Abel? Ishmael and Isaac? Esau and Jacob? Joseph and his brothers? Maybe all of them?

3.4 The Clue of 'Cana'

It's invaluable to know the exact locations where Jesus interacted with different people. Most of us are unaware that, for the sake of the land itself, it was crucial for Him to encounter the Samaritan woman at Sychar and not, for example, at Sebaste. He could heal *her* anywhere anytime, of course, but by choosing to meet her at Jacob's well, He also had the opportunity to heal *the land* whose history was embodied by her life. She was the perfect representative of the past for that particular location. She was, in a sense, the physical manifestation of the *spirit of the place*.

Without going into her details until a later volume, suffice it to say that the history of any locality is vital to any deep understanding of the work of Jesus in that specific place. We all too often miss how profound His work was because we fail to note the geographic clues provided by the gospel writers. But there are further clues provided in the names themselves: as the prophets so often declared, the destiny of towns is poetically proclaimed in their names.[79]

Cana means *reeds*. However as we focus, not so much on the meaning of the word as its sound, we should recognise that 'Cana' is an echo of both Cain and Canaan.

Noah's grandson Canaan gave his name to the land encompassing present day Israel and much of Lebanon. Michael Astour suggests that, in the ancient kingdoms and city-states outside of this special stretch of land, the territory was known as both Canaan and Canaa.[80] He contends that these words, along with the Greek

---

[79] See, for example, Micah 1:10–16
[80] Michael C. Astour, The Origin of the Terms "Canaan," "Phoenician," and "Purple", *Journal of Near Eastern Studies*, Vol. 24, No. 4, Erich F. Schmidt Memorial Issue. Part Two (Oct., 1965), jstor.org/stable/543644 (accessed 20 February 2023)

term 'Phoenicia', all meant *land of purple*, and principally referred to the red and purple dyes produced from sea snails found on the coast near Tyre.[81] This dye became one of the principal luxury goods hawked by trading seafarers of the Phoenician empire. With his monopoly on production, the king of Tyre became so wealthy through his trading ventures that he was compared by Ezekiel to the rebel cherub cast out of Eden for the merchandising of souls.

The dye was variously known as Tyrian purple, Phoenician red, Phoenician purple, royal purple, imperial purple or imperial dye. The land of Canaan moreover was also renowned for its superior wines—and grape skins can produce a red-purple vegetable dye.

So does the name Cana encode a double meaning of *reeds*[82] as well as *purple*? Is it a clue for us that Jesus, in turning water into wine, also changed the colour to a royal red-purple hue?

Now Canaan—the person rather than the land—is first mentioned in the disastrous aftermath of Noah's drinking session that occurred after the flood. Ham somehow dishonoured Noah but for some mysterious and unspecified reason, Noah cursed Ham's son Canaan in retaliation for this violation, rather than the perpetrator himself.

Of course, because of the obvious link between the wine at Cana and the wine Noah produced, it's tempting to pursue a line of inquiry that focusses entirely on Canaan. But let's not overlook

---

81 The Greeks actually called Phoenicia the 'Kingdom of the Blood-Red Men', referring to the red-purple colour.

82 A *reed*, 'qaneh', is not normally solitary but occurs in a bunch, perhaps influenced by the similarity of sound with 'kana', a *bundle* or *pack*. In the original Hebrew, 'kana' also means *to be humble*. Canaan, the name of the son of Ham and the word for *merchant*, was derived from 'kana', *humble*. Noah's curse takes *humble* and crushes it to *slave*.

Cain. The link to wine isn't entirely missing from his story. Yes, he was a man of the soil and his offering to God was of fruit, not of flock. But that's not the connection. It's that after killing Abel, he was exiled to the land of Nod.[83] This name rhymes with 'noyd', *wineskin*.[84] And since any line of inquiry involving either Cain or Canaan is a poetic one, rather than etymological in nature, it would be unwise to discard one option just because it seems less likely.

Nod was east of Eden, and *east* in Hebrew also means *time before*.[85] Here we have yet another time aspect unrelated to the ones we've already looked at. How does it relate to the *appointed hour* Jesus spoke of to His mother? Is there anything Cana, Cain and Canaan have in common?

As we've seen, Cana is usually translated *reeds*[86] and reeds symbolises *brothers*. Cain certainly had brother issues. And certainly the story where Canaan is first mentioned is about brother issues too. Not to mention slavery and dispossession.

Brother issues, slavery, dispossession, family dysfunction: actually the first person who springs to mind with this combination is Joseph of Egypt.

---

83   Nod is thought to mean *wandering*.
84   God is a poet. Paul says so in the Greek of Ephesians 2:10 and John tells us repeatedly in the very last lines of his gospel—appropriately in the chiastic parallel to his opening line about the Word. Jokes and poetry are, of course, the first casualties of translation. So, our current Bible versions give very little indication of the rich wordplay that goes on in Scripture. Rhymes—both head rhyme and tail rhyme, assonances, alliteration, acrostics, cognates, puns, and double—sometimes even triple—meanings all shed light on the message.
85   The very next word in the Biblical text after 'Nod' is a pun with a double meaning involving *place* and *time*. Scripture is so poetic that our highly analytic translations offer us, at best, partial understanding.
86   The ordinary reed found in Israel has the botanical name 'arundo donax', and was used in bygone days for walking-sticks, measuring-rods, fishing-rods, and musical pipes. Its flowers are produced in late summer and are a dense, dark purple.

3.5 The Lifting Up of the Third Day

An obscure prophecy about Jesus occurred at a critical moment in the life of Joseph, favourite son of Jacob. He was imprisoned in Egypt, locked away because he'd been sold as a slave by his brothers and subsequently falsely accused by his boss' wife. There he met a cupbearer who, two years later, would change his life.

> *Pharaoh was so angry with his two officers—his senior security advisor[87] and his head chef—that he locked them up in the prison dungeon... the very place where Joseph was imprisoned. The captain of the guard entrusted them to Joseph's custody...*
>
> *Each had a dream... When Joseph came to see them in the morning, he noticed how downcast they looked! ...So he asked... 'Why are you so sad today?'*
>
> *'We had a dream,' they replied, 'but there's no one to interpret it.'*
>
> *'Interpretations belong to God,'[88] Joseph told them, 'so please tell me your stories.'*

---

[87] Most translations render this as *cupbearer*—this servant tested Pharaoh's food and drink for poison before it was offered to him. Most translations also render 'head chef' as *baker*.

So the senior security advisor related his dream to Joseph. 'In my dream,' he said, 'all of a sudden there was a vine in front of me! On the vine were three branches that budded. Blossoms shot out, and clusters grew up that produced ripe grapes. Then, with Pharaoh's cup in my hand, I took the grapes, squeezed them into Pharaoh's cup, then handed the cup directly to Pharaoh.'

Then Joseph told him, 'This is what your dream means: The three branches are three days. Within three days, Pharaoh will encourage you and return you to your responsibilities. You'll attend to Pharaoh's personal wine cup, just as you did when you were his senior security advisor...'

When the head chef heard that the interpretation was good, he told Joseph, 'I was also in my dream... there were three baskets with white bread stacked on top of my head. There were all kinds of food in the basket that was on top, including baked food for Pharaoh. The birds were eating them from the basket on my head.'

Joseph replied, 'This is what your dream means: The three baskets are also three days. Within three more days, Pharaoh will behead you and hang you on gallows, where birds will eat your flesh from you.'

On the third day, which just happened to be Pharaoh's birthday, he threw a party for all his servants. He lifted the head of both his senior security advisor and of his head chef in front of his servants—that is, he restored his senior security advisor to his former responsibilities, including attending to Pharaoh's personal wine cup, but he beheaded and hanged the head chef, just as Joseph had interpreted.

Genesis 40:2–22[ISV]

---

88 Joseph uses the ambiguous term 'elohim' for God. This can also mean *gods*, *angels* or *divine beings*. The cupbearer and the baker would have fitted the word 'elohim' into their own grid of understanding about the spiritual world.

On the third day… birthday… lifted up…

These are key resurrection themes: third day, newborn from the dead, lifted up—both on the Cross and from the tomb. But also in the story mix are the serving of wine and restoration from shame: essential elements found in the Cana episode.

3.6 Detour into Design

It's difficult for those of us who are thoroughly imbued with a postmodern worldview to learn to read any writing styled using a chiastic format. Throw into the mix the numerical literary design favoured by the Greeks, and it becomes even harder. From the very beginning of their education, Greek boys were taught that elegant verbal structures required mathematical patterning—a concept that was neither novel nor even limited to the classical world. It existed for many thousands of years across both Europe and Asia until its sudden demise, at least in the west, around the sixteenth century.

John's gospel is a fusion of Greek and Hebrew literary styles, but with a subversive edge to it. No Greek writer trained in the art of combining graceful words and ideal arithmetic would ever start a piece of writing with seventeen words about the *logos*. It's unthinkable. Shocking. Offensive.

But, as far as statements go that the gospel is *not* in accord with Platonic, Pythagorean or Gnostic sensibilities, it's an opening salvo that sets the record straight right from the start. No one at the time would have been under the illusion of later centuries—that John was demonstrating *pro*-Gnostic sentiment. Nor would they have thought that John was an uncultured Galilean who made a mistake and used seventeen by accident. It's clearly deliberate because, as Maarten Menken shows, the syllable count for the words spoken by Jesus' mother is 17. Moreover, the syllable count for all speaking characters apart from Jesus is 153 out of a total of exactly 1000.[89]

And furthermore, alluding once more to all the various notions of time in the Cana story, that pericope is made up of 365 syllables, the number of days in a solar year. As far as the literati of his era would have been concerned, John was very explicit: if any reader missed the fact the sign at Cana was about time, John coded it into the syllables.

Now despite his subversion of the norms, John also paid careful attention to Greek literary conventions. After all, the people of Israel had been subjected to Greek culture and language for centuries—ever since Alexander the Great had conquered the country in 332 BC. Moreover, Greek was the lingua franca of the ancient world, even more so than Latin—it continued to prevail despite the Roman takeover of Judea and Galilee. To send the gospel to the widest possible audience, the Greek language was a natural choice.

The ideal Greek mathematical patterning was based on the human body. John uses instead the poetic form of chiasmus, favoured by the prophets, as his primary structure. For his Jewish audience, the word 'Cana' with its connotation of *reeds* would have evoked, as well as many other stories, that of Moses found by the Egyptian

---

[89] This syllable count is for John 1:35–2:11. Syllable counts, particularly for stressed syllables, are exceedingly important in determining whether a lyric is built into the design. Poems and songs emphasise syllables rather than words. There are, of course, multiples of seven as well: verses 3–4 have 28 words and 9–10 have 49 words for a total of 77. See: Maarten JJ Menken, *Numerical Literary Techniques in John: The Fourth Evangelist's Use of Numbers of Words and Syllables*, Brill 1985

princess Bithiah in a basket amongst the reeds of the Nile.[90] Later he led the Israelites out of Egypt by way of the Sea of Reeds.

But before he was able to do so, he had to persuade Pharaoh to let the people go. His demonstrations of God's power culminated in a series of ten plagues. The first of these plagues was changing the Nile into a river of blood: turning water into blood. At Cana, the *place of reeds*, Jesus turns water into wine—both reminiscent of that plague but also a reversal of it into a blessing.

John's Jewish readers, primed by this hint in Jesus' first sign, would have been encouraged to look for a parallel between the tenth and last plague in Egypt and the greatest and last sign in John's gospel. Something about the Passover, a firstborn son and an exchange of cursing for blessing.

---

90   For the name Bithiah as the identity of Pharaoh's daughter, see 1 Chronicles 4:17–18. Also spelled Bit-Yah or Batyah. She cannot have been born with this name as it means *daughter of Yahweh*.

3.7 Behold the New Messiah

The Egyptian princess Bithiah named her adopted son Moses because he was *drawn from the water*. Moses probably has an inbuilt dedication to the Nile as the river-god, similar to Thutmose, *born of Thoth;*[91] Ptahmose, *Ptah*[92] *is born;* Ramose, *Ra*[93] *bore him;* Ahmose, *Iah*[94] *gave him birth*. However, it also sounds like the Hebrew for 'messiah', *anointed one, deliverer of the people*. By reminding his Jewish readers of the first public miracle of Moses—turning water into blood, even in stone vessels[95]—John was effectively saying, 'This is the new messiah.'

Seth Postell points out that 'the New Greater-than Moses, the Redeemer of Israel, can now be identified through these particular signs! While this message is clearly good news for the Gentiles… the packaging of this message is particularly relevant, first and foremost, especially to the Jews.'[96] The 'packaging' involves the chiastic clues about the first and last signs, along with their foreshadowing in the long-ago first and last plagues of Egypt.

---

91   The deity of wisdom and writing.
92   The craftsman god.
93   The sun god.
94   The moon god.
95   Exodus 7:19
96   Seth Postell, 'The miracle at Cana and what it has to do with Moses', devotional, oneforisrael.org, 24 November 2022

In *The Elijah Tapestry*, we've seen that Jesus was identified in John's first and last chapters as the Word, the Light, the Life, Immanuel, the Christ, the new Moses, the new Jacob, the new Israel, the new Joshua, the Son of Man, the Son of God, the war messiah known as the 'Son of Joseph', the priestly messiah like Melchizedek, and also the Elijah-who-is-to-come.

As we move into the second and second-last chapters, John reinforces these—the new Moses, the new Joshua, the Christ (or Messiah), the new Phinehas (who was the original war messiah). However, he also expands his identification of Jesus to include the new Noah, the new Joseph, and, most importantly, the new Adam.

Jesus mended the brokenness and damage that these men, great leaders that they were, inflicted on the world through their disobedience, defiance or failure to complete the task given to them.

This is John's message to his Jewish readers: Jesus has inaugurated the messianic age. The promise of Isaiah is fulfilled in Him:

> *On this mountain, the Lord of Armies will prepare for all the peoples a feast of choice meat, a feast with aged wine, prime cuts of choice meat, fine vintage wine.*
>
> Isaiah 25:6^{CSB}

This highly poetic tongue-twisting prophecy, 'shamarim shamanim mamuhayim shamarim mazuqaqim'—*aged wine, prime cuts of choice meat, fine vintage wine*—contains a stylish pun. The Hebrew word 'shamarim' is not only *fine wine* but also wordplay for *keepers, stewards* or *watchers*. This refers to the original assignment given to Adam and Eve: guard and protect the Edenic garden.

At Cana there was fine wine. In the garden outside the tomb, there were many watchers—some human and some angelic.

3.8 Reeds and Wicks

WINE WAS A PRECIOUS COMMODITY in the ancient world. People drank it in preference to water which, when it came from wells or pools, would often be contaminated. Wine's antibacterial properties aided digestion and its antioxidants promoted health. Paul advised Timothy:

> *Stop drinking only water, and use a little wine because of your stomach and your frequent illnesses.*
>
> 1 Timothy 5:23[NIV]

The superior wines of the land of Canaan were exported across the Mediterranean in clay amphorae. A lattice of reeds in wet clay was allowed to dry on the tops of the jars and this formed a seal for transporting the containers.

Reeds and wine therefore go together. They are not an unusual combination. And reeds are significant to a prophecy about the Messiah:

> *A bruised reed He will not break, and a smouldering wick He will not snuff out, till He has brought justice through to victory.*
>
> Matthew 12:20[NIV]

Matthew reports Jesus quoting this verse from the prophet Isaiah[97] after He retired to the wilderness once the Pharisees began to harass Him about healing on the Sabbath and allowing His disciples to pluck grain on the Sabbath. In the original of Isaiah's oracle, the word for *reed* is 'qaneh'.

The first time 'qaneh' is used in Scripture is when Pharaoh has a dream about seven plump heads of grain growing on a single stalk. He later uses the same word to tell Joseph what he saw: seven heads on grain on a single 'qaneh' that were swallowed up by seven thin heads of grain, blighted by the east wind—the wind from the *time before*.

The term 'qaneh' is used many times refer to the ornamentation of the lampstand for the Tabernacle. God instructs Moses:

> *Make a lampstand of pure gold. Hammer out its base and shaft, and make its flowerlike cups, buds and blossoms of one piece with them. Six branches are to extend from the sides of the lampstand—three on one side and three on the other.*
>
> Exodus 25:31–32^{NIV}

Each of the six *branches* of the menorah coming out from the central shaft is here referred to as a 'qaneh'. This links the story of Cana straight back to the sevenfold mention of light and the subtle allusion to the menorah in John 1:4–9. It's a lovely, gentle lyrical touch.

So we can see that *reed, stalk* or *branch* are all ways of thinking about 'qaneh'. And perhaps the menorah gives us an insight into why the Israelites saw *reeds* as being evocative of *brothers*. Like an inverted diagram of a 'family tree' with the parents imaged as the

---

97 *A bruised reed he will not break, and a smouldering wick he will not snuff out. In faithfulness he will bring forth justice.* Isaiah 42:3NIV

central trunk, each of the six siblings emerge as light-bringers to the household.

Perhaps John is, with the faintest, most delicate of allusions, actually referring back to that prophecy of Isaiah about the bruised reed and the smouldering wick. After all, one partnering of a reed and a wick together was the golden menorah.

3.9 Bridal Scent

Reed, stalk and branch are not the only ways of thinking about 'qaneh'. When God gave Moses instructions for the interior design of the Tabernacle, He didn't include just directions on the way it should look. There were also recipes for the way it should smell.

> *Take the finest spices: of liquid myrrh 500 shekels, and of sweet-smelling cinnamon half as much, that is, 250, and 250 of aromatic cane and 500 of cassia, according to the shekel of the sanctuary, and a hin of olive oil. And you shall make of these a sacred anointing oil blended as by the perfumer; it shall be a holy anointing oil.*
>
> Exodus 30:23–25[ESV]

Aromatic cane or sweet cane, sometimes called *calamus*, was a special ingredient for the fragrant oil used to anoint the tent, the ark, the table, the utensils, the menorah, the altar of incense, the altar of burnt offering and the brass basin.

We're moving through a matrix of interconnected ideas here: starting with the sevenfold mention of light in the first chapter and the image of the menorah associated with it, we've travelled with the six 'qaneh'-branches and breathed in the 'qaneh'-perfume that anoints them. After the account of the wedding at Cana comes the retelling of the cleansing of the Temple courts because of issues involving the *sanctuary shekel*. These 'qaneh' references should remind us of that sacred precinct where the golden menorah and its 'qaneh' stood, while the aroma of 'qaneh' wafted through the Temple complex.

The perfume of 'qaneh' was, appropriately for the celebration at Cana, a bridal motif.

> *You are a garden locked up, my sister, my bride; you are a spring enclosed, a sealed fountain.*
>
> *Your plants are an orchard of pomegranates with choice fruits, with henna and nard, nard and saffron, calamus and cinnamon, with every kind of incense tree, with myrrh and aloes and all the finest spices.*
>
> Song of Songs 4:12–14^{NIV}

Here, *calamus*—mentioned between saffron and cinnamon, and accompanied by myrrh and aloes—is 'qaneh'.

These spices are significant because, although calamus is not mentioned by name in the chiastic parallel to Cana—the scene in the garden outside Jesus' tomb—we know that Mary was carrying myrrh, spices and aloes or balm. Moreover the air would have been redolent with myrrh since Nicodemus had brought a veritable fortune of that particular aromatic oil there.

This is very significant because myrrh was *not* associated with funerals in Jewish culture. The Israelites did not, as a rule, embalm their dead. That was an Egyptian practice. The Jews buried the deceased the same day as they passed away. Myrrh was not normally associated with such rites. So it was probably a shock to those present when Mary anointed Jesus at Bethany that He said it was for His burial.

The reason it would have been so startling was because myrrh was known as 'oil of joy'. It was traditionally associated with the consummation of a marriage.

3.10 Mountains of Spices

> *You who sit in the gardens, companions are listening for your voice, but let me hear it.*
>
> *Come quickly, my beloved, and be like a gazelle or a young stag on the mountains of spices.*
>
> Song of Songs 8:13–14[ISV]

These are the very last lines of Solomon's Song of Songs, an erotic love poem that has often been interpreted as an allegory[98] of Christ as the Bridegroom of the church. This passage of Scripture is customarily read on the first night of Passover at the end of the Seder. It thus attains enormous significance in terms of the words of Jesus on the Cross and His subsequent burial.

Now the 'mountains of spices' were far from metaphorical. Nicodemus and Joseph of Arimathea wrapped the body of Jesus in a simply enormous quantity of spice and myrrh, contrary to

---

98 Allegory, in my view, is not the right term. There's far too much prophecy involved.

the burial rites John describes for Lazarus.[99] Their actions seem more in keeping with Egyptian embalming—yet that cannot be the case since such techniques, which involved the removal of organs, were considered by the Jews to desecrate the body.

The mountain of spices was therefore new and different. Nicodemus seems to have recognised it wasn't a funeral but a wedding and prepared accordingly. The young man who could be likened to a gazelle or a stag on the mountain of spices was coming. So too, though Nicodemus could hardly have foreseen it, was the woman who sat in the garden as her companions listened for her voice while this same young man came to find her.

The word for *young stag* in the last line of the Song of Songs is ambiguous. It could also be *ram, oak, lofty tree, prominent pillar, chieftain, captain, powerful helper*. Behind these different possible translations is the common notion: *a strong leader of its kind*. This indicates we're not so much looking for a stag on a fragrant hill as a *strong leader* surrounded by lots of aromatic spice.

The first candidate who might qualify is not actually Jesus. Rather it's Joseph, son of Jacob. His brothers had thrown him down a pit, intending to kill him. But when they saw some spice-traders heading their way, they rethought their plan.

---

99 In *Hunting for the Tree of Life: A Spiritual Journey in the Garden Traditions*, Maria Theresa de Donato and Anneli Sinkko point out that an honourable Jewish burial involved washing, anointing, wrapping with spices. However, Arie Uittenbogaard suggests that John's extensive description of the scene outside the tomb of Lazarus is to give the reader a swift education in the 'burial customs of the Jews'. He points out that John carefully links as well as contrasts the burial of Lazarus (and the stinking body) to the scene with Mary of Bethany anointing Jesus (where the fragrance permeated the house). See: abarim-publications.com/Meaning/Nicodemus.html (accessed 6 February 2023)

> *They looked up and saw a caravan of Ishmaelites coming from Gilead. Their camels were carrying spices, balm, and myrrh down to Egypt.*
>
> Genesis 37:25^{NET}

Joseph was sold as a slave to his cousins.[100] On the way down to Egypt, he'd have been kept with the baggage. His clothing would have smelled of myrrh and spice. There, in the land that symbolised 'death' for the Israelites, Joseph suffered unjustly until the time came when he was elevated to rulership and given the name Zaphenath-Paneah, *Saviour of the World*.

Likewise, Jesus—whom Joseph foreshadowed—went down into death surrounded by the aroma of myrrh and spices.

> *Nicodemus… went with Joseph [of Arimathea], taking with him about one hundred pounds*[101] *of spices, a mixture of myrrh and aloes. The two men took Jesus' body and wrapped it in linen cloths with the spices.*
>
> John 19:39–40^{GNT}

Less than a week previously, Mary of Bethany had been castigated for lavishing *one* bottle of spikenard and myrrh on Jesus. Too wasteful, too extravagant, too profligate—those were the criticisms.

Yet Nicodemus goes all out with one *hundred* litra, a veritable mountain in spice-terms.

---

100 The traders are variously described as Ishmaelites, Midianites and Medanites. It seems like a business partnership had been formed by families descended—perhaps even inter-married—from three of Abraham's sons: Ishmael, Midian and Medan. These men were all Joseph's great-uncles.

101 Roman pounds or *litra*.

3.11 Lightning and the Mountain Stag

Just a few days before my dad passed away, he witnessed a breath-taking thunderstorm. Three low-pressure weather cells rammed each other and he observed spectacular splinters of lightning arcing between dark brooding cloud fronts as they collided. My mother later said she thought God was playfully saying to my dad, 'Think you know about electricity? Let Me show you what I can do.'

Gene Eby recognised that the water-wine transformation involved mega-voltages. Back in the first century that understanding shouldn't have been possible for anyone, no matter how scientific their bent. Electricity, as we currently know it, simply didn't enter people's thinking.

They did know that rubbing amber with wool produced tiny sparks, attracting hair and the like.[102] In fact, our word *electricity* comes from the ancient Greek for *amber*, 'elektron'. However as far as multi-million-volt discharges go, their only experience of it would have been lightning—those wild dazzling spears thrown from heaven as black, roiling clouds race by overhead. Yet somehow, despite his obvious ignorance, John was inspired

---

102   This is static electricity, and it is different to the alternating current that supplies our homes and businesses.

to link those stone pots sizzling and zizzling with high-voltage electricity to an image connected with lightning.

Before I explain that connection, let's look at the more common lords of lightning in different cultures. Thor is the hammer-god of Norse mythology, wielder of lightning and thunder. His Greek counterpart is Zeus, and his Roman equivalent Jupiter, both chiefs of their respective pantheons. The corresponding Canaanite deity is Baal-Hadad, the same storm-god that Elijah defeated at Mount Carmel.

These deities are relatively well-known, but there is another far more obscure one—mentioned seven times in the Hebrew Scripture—who was considered a commander of lightning and also regarded as a gatekeeper of the underworld. This godling, symbolised as a stag, is Resheph,[103] allied with the goddess Anat.

Resheph is specifically mentioned in the Song of Songs, just a few verses before the famous last line:

> *Make haste, my beloved, and be like a gazelle or a young stag on the mountains of spices.*
>
> Song of Solomon 8:14[ESV]

However, as we've seen, the translation *stag* is not the only possible rendering of the Hebrew word—it basically means *a strong leader, first and foremost of its kind*. And that's precisely what Jesus was as the firstborn from the dead, laid in the tomb with a mountain of spices.

---

103 Resheph is primarily a deity of scorching heat widely known across the ancient world but very obscure in twenty-first century commentaries. As is often the case with idols or foreign deities, it is reduced to a function in most modern versions of the Bible. It is mentioned in Deuteronomy 32:24 where it is translated *pestilence*; Job 5:7 *flying sparks*; Psalm 76:3 *burning arrows*; Psalm 78:48 *sirocco*; Song of Songs 8:6 *burning coals*; Habakkuk 3:5 *sirocco*. See: Anne Hamilton and Irenie Senior, *Dealing with Resheph: Spirit of Trouble*, Armour Books 2020

And it *was* a veritable 'mountain'. Nicodemus supplied one hundred times the myrrh that Mary had been criticised for squandering so wastefully and extravagantly in anointing Jesus. The women brought much spice as well. Altogether it was a staggering, unrestrained amount.

From the very beginning of his gospel, John tells us that Jesus constantly warred against Resheph, the stag-god, lightning-wielder and doorkeeper of dawn who guarded the gates of the underworld. It's a theme he will return to, more than once, in later chapters. After all Resheph counterfeited Jesus, the lightning-tamer and strong leader who holds the keys of Death and of hell.

When the wine ran out, Jesus' mother said to Him, 'They have no more wine.'

PART 4

So she came
running to
Simon Peter and
the other disciple,
the one whom
Jesus loved.
'They have taken the Lord
out of the tomb,' she said,
'and we do not know where
they have put Him!'

'Because they have taken
my Lord away,' she said,
'and I do not know
where they have
put Him.'

JOHN 20:2; 13 BSB

4.1 Houston, We Have a Problem

When the wine ran out, Jesus' mother said to Him, 'They have no more wine.'

John 2:3[BSB]

So she came running to Simon Peter and the other disciple, the one whom Jesus loved. 'They have taken the Lord out of the tomb,' she said, 'and we do not know where they have put Him!'

John 20:2[BSB]

'Because they have taken my Lord away,' she said, 'and I do not know where they have put Him.'

John 20:13[BSB]

When my niece, appropriately named Mary, was very young she'd become very excited when her mother and father announced that a babysitter was coming. Her eyes would light up. 'Are you going to a wetting?' she'd lisp.[104]

Now wettings and weddings are exactly the problems outlined by John. And both the biblical Marys noticed the issue. In each case a mysterious 'they' are involved. In the first instance, we can easily identify these anonymous people: the hosts of the wedding.

But who are the 'they' that the Magdalene is thinking of? Initially it may seem she is contemplating grave robbers. But is it possible

---

104   'Wettings' meant that small and pretty bags of iced fruit cake would turn up next day.

she was referring to hosts of a different kind—the angels of the Lord of hosts? Or perhaps even to the Father and the Spirit as Hosts of a divine wedding?

There's so much Bridegroom imagery scattered throughout John's gospel that this possibility is not out of the question. Certainly, whether they were aware of it or not, Joseph of Arimathea and Nicodemus, along with the women, prepared a mountain of spices to fulfil the prophecy of a wedding, not a funeral.

We're apt to believe that none of Jesus' followers had faith He would be raised from the dead. However, all through John's account are indications that some of His followers were hopeful He would indeed return from the grave. Even here in Mary's statement we see faint traces of that hope.

The word usually translated *taken* also means *raised* or *lifted*. Is she talking about a body? She never uses a term that suggests she's looking for a lifeless corpse. So is she already expressing the hope He has been *raised* from the dead? Moreover, the word for *put* or *laid down* also means *appointed* or *foundationally established*. It speaks not so much to the notion of simply putting something down, but of having chosen and carefully selected a place to settle.

It's possible Mary was weeping and lamenting loss of relationship, rather than loss of life: *He's gone and we don't know where*. So she enlists the help of Peter and John. In doing so, she fulfils yet another aspect of the Song of Songs.

> *Where has your love gone, most beautiful of women?*
> *Which way has he turned? We will seek him with you.*
>
> Song of Songs 6:1[CSB]

The mountain of spices for the strong leader was built by some of His friends and now others are called out to search for the missing Bridegroom.

4.2 Wedding Perfume

Jesus referred to Himself as 'the Bridegroom'. When the teachers and Pharisees queried Him about the unorthodox behaviour of His disciples, He said:

> *'Can you make the friends of the bridegroom fast while he is with them? But the time will come when the bridegroom will be taken from them; in those days they will fast.'*
>
> Luke 5:34–35^{NIV}

This motif of the Bridegroom links the second and third chapters of John's gospel. Not only does the apostle report the words of the wedding supervisor to the bridegroom here in the second chapter, but three times in the third chapter he quotes John the Baptiser calling Jesus 'the Bridegroom'.[105] This profoundly significant

---

[105] CS Lewis points out that the divine bridegroom is recurrent theme in pagan religion. A ritual of 'holy marriage' with the goddess was a regular feature. He contends that Christ transcends, and thus abrogates, as well as fulfils both Paganism and Judaism in this regard. Furthermore, for 'the mystics, God is the Bridegroom of the individual soul. For the pagans, the god is the bridegroom of the mother-goddess, the earth, but his union with her also makes fertile the whole tribe and its livestock, so that in that sense he is their bridegroom too. The Judaic conception is... the Bride of God is the whole nation, Israel. ...Finally... the Bride becomes the Church, "the whole blessed company of faithful people."' See: CS Lewis, *Reflections on the Psalms*, Harcourt Brace 1958

theme is highly visible at the beginning of the gospel but almost invisible at its end.

Yet the design allows us to realise, through the chiasmus, that the death of Jesus mysteriously involves the consummation of a marriage.

Brian Simmons points out that the final words of Jesus on the Cross, *'It is finished,'* have a much deeper meaning than simply a declaration that a task is accomplished, a mission is completed, a calling is fulfilled. In Aramaic, *'It is finished,'* is the joyful cry of a bridegroom on his wedding night at the consummation of a marriage: *'Kalot!'*

All that myrrh—the 'oil of joy' traditionally associated with such a new and wondrous moment of covenantal oneness—together with the aromatic mountain of spices that Nicodemus, Joseph of Arimathea and the 'bridesmaids'[106] created, indicates a splendid and sumptuous celebration was underway. A royal wedding, culminating in the union of the King of the Universe with His newly-created bride, required—as Nicodemus must have suddenly realised—enough oil of joy to make a statement, to testify to the uniqueness of such extraordinary nuptials.

Myrrh isn't about funerary rites. Arie Uittenbogaard indicates that, in the story of the raising of Lazarus, we are given a swift education into Jewish burial customs. They do not involve precious oils of any kind. Martha was pointedly distressed when Jesus suggested opening the tomb. 'He'll stink!' she exclaimed of her brother. There was no wafting perfume in the vicinity of Lazarus'

---

106   Mary Magdalene, Salome, Joanna, Mary the mother of James and Joseph, and at least one other woman. The various gospel accounts mention different women, though Mary Magdalene is given prominence. It would be very interesting if the final tally is five, suggesting that Jesus' parable about the wise and foolish bridesmaids was intended to be prophetic.

tomb. Not like there was throughout the house when Martha's sister, Mary, anointed Jesus with spikenard and myrrh. But there would have been the scent of myrrh everywhere around the tomb of Jesus, given the staggering amount of it that Nicodemus had acquired.

Uittenbogaard states: 'With his hundred *litre* of myrrh-oil… Nicodemus unmistakably declared that the marriage of God and mankind had been consummated. He never went there to bury Christ; he went there to see Him be "born again," just as Jesus had explained him when the whole Nicodemus cycle started (John 3:3). The only other time that word σμυρνα (*smurna*) occurs in the gospels is in the nativity story, when the magi from the east gave it to Mary and Jesus when He was born the first time (Matthew 2:11).'[107]

---

107 Arie Uittenbogaard, abarim-publications.com/Meaning/Nicodemus.html (accessed 22 November 2022)

4.3 The Messiah's Marriage

The parallelism between the wedding at Cana and the distinctive nuptial references at the tomb of Jesus emphasise an earth-shaking surprise: from the Last Supper, all through His death and burial right up to His meeting with Mary Magdalene in the garden outside the tomb, we're reading about a wedding, not a death.

The climax—the words of Jesus, *'Kalot! It is finished!'*—is not a finale, but a consummation.[108] As Nicodemus stood by the Cross, seeing the blood and water emerge from the pierced side of Jesus, he was obviously reminded of their conversation about new birth. Blood and water, after all, accompany a natural birth.

There must have been a moment, a mind-sparking frisson of inspiration, when Nicodemus realised just what he'd seen. Jesus had told him that he had to be born again of water and the spirit—but 'spirit' in Greek can also indicate 'blood'.[109] Perhaps, as he remembered Jesus' words, his first thought was to dismiss the idea that he'd just been present at a birth because it was too

---

108   'Tetelestai', the Greek word translated in the gospels as *'It is finished,'* can also have the meaning, *'It is consummated.'*
109   Not all Greek words for *spirit* can also mean *blood*, but the word, 'haima', used in reference to the blood that flowed from the pierced side of Jesus can indeed do so.

absurd, too outrageous. Birth doesn't happen through the pierced side of a man.

Then it must have dawned on him. There was once, *just once*, in the entire history of the world when such a birth had actually occurred: when Eve was taken from the side of the first man. Nicodemus has to have realised he was watching the birth of the Bride of Christ, the new Eve.[110] Just as the bride of the First Adam was born from under his heart, so too was the Bride of the Second Adam.

To be 'born again' meant to enter by faith into that wound in the side of Jesus and be brought forth as His child, His Bride, His church. And when Nicodemus understood, he didn't stint about any demonstration of faith. The chances he had a hundred *litra* of myrrh back at home are vanishingly small. He would have had to have sent his servants out, scouring every oil shop in Jerusalem for myrrh and buying it up for the wedding of the Lamb.[111] Nicodemus had become, no doubt to his immense surprise, the 'Friend of the Bridegroom' responsible for ensuring the wedding ran smoothly.

Just as the unnamed table-master at Cana was responsible for ensuring the festivities went well, Nicodemus assumed a similar role at the wedding outside the gates of Jerusalem.

And so it was that Mary Magdalene, one of the bridesmaids awaiting the coming of the Bridegroom, winds up representing the Bride, the new Eve.

---

110 As a teacher of the Law, he would have been conscious that the reading after the Passover meal—extending across the day of Passover when Jesus was crucified—was the bridal canticle, *The Song of Songs*.

111 In a single afternoon, he has to have bought a million dollars' worth of myrrh at today's rate.

Back in Eden, God the Gardener had come in the cool of the day looking for humanity, who had hidden from Him. 'Where are you?' He called.

Now, outside the tomb, in the cool of the morning, Mary as a representative of humanity basically asks the hidden God, dressed as a gardener, 'Where are You?'

The story of Eden reversed illustrates how radically Jesus broke death's curse.

4.4 THE WAR AGAINST ALL

JESUS WASN'T JUST TARGETING THOSE thirty Canaanite godlings at Cana. He had in mind all the 'genii locorum',[112] *local spirits*—principalities who ruled cities, regions and territories. He also aimed to overthrow the other ranks in the hierarchy of governance—the powers and world-rulers mentioned in Paul's letter to the Ephesians.

Irenaeus, a student of John's disciple Polycarp, noted that the church Paul had begun in Ephesus was continued by John. There John encountered Cerinthus, an early Gnostic, whose teaching so horrified him that he finally decided to write his own gospel 'to remove that error which by Cerinthus had been disseminated among men'[113] as well as defend the faith against the Nicolaitans and Gnostics.

Because John was in Ephesus, he would have naturally been encouraged to address the most pressing issues there. What was the *genius loci* of Ephesus? What were its deepest spiritual concerns?

---

112 Genius loci, *spirit of a place*; genii loci, *spirits of a place*; genii locurum, *spirits of places*.
113 Irenaeus, Bishop of Lugdunum, *Against Heresies (Book III, Chapter 11)*, newadvent.org/fathers/0103311.htm (accessed 11 July 2021)

Clinton Arnold points out that Ephesians is the only one of Paul's letters that fails to highlight, front and centre, some local problem. He suggests it was simply unnecessary: absolutely everyone in the ancient classical world knew what Ephesus stood for—magic and sorcery.[114] There the seven sons of Sceva did a roaring trade in delivering people from evil spirits by invoking the *'name of Jesus, whom Paul preaches'*[115] until one particular spirit overpowered them, stripped them naked and battered them senseless. This widely reported spectacle brought about a renewed repentance amongst believers:

> *Many who became believers confessed their sinful practices. A number of them who had been practicing sorcery brought their incantation books and burned them at a public bonfire. The value of the books was several million dollars.*
>
> Acts 19:18–19[NLT]

The Ephesians were sophisticated, wealthy people who knew of the elemental *power of words*. Magic incantation is simply the use of the creative power God invested into words in ways contrary to His will. No wonder John begins his gospel with *The Word*. No wonder he defined so many of the miracles of Jesus as 'signs', so they wouldn't be mistaken for magic. No wonder there is such a strong undercurrent of opposition to spiritual potentates in his gospel.

I think there are several reasons for not naming these entities.

First, the Ephesians would have known anyway.

Second, to name 'Dionysius' might have been, for some people, to exclude 'Bacchus'—and that wasn't the intention.

---

114 Clinton E. Arnold, *Ephesians: Power and Magic : The Concept of Power in Ephesians in Light of Its Historical Setting*, Baker Publishing Group 1997

115 Acts 19:13[NLT]

Third, the 'signs' of Jesus were immensely complex, involving not only attacks on the Canaanite divinities but also vast swathes of the Greek and Roman pantheons.

Fourth, unnaming is the most powerful of all dispossessions. Naming was a royal prerogative in ancient times—so Adam's privilege, granted by God, indicates his regal status. The lack of names for the identification of these spirits is not unique—'the satan' is a title, not a name. So perhaps his cohorts are stripped of names in John's account, since ultimately all names and titles are the property of God.

4.5 The Rulers of This Age

Paul was, in some respects, quite vague when he used the overarching term 'principalities, powers and world-rulers' to describe the spiritual enemies of God and of humanity. Similarly, John was not particularly specific when he wrote of Jesus challenging a variety of pantheons across the contemporary world. But that doesn't mean John was hiding it. It seems concealed to us because the common knowledge of the twenty-first century is different from that of the first. Jesus was in a covert war from His very first miracle. It only became truly overt with an actual declaration of war three years after Cana when He announced He was building His church.

Nevertheless, even before that moment, He was very intentional about reclaiming honorific titles for His Father through His miracles and words. When, for example, He walked on water He was demonstrating that it was not Asherah, so-called 'mistress of serpents' and 'mother of young lions', who had the right to call herself, 'She Who Walks On Water'. Rather this was a title usurped from the Lord of Heaven Himself—and which He had originally shown to be His own when His Spirit moved over the face of the waters in the time before Time, and which He had reiterated was His when He closed the door of the ark of Noah and set it 'walking'[115] on the waters of the Flood.

---

116 Genesis 7:18—the word often translated *float* in this verse is the ordinary word for *walk*.

It's easy to miss the intense level of warfare conducted by Jesus. He opened one battlefront after another, storming the strongholds of principalities who had been given charge of the nations after the Flood.

> *When the Most High gave to the nations their inheritance, when He divided mankind, He fixed the borders of the peoples according to the number of the sons of God.*
>
> Deuteronomy 32:8 ESV

A lot of variation exists in the last words of this verse. Apparently at some stage around a thousand years ago, an influential editor of the Hebrew Masoretic text decided to sanitise the wording and changed 'sons of God' to 'sons of Israel'.

Now this didn't change the number—which, according to the Table of Nations in Genesis 10, was seventy. There were seventy people who went down with Jacob to Egypt, and there were also seventy angel-princes set over the nations of the world—however, their existence is better attested in Canaanite mythology than in the Hebrew Scriptures. After the incident at the Tower of Babel, God reserved Israel to Himself and chose Abram and Sarai to be the beginnings of the family He called His own, while at the same time allowing the peoples of the world to choose their own spiritual ruler from amongst the angel guardians.

So, while the editorial change didn't alter the number, it did remove the supernatural overtones involved with national boundaries, as well as laying the seeds for the idea that monotheism means there are no other gods, rather than that Yahweh is unique and uncreated.

4.6 The Image of God

We're called to be children of God, whatever our nationality. As Paul pointed out in his speech to the people of Athens:

> *From one man*[117] *He made all the nations, that they should inhabit the whole earth; and He marked out their appointed times in history and the boundaries of their lands… 'For in Him we live and move and have our being.' As some of your own poets have said, 'We are His offspring.'*
>
> Acts 17:26–28[NIV]

Paul's first quote here is from the Cretan philosopher Epimenides and his second from his own countryman, the Stoic philosopher Aratus. Paul's acquaintance with the literary scene of his age is attested by his ability to cite these lesser-known writers.

Because of this, the magnitude and complexity of the emotional and spiritual devastation he experienced on the road to Damascus would have been overwhelming. He was heading there, with letters of authority from the chief priests, preparing a new phase of persecution for the Christians, when he had a vision of Jesus

---

[117] Although we might instinctively think Adam here, with the mention of 'nations', Paul is more likely making an oblique reference to Noah and the Table of Nations in Genesis 10.

who—incredibly—quoted part of a line from *The Bacchae*, a play by Euripides, written almost five centuries previously.

Paul testifies to King Agrippa of his own conversion:

> *I heard a voice saying to me in Aramaic, 'Saul, Saul, why do you persecute Me? It is hard for you to kick against the goads.'*
>
> Acts 26:14^{NIV}

To 'kick against the goads' was a common Greek proverb. In the drama by Euripides, the king of Thebes orders his soldiers to arrest anyone worshipping Dionysius, the wine-god who is the son of Zeus and a mortal woman. Dionysius eventually appears as a bright light—the king thinks there are two suns in the sky—calling his persecutor to account[118] with this rebuke, 'You disregard my words of warning… and kick against the goads, a man defying god.'[119]

The parallels are substantial: Paul has orders to arrest the worshippers of Jesus, the son of God and of a mortal woman. He too is blinded by a bright light, just as the king of Thebes was; some words spoken are the same.

It's delightful that Jesus appreciates Greek drama so keenly and can use it so aptly. This tiny razor-sharp fragment cut through the

---

118   quora.com/What-is-the-connection-between-Pauls-Damascus-road-encounter-and-the-play-The-Bacchae-by-Euripides (accessed 11 December 2022)

119   At hermeneutics.stackexchange.com/questions/15474/did-luke-base-the-story-of-pauls-conversion-on-the-ancient-play-the-bacchae-b, Dick Harfield comments that, 'in "kick against the goads" [*pros kentra laktizein*], Luke retains the plural form of the noun 'kentra' which, while maintaining the meter in the *Bacchae*, seems out of place in Acts. Not only are these words surprisingly similar, but Acts says that Jesus quoted a Greek proverb to Paul while speaking Aramaic… Even the situations are similar, with Jesus as the persecuted God in Acts and Dionysus the persecuted god in the *Bacchae*.' (accessed 11 December 2022)

rationalisations and inbuilt denials of Saul's faith-edifice. Jesus' quote is vastly more horrifying than simply implying, 'Saul, you're a man defying God.'[120] It's saying, 'Saul, in your heart of hearts, your image of God is Dionysius—the wine-god who inspires mutilation and homicide.'

Saul's image of God was savage, bloodthirsty, uncaring, abusive. His behaviour matched that image. For us too, the image of God that resides in our hearts is matched by our behaviour.

---

120 Jesus didn't need to actually say these words from the play, 'a man defying god.' In the best rabbinical vein, He quoted part of a line and left His student to mentally fill in the rest.

4.7 The Sons of Zeus

SAUL WASN'T THE ONLY ONE WITH an image-of-God problem. We're created to be imagers of God but when our own internal image of God is skewed, the way we image Him will be too.

John, during his early years, wasn't far behind Saul in acting as if his heart was inclined to identify with Zeus. Jesus was about to enter Jericho when James and John—or perhaps their mother—asked Him to grant a favour. They wanted to sit at His right and left hand when He came into His kingdom. This produced an uproar amongst the other disciples who, perhaps, quite apart from any question of promotion, cottoned on to the pagan overtones of this request.

Jesus certainly did, because He rebuked them for thinking in the way Gentile rulers operate. And I believe He was thinking *spiritual* rulers rather than *human* ones.

Now this incident occurred not long after the Transfiguration. Both James and John had witnessed Jesus in His glory and heard the voice of the Father out of the cloud. Obviously they'd been mulling over the vision, trying to create some sort of reference grid for understanding the experience. We might think they'd slot it into the radiant cloud accompanying God's visitation with Moses on the summit of Mount Sinai. But no.

As Jeremiah said, the heart is wicked and deceitful above all things and, in their minds, the image they'd conjured was apparently Zeus, the ruler of Olympus. Not totally unexpected—after all, Mount Hermon, the peak of the Transfiguration, was the Canaanite version of Greek Olympus. The ruler of the seventy principalities who had their palaces on its snow-clad slopes was Baal-Hadad, the local counterpart of Zeus. These storm-gods both wield weapons of wild lightning and deafening thunder.

At the start of this book, I recounted the story of Gene Eby who was inspired to believe that a ceramic insulator had to exist that would carry millions of volts—simply because the stone pots Jesus used at Cana had to be able to withstand that sort of power. Jesus isn't wielding lightning bolts in that story—He's taming them.

And further He clearly understood how James and John thought because, even before they came to Him with their request to sit at His right and left hand, He'd dubbed them 'Sons of Thunder'. This alludes to the mythological twins, Castor and Pollux, who were often represented in art as sitting on either side of the throne of Zeus. The term 'Sons of Thunder' is reminiscent of the title 'Dioscuri', *sons of Zeus*, given to Castor and Pollux, better known in their guise as the constellation and star sign Gemini.

The story of the two brothers, James and John, counterpoints the Dioscuri. Most scholars think they were dubbed 'Boanerges', *sons of thunder*, because they wanted to call down fire from heaven on a Samaritan village. That event occurred right in this same time period: somewhen between the Transfiguration and getting to Jericho.

But Jesus doesn't want them to image God like the lustful lightning-zapper, Zeus. Even though they'd known Jesus for several years at this stage, they still had no idea what God is like. Their thinking was so far off that it must have frustrated Him immensely. Most likely, they didn't even realise how deeply their view of Jesus and the Father was influenced by tales of the Greeks who had been overlords of Israel for centuries before the Romans.

So He called it out bluntly. Just as He called Paul's deep-seated idolatry out into the open.

Jesus continues to do this for us today. But generally, we ignore His rebukes because we don't really believe He'd ever wield a surgical knife.

4.8 'WHERE IS THE LORD?'

DURING THE DAYS OF ELIJAH, the king of Israel was encouraged by his Phoenician wife to invite 450 prophets of Baal and 400 prophets of Asherah to his court as advisers and influencers. Elijah confronted these prophets on Mount Carmel, but it isn't revealed which Baal he was opposing. However, it was clearly the rain-bringer, Baal-Hadad, the son of Asherah. Hadad was not only the ruler of the seventy 'young lions', he was called the 'cloud-rider'.

Elijah informed the king of Israel at the beginning of his ministry that no rain would fall again until he gave the word.[121] This was an open challenge to Baal-Hadad: if he were truly the storm-bringer, then Elijah's silence shouldn't make a jot of difference.

Now Ahab, the king of Israel, had married a wife to secure a political alliance with the maritime trading empire centred at Tyre and Sidon.[122] His bride was Jezebel and her father, the priest Ethbaal, bestowed on her a name straight from the liturgical rites of Baal-Hadad. 'Jezebel' means *where is the prince?* or *where is the lord?* It was the cry of faithful worshippers who gathered at the

---

121 1 Kings 17:1
122 Although 1 Kings 16:31 only identifies him as the king of Sidon, Josephus also adds in Tyre. He was a priest of Baal who assassinated Pheles, the king of Tyre, and took his throne for 32 years.

start of spring to welcome Baal-Hadad as he returned from his winter sojourn in the underworld. The worshippers would stand outside a cave, chanting and waiting, ready to greet the prince as he appeared. 'Where is the Lord?' was their ritual call.

That cry originated with the goddess Anat. After Baal had been killed, his sister Anat went about mourning and looking for him. Eventually finding her brother's body, she took it to his mountain abode and buried it. After three days, she went looking for it and finding that Mot, the lord of death, had taken it, she attacked him viciously. The fact that Mot is also her brother doesn't factor into her behaviour. She's completely without mercy. She splits him, winnows him, burns him, grinds him. She made absolutely sure that Death was dead. After that, she went about, still searching for Baal and calling, 'Iy zbl B'l arṣ?', *Where is the Prince, Lord of the Earth?*[123]

Part of her cry, 'Iy zbl', entered the religious rites of Baal and ultimately became the name 'Jezebel'. It's no coincidence that so much of this story is reminiscent of the resurrection of Jesus. He ripped Baal's claims apart, stitch by stitch.

Elijah had started the ripping, but had not completed it. Back in his day, three years of drought went by before Jezebel's husband, Ahab, agreed to a showdown between Yahweh and Baal-Hadad. Yahweh demonstrated His power on Mount Carmel, and torrents of flooding rain came in from the sea. However, Jezebel was livid over the massacre of the prophets of Baal. She messaged Elijah:

> *May the gods deal with me, be it ever so severely, if by this time tomorrow I do not make your life like that of one of them.*
>
> 1 Kings 19:2[NIV]

---

123 See: smokingaziggurat.com/he-will-swallow-up-death-for-ever-struggles-with-death-in-the-baal-epic-and-the-bible/ (accessed 22 December 2023)

The substance of Jezebel's death threat was a call for the brothers and sisters of Baal-Hadad to avenge the insult to their family honour. She'd upped the ante and basically told Elijah he might be able to take on one of the 'young lions', but how did he feel about *all* of them massed against him? All, including the ferocious Anat.

As it transpired, he felt terrified. He panicked and fled. Even after his encounter with God at Horeb, he was still so unsettled he never truly resumed his prophetic office.[124]

Now Jezebel's daughter Athaliah was married to Joram, king of Judah. Athaliah took after her opportunistic grandfather Ethbaal. After Joram died, she seized the throne at the time her son Ahaziah was killed. She assassinated all but one of the remaining royal males, ruling for seven years until the rightful heir to the throne was brought out of hiding.[125]

Now the genealogy in the first chapter of Matthew's gospel skips several generations. It mentions Joram, but not Ahaziah, Joash or Amaziah. It therefore occludes Athaliah and the three generations after her, obscuring the fact that Jesus' ancestry contains both Athaliah and Jezebel.

Jesus not only had to deal with this aspect of His bloodline, He also had to mend the historical rifts and generational trauma Jezebel brought to the land and its people. In addition, He had to deal with Baal-Hadad and the other 'young lions' of the Canaanite pantheon as well as their 'mother' Asherah.

Now Mary Magdalene spoke three times of her concern regarding where the Lord was *raised, lifted* and *taken*. We might not notice

---

[124] As pointed out in the first book in this series, *The Elijah Tapestry*, his failure had immense repercussions. His mantle passed to Elisha, then Jonah, then John the Baptiser, then to Jesus who handed it to Simon Peter to complete the assignment of preaching to the Gentiles that Elijah had forsaken through his unwillingness to anoint Hazael.

[125] 2 Chronicles 22–23

one query but, by the third occasion, we should realise she was articulating a significant question. She said much the same thing to Peter and John as she did to the angels and she even asked Jesus Himself, believing He was the gardener. Her basic question, *'Where is the Lord?'* has multiple overtones. It reflects the search of the bride and bridesmaids for the bridegroom in the *Song of Songs*. Yet it was also the cry of the worshippers of the 'Cloud-rider'—a title Jesus reclaimed from Baal-Hadad for Himself while on trial in the court of Caiaphas.

The war of Jesus against Baal-Hadad involves total despoilation—names, titles, liturgy, symbols, ritual, a storyline involving a return from death after a sojourn in the underworld—all are seized and reclaimed for their rightful Owner. Nothing is left to the leader of the young lions. Elijah had presided over the slaughter of the prophets of Baal-Hadad but Jesus went even deeper in removing his influence: He took back everything the counterfeit Cloud-rider had stolen. He ransacked Canaanite religion.

He was helped by Mary Magdalene who, like Anat, mourned and buried her lord then three days later went looking for him while asking continually, 'Where is the Lord?'

The Lord of all was never the lightning-lord, Baal-Hadad—nor his Greek counterpart, Zeus. In razing their influence across the nation of Israel, Jesus of Nazareth automatically healed the defilement that permeated His bloodline.

The Israelites tended to use Baal-Hadad's alternative name, Rimmon. Thought to mean *thunder*,[126] Rimmon was the name of the storm-god in Damascus.[127]

---

126 It can also mean *pomegranate*.
127 The father of one of several Syrian kings called Ben-Hadad, *son of the cloud-rider, Baal-Hadad*, was Tabrimmon, *Rimmon is good*, thus showing the dedication to the same deity from one generation to the next.

After he was healed from leprosy, the Aramean army commander Naaman informed Elisha of his obligation to escort his master into Rimmon's temple in Damascus. He asked in advance for forgiveness, since his intention from then on was to worship only Yahweh.

If there's any lingering doubt about the connection between the death and resurrection of Jesus and the rites of Baal-Hadad, then Zechariah's prophecy should dispel them. Zechariah makes an explicit link between deep mourning for Hadad-Rimmon and the death of Jesus:

> *Then I will pour out... on the people of Jerusalem a spirit of grace and prayer, and they will look on Me, the One they have pierced. They will mourn... and grieve bitterly for Him as one grieves for a firstborn son.*
>
> *On that day the wailing in Jerusalem will be as great as the wailing of Hadad-rimmon in the plain of Megiddo.*
>
> Zechariah 12:10–11^{BSB}

Both the angels and Jesus Himself draw attention to the weeping of Mary in the garden. Her action, however, is integral to the takedown of Baal-Hadad and all associated with this fallen angelic prince.

---

128   Hadad-Rimmon is thought to be the town where King Josiah was shot by the archers of Pharaoh Necho, though neither Chronicles nor Kings mentions the exact location. Alternatively, it is thought to be a double lament: first for Josiah and second for the genocide in which only six hundred men of the tribe of Benjamin survived by fleeing to the Rock of Rimmon, a cave in the wilderness near Gibeah. Certainly it is fitting to describe Josiah as 'pierced' since he was shot by an arrow, but regardless of these possibilities, the name Hadad-Rimmon serves the purpose in Zechariah's prophecy of showing Jesus' comprehensive defeat of the head of the Canaanite pantheon under whatever guise or name.

PART

John 2:4-5 BSB

'Woman, why does this concern us?' Jesus replied. 'My hour has not yet come.' His mother said to the servants, 'Do whatever He tells you.'

FIVE

John 20:3-6 BSB

Then Peter and the other disciple set out for the tomb.
The two were running together,
but the other disciple outran Peter
and reached the tomb first. He bent down and looked in
at the linen cloths lying there, but he did not go in.
Simon Peter arrived just after him.
He entered the tomb and saw the linen cloths lying there.

5.1 'WOMAN'

> 'Woman, why does this concern us?' Jesus replied. 'My hour has not yet come.'
>
> His mother said to the servants, 'Do whatever He tells you.'
>
> John 2:4–5[BSB]

> 'Woman, why are you weeping?' they asked...
>
> 'Woman, why are you weeping?' Jesus asked. 'Whom are you seeking?'
>
> John 20:13;15[BSB]

SCHOLARLY INTERPRETATION OF SCRIPTURE rarely includes the thought that the rules for writing detective novels can apply to the text. David Steinmetz, however, in *Miss Marple Reads the Bible*[129] suggests this is sometimes a fruitful approach. Behind certain baffling surface storylines exists a coherent 'second narrative' designed so 'that at the end all of the small parts fall together into an intelligible pattern.'

Any break in pattern, anything out of place, is a salient clue. Julia Hejduk points out that an additional feature of the detective novel with biblical relevance is the Stubborn Fact. 'A solution that accounts for 99 facts but leaves a single, small contradictory

---

129 *Miss Marple Reads the Bible* is actually the title of the second chapter in the more prosaically named *Taking the Long View: Christian Theology in Historical Perspective*. But why be prosaic when you can be memorable?

one must be wrong. Moreover, the Stubborn Fact is usually the key to solving the case, often leading to a radically different interpretation.'[130]

Many commentators indicate it wasn't offensive in the first century to say, 'Woman!' Hejduk, however, points to the Stubborn Fact it was insolent to speak to your mother that way in that society.

So why did Jesus do it? Because this is about *the woman*, not just *any* woman, but THE woman. The first one, the woman so covenantally united with her husband that initially he didn't even give her a name. He simply saw her as the other Adam, *'bone of my bones and flesh of my flesh'*.

Back in the garden, God had declared to the serpent:

> *'I will put enmity between you and the woman, and between your seed and her seed. He will crush your head, and you will strike his heel.'*

Genesis 3:15[BSB]

In the Greek legend of Persephone, Zeus transformed himself into a serpent and ravished her. She bore a horned child Zagreus who was attacked and butchered by the Titans, but this death was also the birth of Dionysius. Consequently he was called 'twice-born', and Jesus' war against him was just as intense as His policy of annihilation against Zeus and Baal-Hadad.

Some authors are tempted, by the realisation the Magdalene represents the Bride of Christ, towards the view she was married to Jesus. John effectively removes that possibility by *also* symbolising Jesus' mother as the new Eve.

---

130 churchlifejournal.nd.edu/articles/the-riddle-at-cana-mary-and-the-biblical-mystery/ (accessed 29 November 2022)

Yet there's still another layer. A Jewish reader of the first century, reading either of these stories in Greek, would have been aware that the dialogue has been translated from Aramaic conversations. The original word for *woman* used by Jesus to address either of the Marys would have been "anath".[131] That would have been a reminder of and pointer to the Canaanite goddess Anat, whose name in Greek was Anath. She is that fierce goddess first mentioned in Scripture during the time of Joseph's governorship of Egypt.

---

131 chaimbentorah.com/2013/01/devotional-john-24/ (accessed 25 August 2023)

5.2 Dreams

OF ALL THE CLUES INTO THE 'SECOND NARRATIVE'—that hidden layer just below the surface—the most important in my view are Scriptural quotes. Sometimes these come from the Greek Septuagint, rather than the original Hebrew. And the translators of twenty-two centuries ago didn't always reach for the same nuances of wording as the translators of today. So, instead of perfect matches, we wind up with strong echoes instead.

That said, in this instance we do have remarkable congruences of wordings. The literal translation of *'Why does this concern us?'* is 'What for you and me?' It's a cultural idiom going back centuries. The widow of Zarephath used it speaking Elijah, some demons used it speaking to Jesus.[132]

Now, as Julia Hejduk points out, when Mary implies Jesus should deal with the wine problem, she's asking Him to assume the bridegroom's responsibilities. It goes much further than fixing a problem. She's asking Him to reveal Himself as the Saviour of the World. Her very next words make that clear: *'Do whatever He tells you.'*

---

132   Mark 5:7

This quote comes from Genesis. When the Egyptians had no food left during the seven-year famine, Pharaoh told them to go to Joseph, the man he'd named Zaphenath-Paneah, 'saviour of the world': *'Do whatever he tells you.'*

Perhaps those words seem to be a little too simple and ordinary to qualify as a distinctive quote we can pin with certainty into the Joseph story. Yet that's the only other time in Scripture when these words occur. And, to confirm it is indeed a quote, there's another snippet of dialogue—just as simple, just as ordinary—that is to be found in the second-last chapter and that, as we're about to see, is first used in the saga of Joseph.

John is unmistakably pointing us to Joseph of Egypt. This is the point of his chiastic parallel—he's informing us that Jesus is more than the Bridegroom, He is also the Saviour of the World, the new Joseph—the One who will rectify Joseph's mistakes and failures. The first Joseph was a dreamer and an interpreter of dreams. Jesus, however, is the one who makes dreams come true.

Joseph, Pharaoh's right-hand man, came to power by correctly interpreting two dreams while he was in prison. When the cupbearer belatedly remembered Joseph's skill after Pharaoh was troubled by a pair of nightmares, Joseph was suddenly catapulted from prison to palace. All because he accurately divined the meaning of the cupbearer's own dream:

> *There was a vine before me, and on the vine were three branches. As it budded, its blossoms opened and its clusters ripened into grapes. Pharaoh's cup was in my hand, and I took the grapes, squeezed them into his cup, and placed the cup in his hand.*
>
> Genesis 40:9–11[BSB]

As happens in a dream, the transitions occur instantly. The vine budded, blossomed and bore fruit in a moment. Immediately the cupbearer squeezed the grapes into a cup and handed it to his master. No season for growing clusters, no months of ripening, no delay for ingathering and pressing, no maturing of wine: it all happens in a smooth swift sequence.

Jesus takes the essence of this dream—with all its preternatural timelessness—bringing it into reality inside six stone pots. Jesus made the cupbearer's impossible dream come true. *Literally*.

5.3 Quoting Genesis

His mother said to the servants, 'Do whatever He tells you.'

John 2:4^{BSB}

'Woman, why are you weeping?' Jesus asked. 'Whom are you seeking?'

John 20:15^{BSB}

Two dialogue quotes, both seemingly mundane and inconsequential, but both straight from the account of Joseph's life.

When extreme hunger came to all the land of Egypt and the people cried out to Pharaoh for food, he told all the Egyptians, 'Go to Joseph and do whatever he tells you.'

Genesis 41:55^{BSB}

When Joseph arrived at Shechem, a man found him wandering around in the fields and asked him, 'What are you looking for?'

Genesis 37:14–15^{NIV}

The question, *'What are you looking for?'* asked by the stranger at Shechem can also mean, *'Who are you looking for?'*

When Jesus, a seeming stranger, is speaking to Mary Magdalene, He poses precisely the same question. The Greek of *'Who are you looking for?'* can also be *'What are you looking for?'*

At the beginning of his gospel John evokes the opening of Genesis, then touches on Jacob's story by mentioning the ladder of angels, before harking back to Joseph. He confirms the first ever-so-subtle allusion with a back-up from the same saga. Joseph replies to the stranger at Shechem:

> 'I'm looking for my brothers...'
> 'They have moved on from here,' the man answered.
>
> Genesis 37:16–17^{NIV}

This interlude with the stranger is, on the surface, completely unnecessary to Joseph's story. It doesn't make the slightest difference to the plotline that Joseph needed directions from a stranger to find his brothers. So much detail is left out of other stories there must be vital reason for the inclusion of this tiny episode. Over the years I've often puzzled over why this stranger is so crucial to the story we have to have his exact words.

John reveals the reason: it's because the stranger is prophetic of Jesus, unrecognised, as He spoke to Mary Magdalene in the garden. Just as the stranger directed Joseph to find his brothers, so Jesus directed Mary Magdalene to do the same. She was called to stand in for Joseph in a mending of an ancient rupture between brothers.

It is not just the reversal of Eden with its restoration of a vertical dimension—the opening of the way between mankind and God—that Mary participates in. She also takes part in the horizontal dimension—the repair of a dysfunctional human family.

5.4 Boundaries

MAKING A DREAM COME TRUE at the level Jesus did seems like magic. It's therefore important to clarify the difference between magic and miracle. Perhaps because he was in magic-obsessed Ephesus, John apparently referenced what Jesus did as 'signs'.

But let's not bypass the issue. One reason our age refuses to believe in miracle is because we don't believe in magic. We invoke science as an explanation for the inexplicable by defaulting to Arthur C. Clarke's dictum that any sufficiently advanced technology is indistinguishable from magic.

Yet the Bible refers to magic as real. When Moses, by the power of God, called down plagues, these events were able to be duplicated at first:

> *The Egyptian magicians did the same things by their secret arts.*
>
> Exodus 7:22^{NIV}

Paul speaks of these sorcerers in what is believed to be his last letter—to Timothy in Ephesus, that hotbed of magic. So Paul's reference to magicians makes sense in the context of Timothy's circumstances:

> *Just as Jannes and Jambres opposed Moses, so these men oppose the truth. They are depraved in mind and their faith is a counterfeit.*
>
> 2 Timothy 3:8[ISV]

Such comments beg the question: what differentiates miracle from magic? The first is encouraged as a sign of faith; the second forbidden as an occult practice. At the risk of over-simplifying, an appropriate core definition of magic is: any attempt to take the creative power God has invested into words and use them against Him, or any attempt to take the redemptive power God has invested into blood and use it against Him.

Now apart from any intent to speak into being something out of line with God's will, one easy way to spot magic is by its boundary-transgressing nature. The satan said to Jesus: *'If you are the Son of God, tell this stone to become bread.'* [133] These temptations in the wilderness had occurred a mere week before the wedding at Cana. They'd happened on Yom Kippur, the Day of Atonement, the same day John the Baptiser was confronted by the leaders sent from Jerusalem. The events of John the Apostle's opening chapter all occur in the week between Yom Kippur and Sukkot.

The satan's temptation involves boundary-crossing. God made plants according to their kinds, fish and birds according to their kinds, beasts according to their kinds.[134] To change stone into bread would transgress these divinely ordained boundaries. Bread does not come from stones.

There's nothing prohibited about multiplying bread from bread as Jesus did in a later sign because that's what normally happens when a seed is planted and a head of grain eventually appears.

---

133 Luke 4:3[NIV]
134 Genesis 1:12; 21; 25

Nor is there anything prohibited about creating wine from water: wine is mostly water.[135] Every day in vineyards, water and trace minerals are transformed by the process of photosynthesis into grapes for the production of wine. Without water and light, there's no wine. This sign performed by Jesus is in complete accord with what the Creator continually does each day in grape vines. In all that Jesus does and did, He maintains the allotted boundaries between kinds.

The theme of the epistle of Jude—a brother of Jesus who was almost certainly present during the wedding at Cana—is about the wreck that follows such boundary-transgression, either by word or action. We invite disaster into our lives and society by ignoring this principle.

Ultimately, a miracle is an intervention by God in which a physical law is unexpectedly overridden but where there is no transgression of moral law or divine sanction. Magic, on the other hand, is an intervention by a human being in which the creative power of words and/or the redemptive power of blood is used to manipulate events, without regard for moral law or divine sanction.

Consider, given these distinctions, the opening of the Red Sea. It's possible to view God's intervention in several ways. One is that God, at the moment Moses lifted his staff, pushed back all the physical laws of ocean, tide, currents and gravity to divide the sea. Alternatively, knowing there would be a window of opportunity at a specific moment in history when the Red Sea would roll back, very much as the prelude to a tsunami, He brought the people of Israel *to the exact spot* where it would happen *at the exact time* it would happen.

---

135 80–90%.

Now, because I believe God keeps His own rules, even physical laws, I prefer the second interpretation.[136] In fact, to me, it's actually the greater miracle—because getting the sea to obey is relatively easy compared to getting millions of people to follow directions.

Thus, the crossing of the Red Sea, like the miracle at Cana, can be understood as a miracle of timing. Both are threshold events, both occur at the beginning of a new era, both are named for *reeds*. The Red Sea is, in Hebrew, 'Yam Suph', often translated *sea of reeds*. Yet 'suph' is poetically evocative of 'saph', *threshold*, reminding us that reeds mark the verge between land and water, while 'yam', *sea*, whispers to us of 'yom', *day*. The 'Yam Suph', on a physical level, speaks of the *sea of reeds*, but on a spiritual one it indicates the *threshold of day*—a new dawn.

Just as Cana does.

Just, in fact, as the empty tomb on the day of resurrection does.

---

136 Now you may wonder how I can say God keeps His own rules, particularly in the light of events like the sun and the moon standing still when Joshua asked for more time (again, *time!*) in his battle against the five Amorite armies. One scientific explanation is that a large celestial body, such as a comet, come close enough to earth for the gravitational interaction to cause a change in our planet's rotation. This would also account for the stones (be they hailstones or meteorites) that dropped out of the sky on the fleeing armies. God is not therefore violating any physical law He has set in place, but overriding one natural principle with another. Once again, it's a matter of timing and of listening. The intervention of God is to inspire Joshua to ask for the impossible on the one day it would be granted in the 'natural' course of events.

5.5. Appointments

'MY HOUR HAS NOT YET COME.'

A repeated theme throughout John's gospel is the consciousness of Jesus about an appointed hour, an assigned time. *'My time is not yet come,'* He told His brothers when they tried to persuade Him to attend the Feast of Tabernacles in Jerusalem—a year or two later.[137] He amplified the idea by explaining that, for them, any time will do, but it isn't so for Him.[138] Jesus did eventually follow them. John then reported the attempts of the authorities to seize Him—thwarted because His time had not come.[139] Similarly, when He was teaching in the Temple courts, no one apprehended Him because, once again, His time had not yet come.[140]

On the other hand, there are times when Jesus declares openly, *'The hour has come.'* He says this in reference to the dead hearing the Son of God,[141] and in regard to worshipping the Father in Spirit and truth.[142] Most mysterious of all is the arrival of the

---

137 John 7:6
138 John 7:8
139 John 7:30
140 John 8:20
141 John 5:25
142 John 4:23

Greeks who want to speak to Jesus and whose request is met with the enigmatic response, *'The hour has come for the Son of Man to be glorified.'*[143] The way John presents the story it appears the advent of these Gentiles was a trigger for Jesus to recognise the hour of His glorification was at hand.

Most mystifying are the declarations that occur during Sukkot in different years: the not-yet-but-now hours. In both cases Jesus expresses initial reluctance to respond to a request by members of His family. First, there's the problem with the wine at Cana and, in a subsequent year, His hesitancy when His brothers urged Him to get moving on some 'brand recognition' by performing some miracles in Jerusalem.

Although the time is not right in either instance, it somehow becomes right. It's made right. It's as if Jesus summons 'kairos', *appointed time,* to supplant 'kronos', *ordinary time.*

This is evident when He showed that He is the Lord of Time by compressing the season of wine-making into the amount of time it took the servants to fill the water pots. It's not so much the water-to-wine transformation that is miraculous—after all, water, trace minerals and light are the primary requirements for grape production and they were all in ready supply—it's the time taken.[144]

Jesus emphasises the time aspect in His statement, *'My hour has not yet come.'* Yet He makes it so. He calls the appointed time to Him, He summons it as simply as He beckoned the servants and attendants, He demonstrates His authority over the hours, days, Sabbaths and seasons right from the start.

No wonder His disciples believed in Him.

---

143 John 12:23[NIV]

144 Quality wine in the twenty-first century is about 87% water, 12% alcohol and 1% flavouring.

5.6 Risk

> *Then Peter and the other disciple set out for the tomb. The two were running together, but the other disciple outran Peter and reached the tomb first. He bent down and looked in at the linen cloths lying there, but he did not go in.*
>
> John 20:3–5[BSB]

The mention of running is so detailed there must be some deeper significance to it.[145] Mary ran to inform the disciples of the angelic message and the missing body, then Peter and John ran to investigate. Is 'running' an evocation of the bride's words in the fourth verse of Song of Songs, *'Let us run together! The king has brought me into his chambers'*?[146]

---

145 There is a possibility that the running motif may be a reference to the Canaanite legend concerning the death of Baal-Hadad. When the news of Baal's death is reported to the assembly of the gods, Bull El in his guise as Latipan, *shroud-face*, remarks that no one can run like Baal or release the lightning at the appointed time. Admittedly this is not only very subtle but it's also questionable if John knew Canaanite myth all that well. However it does link several thematic elements notable in these chiastic sections: running, lightning, appointed time, the death of Baal-Hadad and all of the contrasts Jesus brings into play at His resurrection.

146 Song of Songs 1:4[NASB] Perhaps too, this allusion is stitched together with Psalm 19:5 and the image of the sun as a bridegroom coming forth from his chamber and rejoicing to run his course. The other possible allusion is to the first incident of running in the Bible: Abraham running to greet God and the two angels. Jesus and two angels, after all, are present later in this scene.

John's passage is difficult to interpret because it's so often filtered through our own cultural competitiveness. Most commentators suggest that John was trying to elevate himself at Peter's expense. However, given he was about to reveal that Peter received Elijah's mantle, it might not be a putdown but an explanation. There's a widespread tendency to see John as aggrandising himself here. One commentator even went so far as to suggest that John was pointing out he is more courteous and has more 'tomb etiquette' than rash, brash Peter—as if tombs were opened and unsealed on such a regular basis that 'tomb etiquette' would actually need to exist!

However, if John is preparing his reader for the imminent revelation of Peter as the successor of Elijah, Elisha and Jonah and it's not a criticism, then what is he saying about himself? I think there's a strong possibility it was this: 'Peter was much more courageous than I was. I was cautious, wary. Pilate had placed cursing seals on the tomb to deter grave robbers. I didn't know what they invoked. Just entering was a hazard, perhaps a death sentence. But Peter—the only one of us who'd walked on water—didn't hesitate. He was a risk-taker and went in before me. Eventually, I followed.'

If this is John's point, then he's also suggesting that, whatever precedence in time we might enjoy through reaching an appointed place first, we can miss out through fear. The 'kairos' moment can pass us by. John, of course, didn't lose the chance to enter the tomb and witness its emptiness, but perhaps he came close.

Within these paired chiastic stories, one matching theme is a willingness to risk. There was evidently a risk for Jesus in summoning the 'kairos' moment at Cana. It wasn't the right time to announce Himself publicly.

But risk is also an element of faith. And perhaps that's John's message: he twice came to believe because he risked enough to take a look.

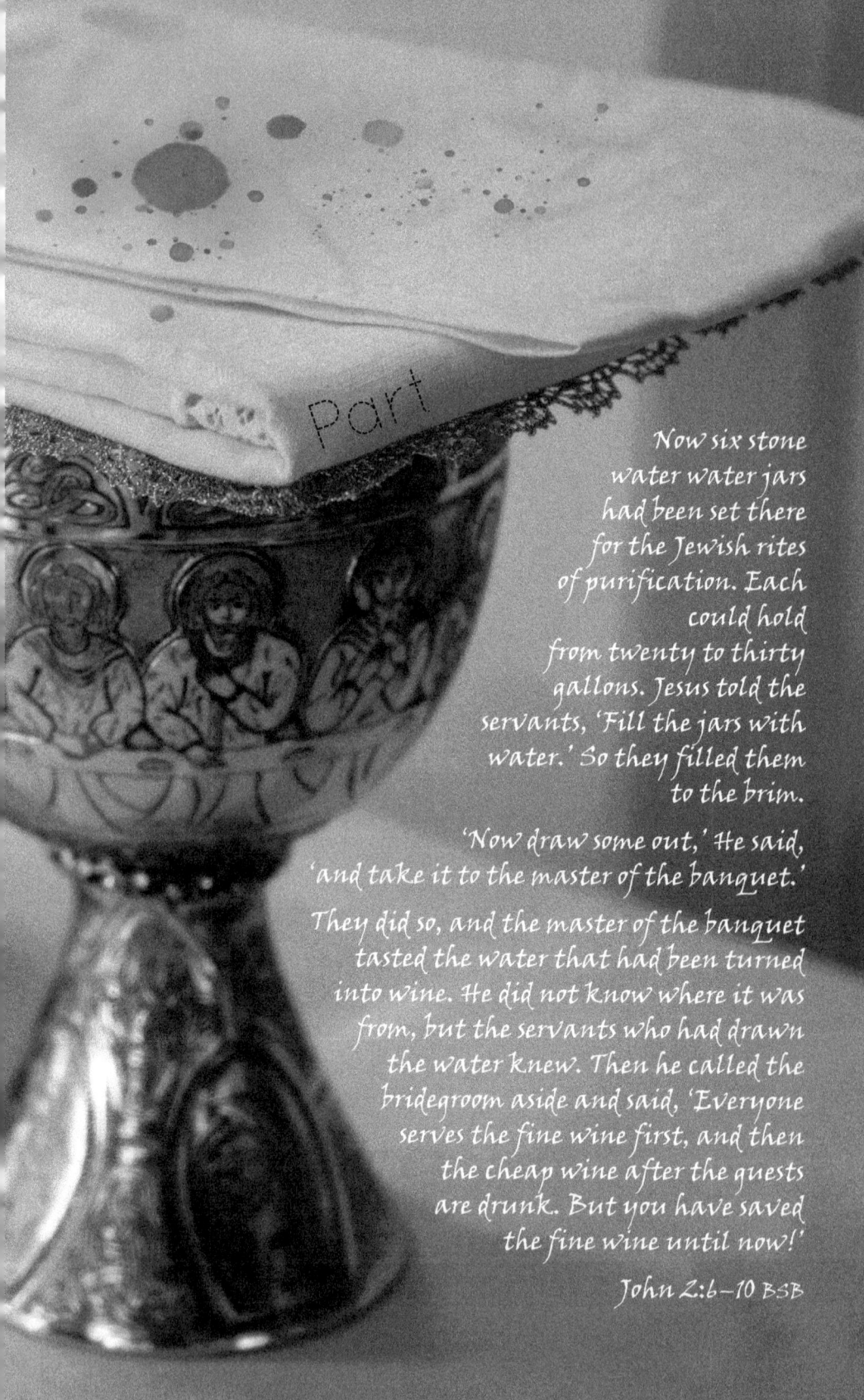

Now six stone water water jars had been set there for the Jewish rites of purification. Each could hold from twenty to thirty gallons. Jesus told the servants, 'Fill the jars with water.' So they filled them to the brim.

'Now draw some out,' He said, 'and take it to the master of the banquet.'

They did so, and the master of the banquet tasted the water that had been turned into wine. He did not know where it was from, but the servants who had drawn the water knew. Then he called the bridegroom aside and said, 'Everyone serves the fine wine first, and then the cheap wine after the guests are drunk. But you have saved the fine wine until now!'

John 2:6–10 BSB

He bent down and looked in
at the linen cloths lying there,
but he did not go in.

Simon Peter arrived just after him.
He entered the tomb and saw
the linen cloths lying there.
The cloth that had been around
Jesus' head was rolled up,
lying separate from
the linen cloths.
Then the other disciple,
who had reached the tomb first,
also went in.

John 20:5-8 BSB

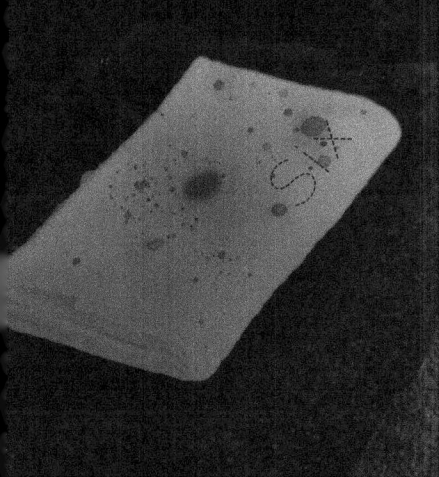

6.1 Fine, Fine Wine

> *On this mountain the Lord Almighty will prepare a feast of rich food for all peoples, a banquet of aged wine—the best of meats and the finest of wines. On this mountain He will destroy the shroud that enfolds all peoples, the sheet that covers all nations; He will swallow up death forever.*
>
> Isaiah 25:6–8[NIV]

WHEN JESUS SAID TO HIS MOTHER, 'My hour has not yet come,' perhaps He was hinting that there was not only an appointed time for Daniel's prophecy to be fulfilled, but Isaiah's too. This wedding in Cana wasn't the appropriate time or place. Isaiah pointed to Jerusalem and the swallowing up of death.

Yet John, in his gospel, links the two. The provision of fine wine for a multitude is, in his chiastic design, paired with the resurrection, with the death of Death.

And Jesus created such a copious supply of wine it was enough for thousands of people. The six stone jars were capable of holding a staggering amount—between 600 and 900 of today's bottles.[147]

---

147 Each pot had room for 2 or 3 metrétés, according to John. In the Greek measuring system of the time, 1 metrétés = 72 sextarii (or 12 chous) = 39.39 litres or 8.75 gallons. Each pot had a net weight (not including the weight of the pot itself) of between 78.78 kg and 118.17 kg.

There was no stinting, no economising, no rationing needed. This quantity does not even take into account the common practice of diluting wine with seawater[148] and adding spices, thereby stretching it even further.

Just as five loaves and two fish were multiplied to satisfy five thousand men—not counting the women and children[149]—this miraculous sign was of the same order. This super-abundance of wine—enough to give thousands of people a substantial cup—is chiastically matched with the mountain of spices created by Nicodemus, Joseph of Arimathea and the women who attended Jesus at the cross. A hundred *litra* of myrrh was an astonishing, extravagant amount. Just as the six pots were unimaginably generous in supply.

However, the wine and myrrh are linked by more than the immensity of provision. Both were symbols of joy. Myrrh was called 'oil of joy' because of its association with the consummation of a marriage. Wine too signified joy because it gladdened the heart.

Here, as John makes clear through his front-and-back pairing, we see Jesus presented as the Ultimate Bridegroom, the Husband of Israel, the Beloved and Lover of all the nations. As evidenced from the interaction between the tablemaster and the groom at the

---

[148] According to Cato the Elder, the seawater was collected far from shore during calm conditions to maximise the salt content. The Talmud prescribes that wine needs to be watered before drinking (though mixtures with ratios less than 1:6 were not considered suitable for ritual use). (slowine.com/the-history-of-mixing-wine-and-seawater/ - accessed 20 December 2022) Undiluted wine was considered only as useful for medicinal purposes. Seawater mixed with wine was called 'wine that smells like flowers' or alternatively *thalassitis*, 'wine of the sea.' Many believed this method of wine-making was invented by Dionysius. (greekreporter.com/2022/05/09/why-ancient-greeks-mixed-wine-with-seawater/ – accessed 20 December 2022)

[149] Matthew 14:21

wedding, it was the responsibility of the groom to ensure enough wine was available throughout the full period of celebration.

Jesus, as the True Bridegroom, provides a wine bursting with paradox: it is, of course, new wine—in keeping with the season—but it is also fine wine. Aged, kept, guarded, preserved—the wine that Isaiah foretold would mark the banquet to celebrate the vanquishing of Death.

6.2 The Unknown Hour

BOTH EXPLICIT AND IMPLICIT TIMING ISSUES occur in the story of the wedding at Cana. A man and woman would be engaged but no one, except the father of the groom, knew when the actual marriage would take place. Once an official agreement was reached with an exchange of gifts and covenantal meal, the prospective groom would go away to build a room for his bride. This room, attached to his family home, had to be approved by his father before the actual marriage could proceed. As a consequence, not even the bridegroom knew when that hour would come—he had to wait for his father's permission.

The wedding was divided into three phases: the contractual agreement, the announcement and the consummation. The marriage was not legally binding until the announcement was made. These phases are marked out in divine time by the appointed feasts: Passover for the agreement and private covenantal meal, Pentecost for the public announcement, Tabernacles for the consummation. These 'mo'edim', *appointed times* or 'kairos' days, portend the betrothal of God with the people of Israel.[150]

---

150 nazareneisrael.org/book/feasts-of-the-seventh-month/chag-sukkot-the-feast-of-tabernacles/ (accessed 6 December 2022)

It would be unlikely for the bride and groom to meet during the betrothal period. A 'friend of the bridegroom' could visit the bride to acquaint her with the ways and character of her husband-to-be. During the wait, the bride made herself ready. She could select up to ten bridesmaids who had to be on hand at a moment's notice. The bridegroom could come for his betrothed at any time, day or night.

Seven shofar blasts would herald his arrival, alerting the bridal party so they could light their lamps. The bridegroom would carry off the bride to his father's house for the wedding feast. Sometimes the bridegroom's friends would collect the bride and take her to meet him.

When Jesus and His disciples were invited to Cana, they probably had as much notice as the bride did. Supposing she was one of Jesus' sisters, Mary's concern is more than adequately explained. Her new son-in-law was about to be shamed. Such a public humiliation in a small village would be hard to live down. It's sometimes thought the extra disciples might have been the cause of the shortage. However, at this point, Jesus only had five followers—hardly 'disciples', except in retrospect. He hadn't yet issued the traditional rabbinic call, 'Follow Me!'

Moreover, one of the five, Nathanael, was a native of Cana and therefore probably invited to the wedding anyway. Whatever the reason for the wine shortage, its lack was common knowledge. If it hadn't been, there'd have been no reason for the disciples to believe in Jesus.

When we realise that the last phase of a wedding happened at an unknown hour, we might consider the first miracle of timing was actually Jesus' arrival in Cana for His sister's nuptials. He'd been away from home for at least seven weeks—He had to travel for a few days from Nazareth to Bethany-beyond-the-Jordan where He was baptised; the Spirit drove Him out into the desert for forty days; and then, after His return to Bethany-beyond-the-Jordan, it was another six days before the wedding at Cana.

Imagine the relief of His mother when she realised that her firstborn son—the one who'd gone to see His cousin, John the Baptiser, and had then mysteriously vanished for so long—had returned just in time for the wedding.

There are multiple overlapping images here of the church as the Betrothed waiting for the Bridegroom to appear at an unknown hour: the sister of Jesus waiting and preparing until the day came for her to be carried off to the groom's home; and, of course, Jesus returning unexpectedly after a long disappearance.

6.3 Time and Body

The usual Christian understanding of 'kairos' involves an *opportune moment*, a *favourable time*, an *auspicious* or *advantageous hour*. This kindly and gentle interpretation sanitises the original concept. Not just *time*-sensitive, 'kairos' was also a vulnerable part of the *body*—a crucial spot targeted with devastating and fatal effect. The most ancient associations of 'kairos' are nuanced as ritual sacrifice.[151]

The original sense of the 'opportune moment' isn't 'seize the day' but a swift and decisive strike. It's not about laying hold, but of piercing and pinning to the spot. This idea of 'kairos' existed from at least a millennium before Christ.

The notion of ritual sacrifice to grasp 'kairos' may lie behind a bizarre episode during the time both David and Ish-bosheth were vying for the throne of Israel. Their rival armies met at the Pool of Gibeon:

---

151 Barbara M.T.P. Baert says: 'Doro Levi's extensive study shows that the Homeric *kairos* was part of a group of related words of uncertain origin: *kèr*: death; *keraïzein*: to plunder, to slaughter; *kèr*: heart; *kèrainein*: to be anxious; *kar*: lock of hair; *keiein*: to split; *keirein*: to cut. All of these related roots have at their kernel the idea of splitting or division, an action of sacrifice in a ritual context.' ias.edu/ideas/baert-kairos (accessed 6 December 2022)

> They sat down, the one on the one side of the pool, and the other on the other… Abner said to Joab, 'Let the young men arise and compete before us.'
>
> And Joab said, 'Let them arise.' Then they arose and passed over by number, twelve for… Ish-bosheth… and twelve of the servants of David. And each caught his opponent by the head and thrust his sword in his opponent's side, so they fell down together. Therefore that place was called Helkath-hazzurim.
>
> 2 Samuel 2:12–16^{ESV}

There are several notable aspects:

- Abner basically says to Joab, 'Let's have a laugh.' In Hebrew, his word for *compete* is related to *laugh, game, lintel* and *threshold*. The later Pythagorean idea of 'kairos' involved a threshold.

- The representatives of each claimant for kingship caught each other by the head. The minor Greek deity, Kairos, was imaged as a bald man with a forelock of hair. To take advantage of a passing opportunity, it was necessary to grab Kairos' forelock.

- The twelve representatives struck each other in a vulnerable spot, just as required by the idea of 'kairos' in the body.

So, I wonder, were the army commanders, Abner and Joab, trying to summon Kairos—or the equivalent deity in Hebrew culture—in order to change the balance of power and advantage their own claimant for the throne?

In Pythagorean mysticism of later centuries, 'kairos' involved a linkage of the perfect time and perfect place—a knot or node in space-time where circumstances were perfectly aligned, everything 'fit' together precisely and the moment to 'strike' was *now*. Ultimately, over many centuries, Kairos came to be understood as a mirror of cosmic perfection, reigning over measure, harmony and equilibrium.

During the wedding at Cana, Jesus challenged this notion of 'kairos', showing Himself not simply Lord of Time but Opportunities as well.

6.4 Threshold Sacrifice

Jesus was on the threshold of His public ministry when He turned water into wine. In pairing this account with the ultimate threshold event in history—His return as Firstborn from the dead—John subtly links 'kairos' with sacrifice.

Barbara Baert comments on Pythagorean worship of Kairos: 'His mystical number is seven, a cyclic "point of crisis." Kairos turns, turns into; he marks the *Wendepunkt*.[152] Kairos is therefore border, threshold, and limit, as well as transition, change, and progress.'[153]

From ancient times, a widespread understanding existed that crossing a threshold required a sacrifice. Whenever hospitality was offered, the guest would be honoured by an invitation to threshold covenant. The blood of the slaughtered animal was painted on the lintel and doorposts signifying this invitation. The guests would accept simply by passing over the blood pooled in the shallow basin carved into the cornerstone under the doorway. If the guests wanted to forgo the invitation, they would strike the blood-stained cornerstone with their feet.

Henry Clay Trumbull points out that the Passover is an example of this rite: it was an invitation to God to pass over the blood

---

152 Turning point.
153 ias.edu/ideas/baert-kairos (accessed 8 December 2022)

on the cornerstone, accept the offered covenant and become the covenant defender of the household.[154]

However threshold covenant went back much earlier than the first Passover. Abraham ran to offer hospitality to God and His angelic companions when he saw them. He killed a fatted calf for a meal. God was near the entrance to the tent, stating He would return in the 'time of life'—surely a 'kairos' moment—and then Sarah would be holding her own child in her arms.

She laughed. Laughter is a common phenomenon associated with thresholds in Scripture. It's ambiguous—sometimes it's positive, sometimes negative. It can mean *joking*, or alternatively *mocking*; it can mean a *playful game*, or *bullying sport*.[155] When Abner said to Joab, 'Let's have a laugh,' his words carry this vagueness until the outcome becomes clear. Both sides however recognise they are presented with an opportunity requiring ritual sacrifice. But who are they making the blood offering to? Not Yahweh, who expressly forbade human sacrifice.

It's easy to think threshold sacrifice no longer applies. But how often do we see people choosing to jump at an opportunity for promotion by 'knifing' any potential rival in the back through rumour, innuendo or even outright lies? It's true we no longer practice blood sacrifice, but the desire for a bloodbath that massacres the reputation of all our opponents may still lurk in our hearts.

Jesus is the all-sufficient sacrifice for passing over any threshold. Yet whether we truly believe that is demonstrated by our behaviour when opportunity arises.

---

154 Henry Clay Trumbull, *The Threshold Covenant, or the Beginning of Religious Rites*, Facsimile Publishing, 1896

155 There are two rhyming words in Hebrew, both meaning *to laugh*: 'sachaq', and 'tsachaq'.

6.5 Neither the Time, Nor the Number

John wrote his gospel, in part, to counter Gnostic infiltration of Christianity. The partnership between Gnosticism and Pythagorean theurgy also made mathematical mysticism a natural target in his writing.

He flung down the gauntlet to Pythagoreanism with his opening sentence of 17 words about the Logos. That was an unthinkable combination for elegant, cultured writing. Then, almost backtracking, he mentions the six pots that Jesus filled. Not *some*, but *six*. Six was such a significant number for the Pythagorean Brotherhood that it might have been wiser to avoid mentioning it.

In my view, 666, the number of a man, and the number of the beast of Revelation,[156] refers to Pythagoras and the teachings of the Pythagorean Brotherhood. It points to reincarnation[157] and thus is a counterfeit of 153, the number indicative of resurrection

---

156 Revelation 13:18

157 The number associated by the Pythagoreans with reincarnation was 6x6x6 or 216. 666 is the 36th triangular number (or 6x6). 6 was regarded as a cyclic number because any number ending in 6 will, when multiplied by 6, result in another number ending in 6.

mentioned in the final chapter of John's gospel. He's hammering home a very long, sharp nail in the Pythagorean coffin.

So why does he briefly resuscitate this philosophy by featuring 6 so prominently? Perhaps because this episode is about time—and, for the Pythagoreans, the number of Kairos, the godling of opportune time, was not six but seven. John thus has at least three messages for his Pythagorean readers in this scene.

First, Jesus is Lord of time—He doesn't have to wait for the appearance of seven to be able to seize the opportune moment. Instead, He can summon 'Kairos' to wait upon Him.

Second, Jesus is the Lord of numbers and numbering. His is the *logos* but so too are all numbers and every branch of mathematics. He created it all. Forget about the so-called 'divine Pythagoras' and his numerical interpretations—2 for female; 3 for male; 4 for justice; 5 for marriage; 6 for perfection; 10 for the tetrakys and manifest deity; 17 for obstruction and abomination; even numbers denoting both feminine and evil; odd numbers masculine and good.

Jesus showed how very wrong that thinking is. In Hebrew thought, six was never regarded as perfection but as falling short of it.

Yet, paradoxically, this idea from Pythagorean-Platonic philosophy of 'perfect' numbers would symbolise for Greek readers the perfection of Jesus. In his first and last chapters, John uses the third 'perfect' number, 496, which is also a triangular number.[158] Likewise, six is both the first 'perfect' number and the

---

158 See *The Elijah Tapestry* for more information on the mathematics of 496.

third triangular number, thus linking the highlighted numbers of these chapters through their common arithmetic features.[159]

Third, the feminine principle is not evil—women are foremost in expressing both faith and faithfulness in these major scenes. They are the ones choosing to believe. Like the women at Sinai who were the first to respond to the giving of the Law, with the men coming at their heels,[160] they are the tip of the spear, the ones driving forward in loyalty, devotion and fidelity. They are confident in the love of Jesus—though not with any sure knowledge of His actions. Neither His mother nor the Magdalene could predict His behaviour or reactions but they were assured of His goodness.

---

[159] The second 'perfect' number is 28, which is also the seventh triangular number. According to the analysis of Maarten Menken in *Numerical Literary Techniques in John: The Fourth Evangelist's Use of Numbers of Words and Syllables*, the number 28 is featured several times in the structure of the first chapter, the most significant of which is the combined total of the words (in Greek) spoken by God, 'The man on whom you see the Spirit descend and rest is He who will baptise with the Holy Spirit,' and the words of the prophecy of Isaiah, 'I am a voice of one calling in the wilderness, "Make straight the way for the Lord."'

[160] See: Anne Hamilton and Natalie Tensen, *More Precious than Pearls*, Armour Books 2016

6.6 The Turn of the Age

IN POPULAR CHRISTIANITY, SIX IS often regarded as symbolising 'man'—going back to the creation of man on the sixth day. This isn't a particularly persuasive argument because various kinds of livestock were also created on the sixth day.

Sometimes the six pots are seen as representing six ages. As the six days of creation represent the time period of God's work in *fashioning*, so the six pots are seen as the culmination of the ages of God's work in *redeeming*.

In Joseph's interpretation of the dreams of Pharaoh's baker and cupbearer, three baskets of bread and three vine branches were each interpreted as symbolising three days. So it would not be unreasonable to follow this example and interpret the six pots as six days or six time periods. This is particularly apropos since the end of the first age and the beginning of the second was marked by the production of new wine—when Noah planted a vineyard after the flood and became so drunk on its produce that he passed out.

Both Joseph and Noah are associated with the beginning of a new epoch—Joseph with the era when the Israelites came to dwell in Egypt and Noah with the transition between the pre-Flood and post-Flood world. Both patriarchs are associated with grace and favour.

In his first epistle, Peter describes grace as 'poikilos', *many-coloured*, reminding us of the rainbow first witnessed by Noah and also of Joseph's coat-of-many-colours. Noah and Joseph were both guardians who preserved life across a cataclysmic period.

Now it's unclear what happened to ruin the harmony of Noah's world. A surface reading suggests that his son Ham saw him lying naked in his tent, but as LJ Thriepland points out, there was never any law against accidental voyeurism—and no explanation as to how Noah immediately knew Ham had done him wrong in 'uncovering his nakedness'.[161] Some scholars take the view, on the basis of Leviticus 20:11, that this wording is a phrase for incest and that Ham had had sexual relations with his mother. Some Jewish sages are of the alternative opinion that Ham had sodomised his father.

Whatever happened, Noah cursed—not Ham, as we might expect—but Ham's son, Canaan. He declares:

> *Canaan is cursed. He will be the lowest of slaves to his brothers.*
>
> Genesis 9:25^{CSB}

The lowest of slaves, literally *a servant of servants, a slave of slaves*—that's what Noah speaks over his grandson. It's the first mention of *slavery* in Scripture, the first time someone is declared to be in bondage to another, dispossessed of the exercise of freewill, and of the fruit of the work of their own hands. Instead of being a steward of creation, with all the royal status that implies, Canaan was to be subject to someone else's whims and desires. And this situation came about because of *new wine*, a word that in Hebrew is derived from the same root as *dispossession* and paradoxically *inheritance*.

---

121 followintruth.com/why-did-noah-curse-canaan (accessed 12 December 2022)

If those six pots do indeed announce the ending of the sixth age and the start of the seventh,[162] then Jesus was mending the past and was undoing the curse of Noah. *New wine* was a significant factor in the dispossession of Canaan, *new wine* became a significant factor in the inheritance won at the Cross as first foreshadowed at Cana. I don't think it's coincidence that Cana and Canaan are so similar, nor that 'qaneh' evokes *brothers* living together side by side in equanimity.

How are *dispossession* and *appointed time* linked? They aren't. Disinheritance and dispossession are not time-bound. They can happen at any time. As Jesus said to His brothers: any time will do.

However, inheritance is time-related: normally it comes after a death and once the executors have finalised the will. It is a process that begins at a time marked by a specific boundary: that of death.

Perhaps we can surmise, given these hints about appointed time and restoring an inheritance that Joseph, the foster-father of Jesus, has indeed passed away and His brothers are concerned, lest they be dispossessed of their share of the patrimony. And in providing a lavish excess of wine—fine wine that could be sold—perhaps Jesus was providing a dowry for His sister.

---

162 Or perhaps the start of the sixth age and end of the fifth.

6.7 Threefold Time

THE FACE OF TIME AT CANA shows itself as varied, paradoxical, wondrously entwined. Echoes of the beginning of a new and fresh age are present, similar to the baptised world after the flood of Noah. But now there's the reversal of a curse.

Just as the meeting with the Magdalene in the garden overturned the curse of Eden, so at Cana we see Jesus upending the curse of slavery and dispossession spoken over the descendants of Canaan. He's removed the potential shame about to be heaped on His hosts by providing a superabundance of 'new', 'mature' wine.

Over and above these hints another age is beginning,[163] Jesus made an explicit time reference when He said His hour had not yet come. Yet that did not limit Him—He summoned 'kairos' to Him. The appointed time is His servant, not His master. As He unravelled the curse of slavery, He commanded Kairos to do His bidding. Then, in a further demonstration of His authority over time—ordinary time, Kronos, on this occasion—He compressed the season for the transformation of water into wine by a factor of many thousands.

---

163   psephizo.com/biblical-studies/what-is-the-meaning-of-the-six-stone-jars-at-the-wedding-in-cana/ (accessed 3 December 2022)

The Cana event is not a simple sign of Jesus as Lord of time—it's highly complex, showing His threefold supremacy over the age, over appointed time and over ordinary time.

Now, Hebrew 'mo'ed' isn't really congruent with Greek 'kairos', *appointed time*. Over the centuries, 'kairos' has become so emasculated it's lost its original sense of swift, forcefully seized sacrifice. Moreover it's vastly different from the overtones of community and assembly associated with 'mo'ed'.

Perhaps the Hebrew word that applies more accurately to the older, darker concept of 'kairos' is 'eth', derived from 'anah', *announce* or *testify*. There's another meaning for 'anah'—*defile* or *bow down*—and this alternative meaning connects to "anat', as in Beth-'Anat, *house of Anat*, a Galilean village just north of Cana.

Anat is that Canaanite warrior goddess who revelled in bloodshed and mayhem. When her brother Hadad died, she buried him and then went looking for him.

Let me repeat that so we can see how out-of-sequence it is: she *buried him and then went looking for him*—after he was dead. As mentioned previously, Mary Magdalene does precisely this. Can you see how Jesus treated Baal's epic? When I commented previously that He stripped Hadad even of his legend and liturgy, I meant it. Seriously.

The Magdalene is not only an archetype of the new Eve[164] and of Jezebel, she also counterpoints Anat, the blood-thirsty sword-slashing sister of the storm-god who was called forth from the underworld at the end of each winter with ritual cries of: 'Where is the Lord? Where is the Prince?'

---

164   As was Jesus' mother, Mary.

Even the language Jesus used points to this. In addressing Mary as *'woman'*, He would have used the Aramaic word, "anath". Although it's Aramaic, it also happens to be the Greek way of spelling Anat. We're looking at multi-lingual coded puns that reveal Jesus was conducting a targeted war.

This specialised skirmish was far from unique. Jesus conducted a similar battle scenario when He confronted the harvest-god Tammuz, the so-called 'Bread of Life', on the same day He challenged the goddess, Asherah, for the title 'The One Who Walks on Water'.

Every 'sign' that John unfurled in his gospel is also a war banner and battle-standard.

6.8 Anat and Kairos

BOTH KAIROS AND ANAT WERE DEPICTED with wings. Kairos was armed with a razor blade and a pair of scales. Anat was armed with a spear and a weaving spindle, or a bow and arrows.

Doro Levi's study of the words connected with 'kairos'—*kèr:* death; *keraïzein:* to plunder, to slaughter; *kèr:* heart; *kèrainein:* to be anxious; *kar:* lock of hair; *keiein:* to split; *keirein:* to cut—are not only evocative of a famous story about Anat, but are rooted in the idea of *splitting* or *division*, an action of sacrifice in a ritual context.

After the death of Baal-Hadad, seven years of drought then followed while Anat searched for his killer. Mot, *Death*, is the culprit and, when she finds him, she splits, cuts, winnows, grinds and sows him like corn. In doing so, she becomes Mot's conqueror, and thus the vanquisher of Death. In overpowering Mot, she doesn't simply slaughter him but ritually sacrifices him. All of which is reminiscent of the cluster of words connected with 'kairos'.

Now, clearly, if Jesus took on Baal-Hadad the cloud-rider and Mot the death-lord, He would surely have had to finish off the Canaanite pantheon by overcoming Anat. Her claim to fame, after all, was that she was the killer of Death—so how can Jesus vanquish Death and not vanquish Anat, goddess of *opportunity and appointed time*, and the one who claimed to have already conquered Death?

All the faint and subtle clues that point to Anat in both the Cana story and the incident outside the tomb indicate that Jesus made a clean sweep of all the old gods.

Back when the Israelites were worshipping Asherah, the Canaanites who still lived in the land had moved on in their spiritual allegiance and begun to worship Anat. Now Anat had a twin sister in their lore. Very little is known about her except her name and the fact she was of a more temperate disposition than her violent sister. The name of Anat's twin was Myrrh.

Isn't that just so apt? I'm sure if we knew more about the legend of Myrrh, the Canaanite goddess, we'd discover Jesus was stripping her liturgy too in that scene outside the tomb.

The presence of twins in these chiastic sections links to the presence of twins in the first and last chapter: the evocation of Jacob and Esau in the paired stories about Nathanael and Thomas, stories that also have a theme of dispossession built into them.

In Greek mythology, Athena was the counterpart of Canaanite Anat—as attested by a bilingual inscription on a stone found in Cyprus and dated to the fourth century before Christ.[165]

---

165   en.wikipedia.org/wiki/Anat_Athena_bilingual

6.9 Anat and Athaliah ᴛᴀᴎᴀ ℮.ð

ATHALIAH WAS THE DAUGHTER OF JEZEBEL and granddaughter of Ethbaal, the Phoenician king who had seized the throne of Tyre and Sidon. Athaliah married Jehoram, the king of Judah. He died two years after marauders from Arabia took all his sons, except for Ahaziah, his youngest.

After Ahaziah had reigned for a year, he took his nephews on a state visit to Samaria. They visited Ahab's son—Ahaziah's cousin Joram, the new ruler of the northern kingdom—and no doubt paid their respects to Jezebel the queen mother. Ahaziah, in his youth and inexperience, was persuaded to join Joram in a war against Hazael, the army commander who had recently suffocated the Syrian king with a wet cloth and usurped his throne.[166]

Now Ahaziah's timing—and, after all, when it comes to 'kairos' or 'eth', it's all about timing—could not have been less favourable.

---

166 2 Kings 8:15.

Jehu had only just been anointed king[167] and tasked with bringing down the House of Ahab. Ahaziah, even though he was king of Judah, was unfortunate enough to have Ahab and Jezebel as his grandparents.

Joram was wounded in the battle and was returning to Samaria with Ahaziah and his nephews, the royal princes of Judah, when they encountered Jehu. None were spared.

> *As soon as Athaliah heard that her son King Ahaziah was dead, she decided to kill any relative who could possibly become king. She would have done just that, but Jehosheba rescued Joash son of Ahaziah.*
>
> 2 Chronicles 22:10–11[CEV]

Athaliah then took the throne by murder, copying her grandfather Ethbaal. Her name, though it doesn't look like it in English, actually begins with 'eth', *opportune time*. This is the Hebrew word that has the same dark overtones as the original sense of 'kairos', a *favourable moment* for *ritual sacrifice*.

Just as Jezebel was named for Baal-Hadad and the cry during the ceremony to bring him back from the underworld, so in turn I suspect Athaliah was named for Baal-Hadad's sister, Anat. The tension in Athaliah's name—'eth' for Anat and 'iah' for Yahweh—was resolved when she chose to rule in her own right instead of as a regent for the heir. Her reign lasted seven years—the number associated, perhaps not coincidentally, with the godling Kairos.

---

167 As noted in *The Elijah Tapestry*, the first book in this series, Jehu was—according to rabbinic tradition—anointed by the youthful prophet and fast runner, Jonah. According to the chronology of 2 Kings, it's clear Elisha did not send off Jonah with instructions to anoint Jehu until after Hazael took the throne of Aram. It's always perilous to attribute motivation, but it does appear it wasn't obedience to the Lord's command that finally prompted Elisha to commission the long-delayed appointment of Jehu. Rather, it was fear of Hazael.

In the garden outside the tomb, Mary Magdalene repeatedly asks the basic question, 'Where is the Lord?' This is fundamentally 'Jezebel' in Canaanite liturgy. But it is also Anat's constant refrain as she searched for her brother during the seven years of drought after he was slain. When Mot, *Death*, won't answer her question about Baal's whereabouts in the underworld, she becomes so furious that she splits, winnows and grinds Mot.

The subtle allusions to Anat, Jezebel and Athaliah in the encounter between Jesus and Mary Magdalene are there to remind us that Jesus is the One who conquered Death. No one else. He is the Lord and the Cloud-rider, not Baal-Hadad. He is also the redeemer of Time and of opportunity. He is the one, and He alone.

6.10 ANAT AND JOSEPH

In the first century, a prophecy of Zechariah about 'Four Craftsmen' had been interpreted to indicate more than one messiah was coming—the royal messiah, the war messiah, the priestly messiah and the Elijah-who-is-to-come. No one expected all those roles to be fulfilled in one person.

> *The Lord showed me four craftsmen… come to terrify [and] cast down the horns of the nations.*
>
> Zechariah 1:20–21^{ESV}

Although the Elijah-who-is-to-come was declared by Jesus to be John the Baptist, I believe I have sufficiently demonstrated in *The Elijah Tapestry* that, after John died, Jesus took his mantle and passed it to Simon Peter to complete Elijah's unfinished work. That's why I'm saying all four craftsmen, not just three of them, were embodied in Jesus.

The expectation was that the royal messiah would be called 'son of David'; the war messiah 'son of Joseph'; the priestly messiah would be of the order of Melchizedek.

John specifically designates Jesus as the 'son of Joseph', using it as a title. The other evangelists simply use 'son of Joseph' to designate Jesus' assumed parentage. John therefore presents the war messiah to his readers. That's his message right from the start when Philip goes to find Nathanael and says:

> *We have found the one Moses wrote about in the Law, and about whom the prophets also wrote—Jesus of Nazareth, the son of Joseph.*
>
> John 1:45^{NIV}

Philip is basically informing Nathanael: 'We've found the war messiah!'

The title 'son of Joseph' as applied to Jesus both fulfilled and defied popular hope. The tag was understood to mean the war messiah would be descended from the patriarch Joseph—the dreamer who'd been given a special coat and who'd so unwisely antagonised his brothers they wanted to kill him. Given the opportunity, they decided to profit instead and sold him as a slave.

On famously interpreting Pharaoh's dreams, Joseph was put in charge of national administration with the specific role of preparing for an upcoming famine. Now any ruler who plucked someone from prison and catapulted him to a position second-in-charge of the entire country would have been extremely foolish not to have put immediate safeguards into place. Joseph might have had an astute plan to save Egypt from ruin but that didn't mean he wouldn't conspire against his master.

We have detailed clues regarding some of the precautions Pharaoh took. First and most significantly, he gave Joseph a new name, Zaphenath-Paneah. Second, he gave him a wife, Asenath, the daughter of a priest in the city of On. Now bestowing a new name may not sound to us today as if it's particularly effective protection against betrayal—but that's because we have lost any understanding of name covenant and the significance of the exchange of names involved. Covenant was how bygone rulers bound vassals to themselves in loyalty—in ancient times the ritual was enacted before a guardian deity as a witness and potential avenger of any covenant violation.

Can we tell who that deity was? I believe so. I also believe we can infer the name of the Pharaoh. Although Zaphenath-Paneah is thought to mean *saviour of the world*, Zaphenath can also mean 'Anat of Zaphon'—a title[168] that would indicate the Pharaoh was a worshipper of Anat. She was particularly popular during the Hyksos period—the era when warrior Canaanite kings invaded Egypt and ruled the land.

In fact one meaning of Asenath, the name of Joseph's wife, is *holy to Anat*.

A Canaanite king would naturally look favourably on a slave from Canaan, and would be inclined to give him a name hailing back to the land of his origin. So who was this Pharaoh? Can we discern that? Given that, for a name covenant, there has to be an exchange of at least part of the name and also given that Zaphon is a placename, rather than a goddess, logically the element is, of course, 'Anat'. There are only three Egyptian rulers whose names contain 'anat' and two of them are Hyksos rulers. Aperanat is the most probable candidate[169] in my view for the Pharaoh who appointed Joseph and who said, when his people came asking for help, 'Do whatever he tells you.'

---

168 'Anat of Saphon' is twice mentioned in offering lists inscribed on tablets from Ugarit. (en.wikipedia.org/wiki/Anat – accessed 13 December 2022)

169 wikipedia.org/wiki/Aperanat (accessed 13 December 2022)

6.11 Joseph the Dispossessor

'Do whatever he tells you.'

Pharaoh's words were to have dire consequences. They were to result in dispossession and deprivation of inheritance—the very things Jesus, millennia later, set about mending at Cana. Joseph had been sold by his brothers into slavery. Dispossessed of home, family, freedom—not to mention fine clothes and fatherly esteem—he served the Egyptian official Potiphar for many years before being falsely accused of rape by Potiphar's wife and winding up in prison.

Joseph knew what it was to have nothing, to be desperate, to be terrified in facing an unknown future. His brothers in later years, when they came to barter for grain during the famine, recalled his anguished pleading with them from the pit as they debated whether he should live or die.[170] He knew what it meant to be stripped and shamed, to lose all prospect of inheritance and see no chance of it ever coming back.

I make this point because I want to ask: what was in Joseph's heart that, in time, he came to dispossess others? Land was the primary means of inheritance back in his day and he not only

---

170 Genesis 42:21

took the opportunity to disinherit the Egyptians—except for the priests—but actually gave the people no way of retrieving their property. In the third year of the famine, the Egyptians came to Joseph and said:

> 'We cannot hide from our lord the fact that since our money is gone and our livestock belongs to you, there is nothing left for our lord except our bodies and our land...' So Joseph bought all the land in Egypt for Pharaoh. The Egyptians, one and all, sold their fields, because the famine was too severe for them. The land became Pharaoh's, and Joseph reduced the people to servitude... Joseph established it as a law concerning land in Egypt—still in force today—that a fifth of the produce belongs to Pharaoh.[171] It was only the land of the priests that did not become Pharaoh's.
>
> Genesis 47:18; 20–21; 26^{NIV}

Hundreds of years later, implied in the phrase *'still in force today'*, the Egyptians were under the yoke of servitude that Joseph established. It was never revoked. It had become permanent.

God decreed otherwise for the Israelites. Possibly because they were so heavily influenced by the Egyptians, He ordained that, in the year of Jubilee, all inheritances of land would be returned to their original owner:

> *The land shall not be sold in perpetuity, for the land is Mine... in all the country you possess, you shall allow a redemption of the land.*
>
> Leviticus 25:23–24^{ESV}

---

[171] The people had already been taxed at this level in the lead-up to the famine, so it was nothing new. It was thus an enforcement of 'permanent famine' measures. The loss of the land was the new aspect. The people effectively became serfs, never able to own their own property again.

Mary's words, *'Do whatever He tells you,'* with their ancient echo of Pharaoh's instruction, are not only a reminder of the role of Joseph as the *saviour of the world* but also of his opportunistic seizure of the 'eth' moment to disinherit an entire population, forcing them into servitude.

We've seen how Athaliah also grasped an 'eth' moment to slaughter all the remaining heirs to the throne of Judah. Curiously there is a connection between her and Joseph of Egypt, through her father Ahab. The parallels between the two men suggest that, if Ahab had followed his true calling in the Lord, he would have been the 'saviour of the world' in his generation.

Both Ahab and Joseph had fathers-in-law who were priests of a sun-god. Both were buried in Samaria. Although Ahab was killed in battle, his body was taken back to his capital. And although Joseph died in Egypt, his bones were taken to Shechem, the original capital of Samaria. His tomb there is still a place of pilgrimage today. Before his death Joseph requested that his bones be taken from Egypt to the plot of land he was given as an inheritance from his father—and so, when the Israelites left Egypt, they took along his casket and carried it through the desert for forty years.

Both Joseph and Ahab lived during a time of drought and famine: but Joseph prepared for it while Ahab blamed Elijah for it. As Joseph dispossessed the Egyptians of their land,[172] so Ahab

---

[172] Rabbi Jonathan Sacks pointed out that Joseph, by acquiring the cattle and all the land for Pharaoh during the course of the famine, as well as allowing the Egyptians to sell themselves into bondage for food, actually created the very political mechanism that a later Pharaoh used to enslave the Hebrews. In addition, Joseph instituted a policy of forced resettlement, later used to great political effect by the Assyrians, by moving the people off their traditional land and shunting them from one end of the country to the other. See: rabbisacks.org/covenant-conversation/mikketz/joseph-and-the-risks-of-power/ (accessed 6 March 2023)

dispossessed Naboth and his sons of their land—true, it was Jezebel who facilitated the seizure of Naboth's vineyard, but it was Ahab who went in to take possession.

These parallels lead me to suspect that Ahab was called, just like Joseph many years before him, to build granaries. Not a palace of pearl.

Yet it also leads me to see that Jesus as the true Saviour of the World offers us a redemption that encompasses all disinheritance, too—both that of revered leaders like Joseph,[173] and also despised ones like Ahab.

---

173 I wonder if Joseph had truly forgiven his brothers. Forgiveness is such a complex work of the heart that, personally, I doubt it. I think he'd have resisted making others suffer as he had, if his forgiveness was complete. When Joseph put on a meal for his brothers, they received one-fifth of Benjamin's portion. Note the number. It's the same as Pharaoh's tax on the people who farm the land they used to own but have been forced to sell to survive. There is no mechanism by which they can get it back. They are serfs forever. So did Joseph simply project his resentment from the brothers he'd been taught to despise onto the Egyptian farmers he'd come to despise? The forced resettlement that breaks a person's ties to the land has been used throughout history to subjugate others. Yes, Joseph should be honoured for the great good that he did. However, the damage he inflicted should not be overlooked.

6.12 Dispossess and Repossess

Dispossession and repossession should be opposites. But they often have an overlapping connotation—repossession usually denotes a loss of something only partially paid for. They are thus similar to Hebrew 'yaresh',[174] *take possession of* and also *dispossess*.

Joseph enslaved the Egyptians. This was followed, all but inevitably, with the reverse: Israelites enslaved by the Egyptians. The principle of 'sowing and reaping' is not unique to Jewish and Christian spirituality. Inescapable karma or kismet, the notion of fate overtaking us and the punishment fitting the crime, the law of cause and effect in classical physics, the notion that

---

[174] 'Yaresh' is the root word for 'tirosh', *new wine*. It is also the root word for *net*, found in John 21:6 (though obviously 'yaresh' is Hebrew, rather than the Greek 'diktuon'.) As pointed out in *The Elijah Tapestry*, there are many clues knotting together the mathematics and wording to develop a restored concept of inheritance in general, and also to include the specific passing on a legacy, as in Peter receiving Elijah's mantle. Now in the second chapter, we see an extension of the chiasmus linking the first and last chapters of John so that it encompasses *new wine* and the blessings that Jesus bestows with a return of inheritance.

beginnings determine endings—these all express the general rule of consequences.[175]

We don't notice 'sowing and reaping' largely because we're ignorant of history. We truncate or brush aside those parts that don't fit into our preferred narrative. We don't want to diminish the haloes we've affixed to our heroes, especially those champions who are our role models. And when it comes to Scripture, we're even more inclined to gloss over the failings of the more revered characters in its pages. How often, for example, is Elijah's defiance of God pointed out? How often is it noted he taught his students to do similarly? How often do we realise his refusal to obey God's direction to anoint Hazael had consequences so prolonged that Jesus—nine *centuries* later—had to set it up for Peter to complete Elijah's assignment?

Why did Jesus take up Elijah's mantle? Because God's agenda wasn't simply about anointing Hazael, it was about gathering the Gentiles into the kingdom of God.

Now Joseph may not have defied God but he was influenced by the 'anah' behind the 'anat' in the name he was given. The sacrificial offering for 'kairos'-opportunity is evident in his dispossession of the Egyptians—and in their natural retaliation, once their own time of opportunity arose. They'd been enslaved on the orders of a Hebrew, so naturally they wanted the Hebrews enslaved in turn. And, human nature being what it is, simple justice wasn't nearly enough. So the murder of baby boys began—in a cycle of sowing

---

[175] In *Snakes in the Temple*, David Orton exemplifies the principle of 'beginnings determine endings' with an illustration about the focus of church on people, instead of worship of God. If we start with man, he points out, we end there too. He exhorts us to find a new starting point. (*Snakes in the Temple*, Sovereign World 2004)

that culminated in a devastating reaping when, eighty years later, all the firstborn males in the land were killed in a single night.[176]

The words of Jesus, *'It is finished!'* applies to sowing and reaping. The power of His Cross enables the relentless escalation of the cycle to end. Consequences may still ensue but the continual repetition of sowing can be over and done with—if we so choose. Repentance is the choice that brings us into alignment with God's will and ends the planting of harm, replacing it with a sowing of blessing.

---

176 Jon Levenson points out that the story of the Pharaoh who enslaves the population of Israelites and orders the death of the baby boys parallels (in reverse order) the story of Joseph who was to be killed but was then enslaved. It may also parallel and distantly reflect the enslavement of Baal to the sea, Yamm, and his annihilation by Mot, *Death*. (See: Jon D. Levenson, *Resurrection and the Restoration of Israel: The Ultimate Victory of the God of Life,* Yale University Press 2006)

6.13 BACK IN EGYPT

THE CANAANITE GODDESS ANAT IS OFTEN equated with the Egyptian goddess Hathor.[177] Anat is sometimes depicted with horns—a link to her brother and father, both of whom were symbolised by a bull. Hathor was always portrayed with cow horns, and considered the mother of Ra, the sun-god, and Horus the sky-god. She was therefore the mother of the pharaohs, who were more than representative of these deities: they were the god in themselves.

Anat and Hathor were both warriors who attacked the enemies of their house and waded knee-deep in blood. In the Egyptian version of the universal flood, Ra, growing old and feeble, felt his authority over humanity was waning. Calling an assembly of the gods, he alleged mankind was plotting against him. He was advised to send the Eye of Ra, the goddess Hathor, against them. She took up the task of elimination with such diligence Ra became alarmed. He didn't want all humanity destroyed. So while Hathor was wading in blood he had seven thousand pots of barley beer made. The beer was dyed with red ochre and poured onto the fields, covering it to a depth of about half a cubit. Hathor was smitten, Narcissus-like, by her own beauty reflected in the red flood at dawn. Bowing down, she drank the beer, became drunk and forgot her battle-rage. And so a remnant of humanity was saved.

---

177   More often, however, she is equated with Neith.

Samuel Hooke suggests the story is meant to explain the origin of barley beer. If so, it not only harks back to Anat's war fury and her vengeance on behalf of the ruler of the gods but also parallels much of the story of Noah, his drunkenness, the saving of a remnant of humanity, and the start of a new age after a cataclysmic disaster.

The blood-red beer also evokes the first plague of Egypt—the waters turning into blood. Moses struck the Nile with his staff, and the river, canals, ponds and reservoirs, even the water stored in stone and wood vessels all turned to blood. Pharaoh's magicians[178] were able to duplicate the feat,[179] so he felt able to ignore the first plague and the sign of God it indicated.

Traditionally the Pharaoh of the Exodus is portrayed in films and popular history as Rameses the Great. This is often vehemently disputed by Egyptologists, particularly since Scripture doesn't specifically identify him.[180]

---

178 This is, of course, a different Pharaoh to the ruler in the Joseph cycle. I believe the Pharaoh in the time of Joseph to be Aperanat; while the Pharaoh of the Exodus is most probably Rameses II.

179 Some skeptics see a contradiction here and wonder how they could do this if all the water was already blood; however, it is explained in Exodus 7:24 that people dug around the Nile, obviously seeking groundwater in the water table. The text of the Hathor legend appears to have been used as incantation for a deceased Pharaoh, so it may have been adapted to the purpose. If it seems like I'm giving too much credence to magic, bear in mind that, as mentioned previously, spells are simply the use of the creative power God invested into words for purposes that defy His will.

180 Though it does leave substantial clues in the names of the treasure-cities, Rameses and Pithom, that the Israelites were forced to build by slave labour. Moreover, the layout of the Tabernacle in the wilderness is the same as the war camp of Rameses II at the Battle of Kadesh. See: thetorah.com/article/the-tabernacle-in-its-ancient-near-eastern-context (accessed 16 July 2023) The 'god-space' in the camp of Rameses was occupied by the Pharaoh himself; the deity he served being Anat.

I would however like to point out a lovely spiritual reversal, involving a 'healing of history', if Rameses is in fact right. He was a devotee of Anat who named his dog and his daughter after her, as well as his horse and his sword.[181] He also perpetuated the custom amongst the royal family for brother-sister marriages and father-daughter marriages and married three of his daughters, including Bint-Anat, the Great Royal Wife whose name means *daughter of Anat*. She had a tomb in the Valley of the Queens, along with statues where she is posed with Rameses.

Now this is a speculation. However, if Bint-Anat were the princess who adopted Moses, we'd be able to identify the daughter of Pharaoh who married into the tribe of Judah and took the name Bithiah, *daughter of Yahweh*.

Rameses with Bint-Anat at his knees.

> Mered's wife Bithiah gave birth to Miriam, Shammai, and Ishbah the father of Eshtemoa. These were the children of Pharaoh's daughter Bithiah.
>
> 1 Chronicles 4:17–18[BSB]

This statement, implying that Bithiah accompanied the Israelites into the wilderness, would seem to contradict Bint-Anat's burial in Egypt—except for the fact her sarcophagus contains a man's body, not a woman's.

And doesn't it make sense, if they were one and the same, that *daughter of Anat* would change to *daughter of Yahweh*—a name

---

181 His dog was 'Anat in vigour' or 'Anat protects', his horse was 'Anat is content' and his sword 'Anat is victorious'.

that Pharaoh's daughter could not possibly have been born with? Now, more wonderful than this possibility, is this: hundreds of years previously another Pharaoh had dubbed Joseph 'Zaphenath-Paneah' and that name has an inbuilt dedication to Anat.

So if the princess were indeed Bint-Anat—and incidentally Pharaoh's *wife!*[182]—then a spiritual and historical reversal was underway: the name covenant with Anat bestowed on a Hebrew

---

182 This might well explain why the Pharaoh pursued the Israelites so recklessly. Perhaps his wife had absconded with his enemies. He might have had five other Great Royal Wives, including three of Bint-Anat's sisters, but that was entirely beside the point when it comes to regnal dignity. Apparently, right from the start, the Pharaoh had suspected Moses' request to go off for three days to worship Yahweh had another agenda. That would mean, if his suspicions were correct, and one of his favourite wives had joined her destiny to the Israelite slave nation, then she wasn't coming back.

Assuming Rameses II was indeed the pursuing Pharaoh, then he would have been in his late nineties at the time. He ruled 67 years, so he cannot have been the murderous Pharaoh at the start of the Exodus story—since it happened 80 years prior to the plagues. So that would have been his grandfather, Rameses I, who was appointed by the previous Pharaoh, the childless Horemheb. Because Rameses I was not of the previous bloodline, he was not obliged to keep any covenants sworn by former rulers. This is the significance of the Scriptural comment, that a king arose who *'knew not Joseph.'* (Exodus 1:8) *'Know'* was often used to describe covenantal relationship, and this statement tells us the covenant of old, sworn to Joseph, was no longer in operation. A new dynasty had come to power.

Nevertheless, Rameses II—being close to twenty at the start of the Exodus story, would have been old enough to have sired children. His firstborn daughter Bint-Anat could well have been a young child, if she is the princess who found Moses in the reeds. And that perhaps would explain a lot—she wasn't old enough to understand the political implications of her actions in desiring to keep a 'living doll', but she was still a princess none of her attendants were willing to gainsay. She would therefore have been very old when she left Egypt, but in those days people were still regularly living to be 120, so it's possible she was not past child-bearing. Sarah after all had Isaac in her nineties. Regardless of whether she was the Great Royal Wife or not, and Bint-Anat or not, the Egyptian princess Bithiah clearly rebelled against her upbringing—even to the point of marrying Mered, whose name means *rebel*.

was dissolved in favour of a name covenant with Yahweh bestowed on an Egyptian.[183]

Turning our attention back to Cana, Jesus' brothers were able to shrug off miraculous demonstrations, just as the Pharaoh of the Exodus had. They were present, after all, at the wedding. Yet His first public sign wasn't sufficient to break open their hard-heartedness and prompt them to believe. Two years later, just before another Sukkot, they urged Him to get moving on His publicity because His disciples—*not* they, His brothers, *but* His disciples—needed more power demonstrations. At that time, just as at Cana, He said, *'My time has not yet come.'*[184]

The net that Jesus repairs at Cana is knotted with threads of history and legend, ritual and record. His mending encompasses all aspects of the past.

---

183 Now, I admit that because of my early mathematical and scientific training, it's easy to be seduced into a mistaken conclusion by its sheer beauty and elegance of formulation. Stephen Hawking admitted once making a significant theoretical mistake for this very reason. So the symmetry of Joseph being given a name dedicated to Anat and joining the royal household of Egypt counterpointed with a princess giving up a name dedicated to Anat and leaving the royal household of Egypt is an irresistible thought. Even if it is mistaken. It seems almost too good to be true. But, on that point, it should be noted that Jesus repeatedly does too-good-to-be-true things just like this when He heals history.

184 John 7:6[ESV]

6.14 Time the Dispossessor

THE HEBREW WORD FOR *APPOINTED TIME* that most closely corresponds with the Greek notion of 'kairos' is 'eth', from 'anah'. As we've noted, 'anah' is closely connected to Anat, a Canaanite goddess who was also immensely popular in Egypt across several centuries from the time of Joseph to the time of Rameses.

Such a derivation—'anah' from 'Anat' or vice versa—may seem strange. However Owen Barfield pointed out that philologists have so often found that words are etymologically based in myth that Max Müller called it 'the disease of language.' Although JRR Tolkien disputed Müller's assessment, saying that the notion can be 'abandoned without regret', it was only because his view of myth was so high and heroic that he was resistant to thinking of it as a 'disease'.[185] Tolkien didn't seem at all averse to the idea that myth is present in the ancestral background of words. He simply objected to the thought that myth is a sickness.

When Joseph was called up from prison to interpret Pharaoh's pair of dreams about seven fat cows devoured by seven scrawny cows, and seven plump heads of grain swallowed up by seven withered heads, he mentions five times that the revelations have a

---

185 JRR Tolkien, *The Monsters and the Critics and Other Essays*, Harper Collins 1983

divine origin. Twice Pharaoh responds along the lines that Joseph is divinely inspired, making seven references in all to heaven.

I am reluctant to agree with the translations that have Pharaoh stating Joseph has the *'Spirit of God'*. Because both Joseph and Pharaoh use the vague term 'elohim' that, beside Yahweh, could mean *gods* or *heavenly beings*,[186] I am also hesitant to commit to Joseph's words as unambiguously saying: *'God has shown Pharaoh what He is about to do.'*[187] In four of the five times Joseph speaks of the source of the dreams and their interpretation, he says 'ha'elohim', THE *elohim*, which I believe is a reference to angels.[188] Joseph says:

> *The reason the dream was given to Pharaoh in two forms is that the matter has been firmly decided by* ha'elohim, *and* ha'elohim *will do it soon.*
>
> Genesis 41:32

It may be tempting to immediately dismiss the possibility that 'ha'elohim' means *angels* in this instance. However, angels do enact judicial verdicts—as noted in another dream in a different era also involving a seven-year calamity.

King Nebuchadnezzar had a nightmare and Daniel warned him to repent quickly because an angelic judgment is imminent:

---

[186] Michael Heiser considers that the true meaning of 'elohim' is not 'God' but 'resident of the heavenly realms', thus encompassing both the Godhead and a wide variety of spirits.

[187] Genesis 41:28[NIV]

[188] See: *Dealing with Kronos: Spirit of Abuse and Time, Strategies for the Threshold* #9, Armour Books 2022. Since it was 'ha'elohim' who asked Abraham to sacrifice his son Isaac, I do not believe we can unequivocally say this was a direction of Yahweh. It is clearly Yahweh who stops the test, since it specifically says so, but it is not clear who asked for the sacrifice in the first place.

> *A watcher, a holy one, came down from heaven. He proclaimed aloud and said thus: 'Chop down the tree… but leave the stump of its roots… Let his mind be changed from a man's, and let a beast's mind be given to him; and let seven periods of time pass over him. The sentence is by the decree of the watchers, the decision by the word of the holy ones, to the end that the living may know that the Most High rules the kingdom of men and gives it to whom He will and sets over it the lowliest of men.*
>
> Daniel 4:13–17^{ESV}

There are similar elements in both Daniel's and Joseph's interpretations: warnings of coming disaster, time to prepare and avert the calamity, a seven-year period, a sentence that will definitely be carried out. Whether Joseph meant to invoke Yahweh or not—and it's highly unlikely he did because 'I Am' was unknown until it was revealed, generations later, at the burning bush—the Pharaoh would have taken his words as *the gods*.

Now if the Pharaoh was Aperanat, he'd have instantly resonated with Joseph's interpretation. Named for Anat, Aperanat would have intimately known her liturgies, legend, titles, rituals and the complex story of her family relationships. As soon as Joseph said:

> *'The seven lean, ugly cows that came up afterward are seven years, and so are the seven worthless heads of grain scorched by the east wind: They are seven years of famine,'* [189]

it would have clicked. With the final words 'seven years of famine', Aperanat would have immediately thought of a corresponding disaster in the epic of his patron. In it, a seven-year famine devastated the earth during the time Baal-Hadad was dead and

---

189 Genesis 41:27^{NIV}

Anat had not yet discovered his whereabouts in the underworld so he could be restored to life.[190]

Aperanat probably even thought Anat was one of the 'ha'elohim' who had sent the warnings. Moreover, given Joseph's ability to download dream interpretation through the power of 'ha'elohim', it would be logical for Aperanat to conclude Joseph was on Anat's wavelength. It was a natural step to rename him with one of her titles, 'Anat of Zaphon'—since it had the additional benefit of being a name covenant with the ruling house of Egypt. Such a covenant brought with it contractual obligations and safeguards favouring Pharaoh. He'd be secure in the knowledge that, if Joseph thought of deceiving him, the prospect of swift vengeance by Anat was a significant deterrent.

Yet names are carriers of both identity and destiny. Back in Joseph's era, a new name meant a new beginning, a new destiny, a new calling. So perhaps it's no coincidence that he became the dispossessor of the Egyptians after he was given an 'Anat' name.

Anat was not simply a warrior goddess who revelled in wanton destruction: she protected her brother Baal-Hadad by vanquishing and dispossessing his enemies. When Baal sent two messengers, *Vine* and *Field*, to inform her he'd invented a wondrous new weapon—lightning—she wondered what new enemy had arisen that he would need such a device. Hadn't she slain Yamm, the Sea? Hadn't she annihilated Nahar, the River? Hadn't she muzzled and thrashed Tannin, the sea monster? Hadn't she killed Lotan, the seven-headed coiling serpent? Hadn't she snuffed out the darlings of the gods, Fire and Flame? Hadn't she destroyed Mot, Death? Hadn't she been the one to smite the Flood, the notorious adversary of Baal?[191]

---

190 She's the one who buried him but she also searches for him.

Now, in other stories, Baal is the conqueror in many of these cases. Yet when Anat gets to speak for herself, she proclaims herself as the one who smashed these enemies and stripped them of their power and possessions. She is the dispossessor *par excellence* for she claims to have even defeated Death.

And it's no wonder her name is related to time, for Time is a dispossessor: of health and wealth, loved ones and loved things— even, if we are not vigilant, of blessings and destiny, hope and joy.

This is why Jesus' actions at Cana are so important: He did not allow the appointed time to dictate to Him, nor allow it to dispossess those around Him. He summoned the appointed time to do His bidding, showing Himself Lord of Time in all its aspects.

---

191 Rev. Prof. John Gray M.A., B.D., Ph.D., *Legacy of Canaan: The Ras Shamra texts and their relevance to the Old Testament,* Series: Vetus Testamentum, Supplements, Volume 5, Brill 1965

6.15 Anat and Deborah

During the time of Joshua, three Canaanite cities were completely devoted to destruction: Jericho and Ai in the south and Hazor in the north. Such cities were intended to remain as ruins forever. Deuteronomy 13:12–16 reveals that such a doom was also reserved for towns in Israel whose inhabitants were enticed by 'sons of Belial' to worship other deities, especially Belial himself, the spirit behind physical, sexual and spiritual abuse. Although the reasons for such interdictions on Canaanite towns are not known, we can surmise from Joshua's curse over Jericho that the *spirit of the place*, what the Romans called the 'genius loci', was one of child sacrifice.

Of course, each city had its different tutelary deity with different rites and sacrifices. There was much in common but there were also substantial differences. It's possible that the declaration of *accursed* and the prohibition on rebuilding only applied to the places where Belial was worshipped. It was some six or seven centuries before Jericho was rebuilt by Hiel of Bethel, but it was only a few years before the Canaanites reestablished Hazor in Upper Galilee. In the time of Joshua, Jabin was king of Hazor. And in the time of the Judges, Jabin was also king of new Hazor. Either this was a hereditary name amongst the overlords of Hazor or, like Pharaoh of Egypt, Araunah of Jebus[192] and Abimelech of Gerar, it was simply a title to designate the ruler of the land.

By the time of Deborah, the Canaanites had once again become a formidable force at Hazor and had been oppressing the Israelites for twenty years. Their cavalry boasted nine hundred iron chariots—the type that would have had three riders each—and their army would have numbered thousands more. The Israelites had no horses and, indeed, would not start to stable and breed them until the time of the third king—Solomon. There were theological motivations at work in this initial decision to deploy only foot-soldiers in battle: in warfare, the leaders would rely on the strength of their horsepower, rather than on the Lord.

Deborah lived in the hill country of Ephraim, suggesting that she was a descendant of the tribe of Joseph. She held court under a palm[193] and people came from all over Israel to receive her judgments. It's unclear whether she was the wife of a man named Lappidoth, *torch*, or whether she simply had the title 'torch-bride'.

In these descriptors alone, there are already counterparts with Anat. When the Canaanite sun-goddess Shapash helped Anat rescue Baal-Hadad from the underworld, she appraises Anat as a torch of the gods as well as a judge of both gods and mankind.[194]

Barak, *lightning*, counterpoints Baal-Hadad, the lightning-wielder, just as Deborah does Baal's warrior-sister, Anat. Perhaps Barak's

---

192 The original name of Jerusalem.

193 Possibly this was the same tree or in the vicinity of the tree near Bethel where the first woman in Scripture named Deborah, the nurse of Isaac's wife Rebekah, was buried. It was called the 'tree of weeping'.

194 herald-magazine.com/2021/01/01/deborah-and-jael-prevail-over-three-canaanite-goddesses/ (accessed 1 September 2023) This excellent article, *Deborah and Jael Prevail Over Three Canaanite Goddesses*, provides considerable detail on other goddesses, besides Anat, that were overcome in this battle.

reluctance to go to war without Deborah at his side indicates not only his fear of the Canaanite war goddesses[195] worshipped by his opponents but also the heart-belief that, because of those goddesses, he needed a woman to make victory possible. Barak thus becomes part of a line of men—Joseph, Elijah, Elisha, Jonah—whose fear of Anat outweighed their trust of God.

In her victory song, Deborah mentions Anat in passing:

> *In the days of Shamgar son of Anath,*
> *in the days of Jael, the highways were abandoned;*
> *travellers took to winding paths.*
> *Villagers in Israel would not fight;*
> *they held back until I, Deborah, arose,*
> *until I arose, a mother in Israel.*
>
> Judges 5:6–7[NIV]

That last phrase, *'a mother in Israel'* is another glancing reference to Anat who was known as the 'mother of gods'. Anat's Egyptian counterpart is usually considered to be the goddess Neith[196] who was often depicted wearing the crown of Lower Egypt that was

---

195 Besides Anat, there was also Astarte, 'Mistress of Horse and Chariot', who was summoned in curses to smash the skulls of various enemies. Ironically, Sisera almost certainly worshipped Astarte but had his skull smashed by a woman. See: herald-magazine.com/2021/01/01/deborah-and-jael-prevail-over-three-canaanite-goddesses/ (accessed 1 September 2023)

196 Anat's relationship to the Egyptian goddess Hathor was functional. The violence of their characters linked them. However the actual names Anat (or Anath), Neith, and Athena (who is the Greek equivalent of Anat) are all linguistically related. Perhaps there is also a relation between Anat and names like Nathan, Nathanael and Jonathan. Nathan means *to give, to put, to set, to fix, to appoint*. Perhaps the notion of *appointed* in respect to *time* derives from a combination of 'nat' and 'eth' in the name Anat. The use of the name Nathanael instead of Bartholomew in John's first chapter might therefore be an initial pointer towards Anat's hidden presence in the second chapter.

adorned with a stylised probiscis to symbolise a bee. One of the meanings of the name Deborah is *bee*.

Also in her victory song, Deborah mentions the stars fighting against Sisera. This could be a literal reference or it may be more metaphorical.

> *From the heavens the stars fought,*
> *from their courses they fought against Sisera.*
>
> Judges 5:6–7[NIV]

This could indicate a meteorite strike, similar to the shower that aided Joshua in his battle with the five Canaanite kings. Or, alternatively, it could be an astrological reference. The Canaanites believed in following signs from the heavens. Thus, there would have been an 'appointed time' for victory.

Yet it is God who rules the stars and decrees appointed times.

Can we miss those times He has chosen for us? Can we move too soon or delay too long and thus lose the opportunities He has given us? Of course we can. But the message of the miracle at Cana is that Jesus can summon back the appointed time for us so we can fulfil the assignments He has given to us and to our family.

6.16 The Folded Cloth

> *The cloth that had been around Jesus' head was rolled up, lying separate from the linen cloths.*
>
> John 20:7^{BSB}

I ONCE HAD AN EDITING JOB THAT involved considerable research. If I suspected the accuracy of any story, I had to look for its origin and decide whether or not it fell into the category of 'Christian urban myth'. The most difficult case ever was that of the 'folded napkin'.

Since the new millennium, Christian devotionals have widely circulated the idea that, when Jewish carpenters of the first century completed a project, they would wash their arms, dry them and then fold their cloth towel to indicate: *It is finished*.

I was surprised I'd never heard of this practice until recent years. So I invested considerable time investigating. As far as I can ascertain, the very first mention of this symbolism occurs in Sigmund Brouwer's novel, *The Weeping Chamber*, published in 1998. If there is a prior instance, I've yet to find it. Significantly I have not yet been able to unearth a single academic article that mentions this alleged workshop practice.

I have therefore concluded that *The Weeping Chamber* is most likely the source of the explanation about the symbolism of the folded cloth. Brouwer finishes his superb work of fiction with this image. It packs a powerful emotional punch, creating an exceedingly memorable ending. In fact, dare I say, it's the 'perfect' ending.

However, it appears to be a work of imagination—a very beautiful and evocative work, admittedly—that wraps Brouwer's finale in a highly charged gospel motif: the moment when John comes to believe Jesus has risen from the dead. The factual basis of Brouwer's scene is, in my view, in serious doubt. Given the ease of discovering other sources in his novel,[197] I'm surprised at the difficulty of uncovering any independent scholarly verification for Brouwer's symbolism of the folded cloth, if it is indeed true.[198]

There is however another possibility for the cloth: that of betrothal. One reinforcement of this potential symbolism occurs in the note that *'six stone water jars had been set there for the Jewish rites of purification.'* It's unclear whether they were to provide water for hand-washing or so that the bride and groom could bathe in a 'mikvah'.

In observant Jewish circles, a 'mikvah' is still considered essential to become ritually pure before marriage. However, it was not just used as preparation for marriage. It was forbidden to come into the presence of God in the Temple without passing through a mikvah.[199] This would also apply to anyone who had become

---

197 For example, Brouwer mentions the verifiable tradition that life is taken from a person by a drop of gall from the sword of the angel of death. He also uses testimony about trial procedure in rabbinical law.

198 This is not to say there is none, just that I have not been able to find it despite diligent searching. If you are aware of a scholarly source citing this tradition, I would really appreciate you contacting me with the details.

199 John specifically mentions that these are stone vessels. By law, earthenware vessels could not be purified but had to be broken. However, stone vessels though much more expensive, could be purified and so were used as containers for such rites. (See, for example, Leviticus 6:38; 11:33; 15:12)

ritually unclean through touching a deceased or diseased person. Women would routinely use a 'mikvah' after menstruation.

'Mikvah', *gathering of waters*, symbolises both a womb and a tomb, as well as rebirth and baptism.[200] 'It is regarded as a pure, unadulterated avenue of connection with God; and for that reason, it is a place where hope is reawakened and strengthened.'[201] In the grave where the body of Jesus lay, we can see far more than symbols of a tomb and womb—we see their realisation and manifestation.

Many other marriage symbols feature in the account of the death and resurrection of Jesus, some already examined and some that will remain until the next book with a closer look into the chiastic sections of John's third and third-last chapters. Still, the napkin that was folded and set aside may be one of these. It's difficult to be sure if the marriage tradition involving the napkin is as old as the first century, yet it's certainly possible. During the signing of the 'ketubah', the marriage contract which stipulates the rights of the couple, a handkerchief or napkin is used as a sign of acceptance. The lifting and transfer of the napkin before signing the ketubah must be observed by official witnesses for the betrothal to be considered valid.[202]

---

200 This connects the scene at Cana back to the previous chapter with its emphasis on John the Baptiser at Bethany-beyond-the-Jordan.

201 See: free.messianicbible.com/feature/mikvah-baptism-the-connection-between-immersion-conversion-and-being-born-again/ (accessed 7 March 2023)

202 See: myjewishlearning.com/article/the-ketubah-text-part-2/ (accessed 7 March 2023) Although this refers to modern betrothal ceremonies, it's possible the tradition goes back a long way. Ketubahs are attested as far back as the fourth century before Christ.

It isn't recorded what happened to the napkin in the tomb that was lying separate. We don't know if it was lifted by one of the disciples or not. The known fact is merely that the cloths from Jesus' body lay there. The description suggests He hadn't been unwrapped, but rather that the shroud simply fell flat as His resurrected body passed through it. Much as He was to pass through walls when He visited His disciples in the Upper Room.

Now John may well have helped Nicodemus and Joseph of Arimathea bring the body of Jesus to the tomb. He'd have instantly recognised anything unusual about those wrappings. He'd also have known that grave robbers—whether thieves or official body-snatchers—wouldn't bother tidying up. They'd take the body in its wrappings. But they were all there.

Fortunately for Jesus, now we come to consider this particular predicament, a young man had lost his linen garment[203] in the garden a few nights previously.

---

203 'One young man who had been following Jesus was wearing a linen cloth around his body. They caught hold of him, but he pulled free of the linen cloth and ran away naked.' Mark 14:51–52[BSB]

6.17 Royal Raiment

Adam was given a garment of skins by God to cover his nakedness—a 'ketonet' of exceptional quality and workmanship. We can be sure of its excellence because the next time we hear of a 'ketonet' in Scripture is when Jacob gifts one to his teenage son Joseph, favouring him so blatantly that his brothers became murderously jealous of him.

Normally, in Joseph's case, 'ketonet' is translated *coat of many colours,* though more accurately it would be a *long-sleeved tunic,* reaching to the ground. Now it wasn't just the richly ornamented coat itself that was a problem, it was also that it was clearly such a gorgeously fashioned garment it indicates Joseph was exempted from manual work. Long sleeves and trailing hems get in the way, after all.

Joseph loses his 'ketonet' when his brothers attack him. They sprinkle it in goat's blood and present it to their father as a silent witness to Joseph's disappearance. They don't speak out any explicit lies, they just let their father assume the worst from the tampered evidence they present. Joseph is later stripped another time: he loses another coat when Potiphar's wife grabs it from him. Once again this is presented as evidence, but on this occasion with lies attached: it's used by Potiphar's wife to make the claim Joseph tried to assault her.[204]

The next time 'ketonet' turns up, it describes the beautiful apparel to be sewn for Aaron and his sons. These are the exquisite garments they don for their ordination as the high priest and his assistants.

David's daughter, the princess Tamar, also wears a 'ketonet' that she tore in grief after she was raped by her brother. And one of David's most trusted allies also wore a 'ketonet'.

In the vast majority of instances where it's described, it's a priestly garment. Yet clearly it's also that worn by royalty. It's costly, distinctive, striking. No doubt the fine garment woven in one piece that belonged to Jesus would have been classed as a 'ketonet'.

> *When the soldiers crucified Jesus, they took His clothes, dividing them into four shares, one for each of them, with the undergarment remaining. This garment was seamless, woven in one piece from top to bottom.*
> *'Let's not tear it,' they said to one another. 'Let's decide by lot who will get it.'*
> *This happened that the Scripture might be fulfilled that said, 'They divided my clothes among them and cast lots for my garment.'*
>
> John 19:23–24[NIV], quoting Psalm 22:18

Jesus lost His fine garments at the Cross. The shame of Adam was revisited. But once again another small reversal occurs. In Eden the divine Gardener came looking for humanity who, in their shame, had sewn fig leaves together. God provided them

---

204 Joseph does not receive a second 'ketonet' as far as we know. The garment he wears when Potiphar's wife tries to seduce him is a 'beged'—she seizes it to substantiate her lie that he tried to molest her. Joseph however is given a fine linen tunic, another 'beged', by Pharaoh.

with a 'ketonet' each but, on the day of resurrection, humanity is the source of provision for Jesus' raiment. Clothes were waiting in the garden. The young man who lost them on the night Jesus was arrested reminds us of similar losses in Scripture—particularly of Joseph and his multi-coloured long-sleeved coat.

And that suggests to me that the linen garment lost by the young man wasn't any ordinary outfit, but prized clothing, fit for a priest and a prince.

Significantly, from the very beginning, a 'ketonet' was associated with loss of status and the father's presence. In many cases—certainly not all, since the priestly examples would be excluded here—it constitutes a symbol of dispossession. Adam and Eve were given a 'ketonet' by God when they were expelled from Eden and the immediate presence of the Lord. After Joseph's 'ketonet' was shredded, he was enslaved and did not see his father again for decades. When David's daughter Tamar tore her 'ketonet', it signified her loss of marriageable status and, as it turned out, also of her father's presence. David knew of her situation but did not send for her or go to her; he did not provide either comfort or justice. The last person specifically mentioned as wearing a 'ketonet', apart from the priests, was David's friend Hushai who tore his costly robe when he went to meet David during Absalom's insurrection. David sent him to foil Absalom's plans, so he too was deprived of the true king's presence. And finally, the loss of His 'ketonet' by Jesus preceded His agonising sense of abandonment by God on the Cross.

Yet all that John writes in his gospel is to say that, whatever dispossession we have experienced because of the lusts or jealousies of others, however unyielding our addiction or enslavement, however deep our loss of family or the presence of a loving, caring father, however much we have been deprived of status or calling or position or birthright, Jesus—the One who turned water into wine, symbolising a return of inheritance—has an appointed time to set it right.

In his first and last chapter, John leaves us a trail of clues to indicate that the mantle that fell from Elijah as he was drawn up to heaven passed, at least in a spiritual sense, from John the Baptiser to Simon, son of Jonah. There's significant ambiguity about whether Jesus meant 'Jonah' or 'John' or both. John the Baptiser, as the Elijah-who-was-to-come, was the heir to Jonah's mantle which had fallen from out of the whirlwind whisking Elijah heavenwards and then picked up by Elisha. The weight of unfulfilled potential on it was immense. It was meant for the ingathering of the Gentiles.

But in the second and second-last chapters, there's a new mantle on display: Joseph's 'ketonet', his coat-of-many-colours. Jesus has taken charge of this mantle too and made it pure, clean and holy. But who does He gift it to? Who is given charge of the mantle that brings with it a governing role to undo dispossession of nations, to restore lost inheritances, to sweep away the trauma of abandonment and to return a band of brothers to their Father's favour?

Let me give one hint. It isn't John.

6.18 The Tablemaster and the Cupbearer

> *'Now draw some out,' He said, 'and take it to the master of the banquet.'*
>
> *They did so, and the master of the banquet tasted the water that had been turned into wine. He did not know where it was from, but the servants who had drawn the water knew. Then he called the bridegroom aside and said, 'Everyone serves the fine wine first, and then the cheap wine after the guests are drunk. But you have saved the fine wine until now!'*
>
> John 2:8–10[BSB]

The Greek term 'architriklinos', *master of the banquet*, is difficult to translate. Literally it is *ruler of a dining room with three couches*. However, his role in wine-tasting suggests that his job as a tablemaster included the responsibilities of a cupbearer or 'oinochooi', *wine-pourer*.

An important aspect of Greek culture, dating from many centuries before Alexander conquered Judea, was the symposium. Originally held after a meal, a symposium was a gathering for *drinking together*, a party and talk-fest for debating and celebrating victories. The vintner, Mihalis Boutaris, commented, 'Inspiration and eloquence were the objectives of the symposium members, and the *oinochooi* had the responsibility to unleash the magical powers of wine to this end.'[205]

It sounds like a job for an enchanter but, in actual fact, the task was much more prosaic. The 'oinochooi' ensured the guests did *not* drink to excess by adjusting the concentration of the wine.[206] He kept the flow of witty conversation and philosophic insight going by making sure everyone was happily mellow, not aggressively inebriated. Seawater, seasoned with honey and resin, was added to the wine to make 'thalassitis'.[207]

The role of the 'oinochooi' was, in many ways, an extension of the ancient position of a cupbearer. In a royal court, a cupbearer tasted the wine before serving it to the king. He wasn't just a quality control expert, sending away anything too vinegary or bitter, he was there to detect poison. If the drink had been tampered with, then the cupbearer would suffer the fatal consequences, not the king. Unless, of course, the cupbearer betrayed his monarch and slipped in some poison after tasting the wine. A cupbearer, in effect, was a specialised bodyguard responsible for high level personal security.

This is why the Pharaoh in Joseph's story was so angry with his cupbearer and baker: one of them had tried to kill him and he wasn't sure who it was. While the investigation proceeded, he had them both locked up.

Now by the time the Greeks developed the symposium, the cupbearer's role wasn't so much about detecting poison as

---

205   scmp.com/magazines/post-magazine/food-drink/article/2094773/greek-wines-rich-history-and-recent-rebirth-and (accessed 22 November 2022)

206   Oinochooi is the modern Greek word for 'sommelier', *master of wine*. Originally it simply meant a person who pours wine.

207   Drinks were made up of two parts wine to five parts water, or one part wine to three parts water.

ensuring the party-goers didn't get sick-drunk. The tablemaster at Cana clearly knew about wine quality, indicating he was fulfilling a cupbearer's role.

Yet Jesus also filled and fulfilled this role—He's the one ultimately responsible for the quality of the wine in those stone jars. He mixed it precisely to His specifications. He's the Divine Wine-Pourer and Cupbearer.

6.19 Cupbearers Amongst the Gods

THE NOTION OF THE 'CUPBEARER' is such a profoundly important theme John returns to it in his fourth chapter. There, during His meeting with the Samaritan woman, Jesus brings about a healing from an historical wound and societal rift partially caused by the cupbearer Nehemiah.[208]

Perhaps we should consider this work of Jesus as inevitable. After all, the role of cupbearer is significant in many stories involving the Greek and Canaanite pantheons—the very deities Jesus was opposing. He had to expose the counterfeits, cleanse the defilements and demonstrate the true nature of cup-bearing.

Anat declared herself willing to be the cupbearer of Baal once he was granted his palace.[209] Her offer may connect to wine-making as well as the wild slaughter she undertakes during the victory feast for Baal's conquest over the chaos-making Sea. Anat sends out an invitation to a banquet. Painting herself in rouge and henna, she locks the doors of the feasting hall and massacres all

---

208 I intend to provide further details in the fourth book in this series. However, if you want an early glimpse of what Jesus does with the idea of the cupbearer, see *Like Wildflowers, Suddenly: Jesus and the Healing of History #01*, Armour Books, 2019

209 Astarte also offers to fill this role.

Baal's enemies. Wearing the heads and hands of these slain foes as trophies, she wades in blood.[210]

Victor Matthews and Don Benjamin explain this detail in the Baal cycle as an analogy to the celebration of the grape harvest: while she is knee-deep in the blood of her enemies, Canaanite farmers would have been knee-deep in a winepress, treading out the juice of their grapes.[211] The cultic celebration of Ra'shu Yeni, the Canaanite New Wine Festival, was associated with this harvest period. Like Sukkot, the Jewish Feast of Tabernacles, it was a week long and, in addition, both involved dwelling in makeshift booths for the duration of the festival.

On 7 October 2023, as Sukkot was winding up, Hamas forces from Gaza breached the border wall, committing atrocities generally condemned around the world. The spiritual fingerprints of Anat were in the timing—that knot or node in space-time where circumstances were perfectly aligned and the moment to 'strike' is *now*—it was not just an auspicious day when Anat had been worshipped in the past during Ra'shu Yeni, but it was also the fiftieth anniversary[212] of the start of the Yom Kippur war when Israel, unexpectedly attacked by a coalition of enemies, had not only defeated them but won back lost territory. Is there a more appropriately perverse day for vengeance by a war goddess than the Jubilee commemoration of a victory in battle?

---

210 As did the Egyptian goddess Hathor in slaying Ra's enemies.
211 Ra'shu Yeni, the New Wine Festival, was held in the twelfth month of the Canaanite year, while Sukkot, the Feast of Tabernacles, was in the first month of the Jewish civic year. Nevertheless they were both celebrated at a similar time.
212 Actually it was the fiftieth anniversary plus one day but I've yet to find a commentator who has made this fine distinction. The Yom Kippur War started on 6 October 1973 and the invasion from Gaza in the early morning of 7 October 2023.

Anat is a chaos agent and the violent slaughter, barbaric targeting of civilians, including children and the elderly during the attack from Gaza shows her to be the spiritual force behind the incursion.

She is not the only violent cupbearer featured in mythological cycles. The sky-ruler of the Hurrian pantheon was overthrown by his cupbearer. Reigning for nine years, he was challenged by the sky-ruler's son Kumarbi who castrated him. The former cupbearer then cursed Kumarbi to give birth and he eventually did—to Teshub, the storm-god, another lightning-wielder, who fought against his father.

A parallel in Greek mythology is the castration of Uranus by his son Kronos. Subsequently frightened by his father's curse that he will be similarly overthrown, Kronos decides to be pro-active in ensuring it never comes to pass. He therefore swallows his children at birth. His wife eventually tricks him with a stone and baby Zeus is saved. Zeus grows up, applies to become his father's cupbearer, then serves him wine mixed with mustard, salt and nectar. This nausea-inducing concoction causes Kronos to vomit up Zeus' siblings. An epic war then begins between Zeus at the head of the younger Olympians and Kronos as the leader of the titans, the elder gods.

Neither of these two stories, on the surface, has any connection with Noah and his family.[213] Yet, once we consider that Jesus was working to heal a curse of dispossession, the common elements might be more obvious: sexual transgression against the father, the cursing of a child, the turn of the age, dispossession and

---

213 Peter, however, made a connection in his second letter when he mentions the fallen angels who fathered the nephilim destroyed in the flood and who were themselves sent to Tartarus (2 Peter 2:4). This is a reference to the lowest level of hell where the titans were imprisoned. Peter thus equates the elder-gods of the Greeks with the fallen angels, commonly called Watchers.

inheritance, wine and cupbearing. For many centuries, one rabbinic viewpoint has been that Ham actually castrated his father. Hence Noah's curse on Canaan: because Noah realises he is dispossessed of more progeny, he speaks out dispossession against the progeny of Ham.

The healing of dispossession therefore encompasses this eon-old dishonour of the father.

PART
JOHN 2:11-16 BSB

Jesus performed this, the first of His signs, at Cana in Galilee.
He thus revealed His glory, and His disciples believed in Him.

After this, He went down to Capernaum with His mother and brothers
and His disciples, and they stayed there a few days.

When the Jewish Passover was near, Jesus went up to Jerusalem.
In the temple courts He found men selling cattle, sheep, and doves,
and money changers seated at their tables.

So He made a whip out of cords and drove all from the temple courts,
both sheep and cattle. He poured out the coins of the money changers
and overturned their tables. To those selling doves He said,
'Get these out of here! How dare you
turn My Father's house into a marketplace!'

SEVEN
JOHN 20:8-12 BSB

And he saw and believed.
For they still did not understand from the Scripture
that Jesus had to rise from the dead.

Then the disciples returned to their homes.

But Mary stood outside the tomb weeping.
And as she wept, she bent down to look into the tomb,
and she saw two angels in white
sitting where the body of Jesus had lain,
one at the head and the other at the feet.

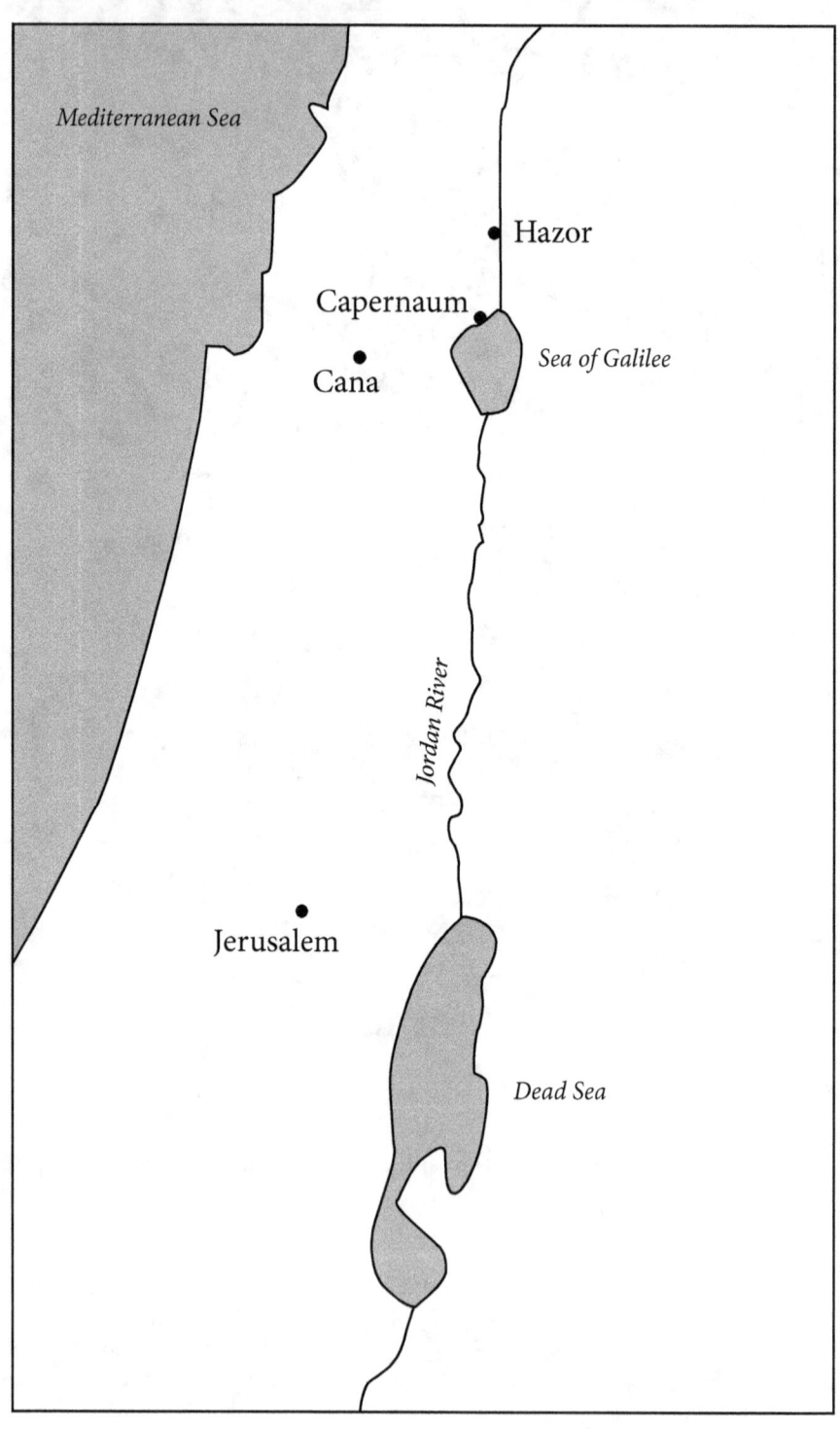

7.1 Belief in the Resurrection

His disciples believed in Him.
John 2:11^{BSB}

And he saw and believed.
John 20:8^{BSB}

What does it mean to believe in the resurrection? Resurrection is, after all, THE distinguishing feature of Christian belief. John addresses various misconceptions about it in his gospel. An entire book could be written on each of these misunderstandings, but I'm just going to summarise them briefly.[214]

Resurrection is NOT immortality of the soul.

Resurrection is not incompatible with the concept of immortality of the soul. However resurrection involves flesh, matter, body. It involves the soul returning to the same, but perfected, DNA. If resurrection were a normal part of earthly experience—even if rare—it would gradually become a cultural expectation, not remain an almost unbelievable, miraculous event. It would no longer be a matter of faith. For most cultures across most eras, belief in immortality of the soul has been widespread. Resurrection, however, has not.

---

214   Most of these categories (if not always the content of them) are taken from Jon D. Levenson's excellent exposition: *Resurrection and the Restoration of Israel: The Ultimate Victory of the God of Life*, Yale University Press 2006

Resurrection is NOT reincarnation.

In John 9:2[NIV], the disciples ask Jesus:

> 'Rabbi, who sinned, this man or his parents, that he was born blind?'

The odd question—suggesting that the man's blindness might be a punishment for his own sin—indicates the disciples were querying if karma from a past life had caught up with the man. Even if they personally didn't hold with reincarnation, they were sufficiently aware of it to pose the question.

Reincarnation was to become a contested issue in the early Christian era. Adherents of the Greek mathematician and religious philosopher, Pythagoras, joined the growing church and brought with them the belief that souls, having survived a person's death, transmigrated to another body. Admiring both Pythagoras and Jesus, some of these disciples decided there were so many commonalities between the two that Jesus was obviously a reincarnation of Pythagoras!

Yet reincarnation and resurrection are incompatible. Resurrection unites the soul with the same body it left at death—now raised up from the dust, returned to life and transformed in glory.

Resurrection is NOT memory.

Despite the thought that life after death is substantially equivalent to 'living on in the remembrance of friends and family' is relatively modern in concept, John tackles it in his second-last chapter. Memory stands apart as a living witness to the resurrection—not as resurrection itself. Mary is not only an eyewitness to the resurrection; her very name—Magdalene, *of the watchtower, the watcher, observer, rememberer*—speaks to her role as a repository of memory. Memory corroborates and authenticates the resurrection but does not embody it.

Resurrection is NOT offspring.

The notion of 'living on through a place in the family tree', either through descendants who share a bloodline or a surname by adoption, is another belief occasionally promoting itself as 'resurrection'. We are certainly offspring of God[215] but to suggest our existence is evidence of the resurrection misses the difference between creation and re-creation. Nominal resurrection—resurrection in name only—is an accommodation to our prevailing cultural rejection of the miraculous. It adopts a worldview devoid of the power of heaven, bereft of God's divine intervention, and totally lacking in the comprehensive defeat of the last enemy, Death.

Resurrection is NOT self-empowerment

Jon Levenson describes the traditional Hebrew formulation of God as the One 'who revives the dead' as being retro-fitted into 'may all blossom into persons who have gained power over our own lives.' In this interpretation, the dead have disappeared, and God's role in 'resurrection' is to grant us success and control in our lives. 'The inversion is striking: an ancient acclamation of divine power in the face of ultimate and unavoidable defeat has been transformed into a thoroughly modern prayer for enhanced personal autonomy.'[216] The ongoing metaphor in the prayer he cites views the dead as vegetation in need of watering, resurrection as rainfall and new life as a flowering in the presence, not of God, but of the sun.

---

215 Acts 17:28
216 Jon D. Levenson, *Resurrection and the Restoration of Israel: The Ultimate Victory of the God of Life*, Yale University Press 2006

This interpretation of resurrection is directly akin to the serpent's promise in Eden: you shall be like gods. You'll be in control, you'll be able to direct circumstances as you please, you'll be empowered to create your own destiny.

Resurrection is NOT individual.

Resurrection is NOT temporary.

Resurrection is true in more than a spiritual sense.

Or rather, it's not *solely* individual. To any society with an atomistic, separatist ideology of the individual—most of western civilisation in the twenty-first century—this is beyond comprehension. We simply cannot put ourselves into the first century cultural mindset where an individual simply didn't exist apart from family, community and nation and where resurrection restricted to the individual wouldn't have made sense. Resurrection that didn't benefit the whole society, that didn't offer a renaissance to every Jew, including those in the Diaspora, wasn't worth the name. It wouldn't have dawned on them that resurrection should embrace the Gentiles, but there was no question about friends, family and neighbours.

It's easy to miss the fact that the resurrection of Jesus was communal in nature.

> *The bodies of many holy people who had died were raised to life. They came out of the tombs after Jesus' resurrection and went into the holy city and appeared to many people.*
>
> Matthew 27:52–53[NIV]

What happened to those resurrected people? Traditional wisdom has it that they died again. A temporary resurrection seems completely pointless to me. I just can't fathom its purpose, so I'm going to express my faith it's a permanent thing. Furthermore, Scripture is noticeably silent on the matter. Did the resurrected ones ascend like Jesus did? Or, are they still here? It's an unsolved mystery.

And a similar mystery—just what was Jesus doing for the forty days between His resurrection and ascension? He clearly didn't spend most of the time with His disciples. They were repeatedly surprised when He turned up, unannounced.

John's portrayal of the resurrection is different from his fellow gospel writers. It's intimately bound up with the wedding at Cana and, consequently, with the Bridegroom of all mankind. For John, it's rebirth, betrothal, marriage, bestowal of inheritance—and applies to individuals, to family, to brothers, disciples and nations.

7.2 Home

After this, He went down to Capernaum with His mother and brothers and His disciples.

John 2:12^{BSB}

Then the disciples returned to their homes.

John 20:10^{BSB}

It's the small details like this that convince me how thorough the chiasmus is. The inconsequential comments that parallel each other and that we might be likely to dismiss as just marking a break between one part of the story and the next. Of course they *do* do that, but sometimes they carry weight far greater than appears on the surface.

What is the significance of the name Capernaum in a story harking back to Noah, Joseph, Canaan and Moses? Capernaum was where Jesus made His home when He was in Galilee. However, as far as 'homes' go in the narrative of the resurrection, it can't be the disciples' places of residence back in the north. Instead it must be where they are staying in Jerusalem or Bethany. The Greek in fact does not contain the word *home*, but says they went back to *their own.*

Nevertheless *home* evokes comfort and rest, just as Capernaum does. The name Capernaum means *village of Nahum*[217] or *village of Noah*. But *village* is a Hebrew pun that can encode a double meaning: it also designates a *young lion* and perhaps even points to *rock, cornerstone* or *threshold*. Nahum means *comfort* and Noah means *rest*. Once again we have echoes of threshold moments in the story of Noah in John's text.

Moreover, the first mention of *comfort* in Scripture occurs when Noah was born. At that time, his father Lamech said:

> *May this one comfort us in the labour and toil of our hands caused by the ground that the Lord has cursed.*
>
> Genesis 5:29^{BSB}

Now, personally, despite what other commentators think about this prophetic utterance over Noah, I don't believe this comfort ever truly came about until Jesus ushered it in. The story of the flood and its aftermath is not a particularly comforting one and certainly not indicative of the *rest* that Lamech named Noah for. Building the ark, provisioning it, moving in all the animals, keeping them fed and looking after their health for months and then starting again in a washed, baptised world does not strike me as restful but stressful.

So with all the subtle links John has given us back to Noah, I think the mention of Capernaum is included to say: the *comfort* promised to humanity nearly three millennia previously has at last, at long last, come to settle in the world. The *rest* and restoration that is long overdue has been actualised and made manifest in the sublimely wonderful Person of Jesus of Nazareth.

---

217 We don't know if Capernaum was the hometown of the prophet Nahum. It's possible but unlikely, since only Jonah is known to have come from Galilee.

7.3 Time Shift

> *When the Jewish Passover was near, Jesus went up to Jerusalem.*
>
> John 2:13[BSB]

Once again, aspects of time are bedrock elements in this section of John's gospel presentation. Tabernacles—Sukkot—is the last divinely sanctioned feast of the sacred year. Passover—Pesach—is the first. There are other festivals, Purim and Hanukkah, between these two, but they are human institutions, not God-appointed.

John is about to relate the incident where Jesus chased the money-changers out of the Temple and, because he does so right after the story of the wedding feast, many commentators have thought there must have been two occasions when this happened: one early in Jesus' ministry and one in the last week before His death, as described in all the synoptic gospels.

However the assumption behind this reasoning is that John is proceeding in chronological order, whereas in fact, as I've shown in this series, he is working chiastically. Matching themes are his signature design, not sequential ordering. His only time-stamp regarding the cleansing of the Temple is: *'when the Jewish Passover was near.'* That matches the events in Matthew, Mark and Luke who also indicate it happened in Passover week.

So, despite the assertions of scholars who favour two dust-ups in the Temple, there is, in my view, just one occasion when Jesus expelled the traders. It was the last major event of His public ministry. John therefore, in shifting his time focus from Cana at Sukkot to Jerusalem approaching Passover three-and-a-half years later, has simply gone straight from first to last, from beginning to end, from start to finish. His account moves directly from the spectacular opening 'sign' that demonstrated the identity of Jesus to the closing 'sign'—the wild meleé that was the fulfillment of an enigmatic and obscure line in Isaiah's prophecy.

Yes, Jesus was active before the wedding at Cana—the first chapter of John's gospel describes Him talking and teaching various men who would become His disciples. And yes, Jesus was active after the Temple cleansing at Jerusalem—those days of talking and teaching are also described by John. But, talking and teaching aside, His *first* public *action* was changing water into wine and His *last* public *action* was driving the money-changers out of the Temple.

This is important because, as we've seen, a possible nuance behind Jesus' reply to His mother's request for Him to do something about the wine is: 'You're asking Me to upset the timing of a prophecy.' By moving straight from the first to the last public action, John is mindful to show how, even with an early start, Daniel's prophecy about the 'cutting off' of the Messiah still fits into the timeline of Jesus' ministry. The exact number of 1290 days certainly no longer points directly to the death of Jesus. And yet, indirectly, it still does.

The prophecy can only still work if the emptying of the Temple courts straightforwardly connects to the empty tomb. And this is exactly John's chiastic match: he directly linked the two together. Yet he also has some very subtle and unexpected themes in parallel play—the demi-god and strong man Herakles finally turns up, Archimedes makes yet another surprise appearance, and while the angelic presence is obvious in the tomb, it's not quite so obvious in the scene where Jesus overturns the tables. However both cherubim and seraphim are alluded to in that skirmish. The expulsion of the traders from the Temple is a foretelling of both the momentous combat of Jesus with Death as well as His imminent victory—a hidden theme that is only brought to the surface by John's chiastic mirroring.

7.4 Archimedes

In the temple courts He found men selling cattle, sheep, and doves, and money changers seated at their tables.

John 2:14^{BSB}

He entered the tomb and saw the linen cloths lying there...

John 20:6^{BSB}

She saw two angels in white... one at the head and the other at the feet.

John 20:12^{BSB}

It may seem odd to connect these verses with Archimedes, the great Greek physicist, mathematician, astronomer, inventor and engineer who was born about three centuries before Jesus died. Apart from one completely unsubtle connection—the 153 fish caught at the post-resurrection breakfast in Galilee and the geometrical theorem discovered by Archimedes called the 'measure of the fish' and involving the number 153—there doesn't seem to be much to link the two.

I'm convinced, however, the John's record of the joke about the 153 fish is there to make his erudite first century readers so conscious of Archimedes that they'll actually notice the less conspicuous references. And perhaps even shout 'Eureka!' when they catch the clues.

Now the king of Syracuse had ordered a fine gold crown. Then, becoming suspicious silver had been substituted in the finished product, he'd tasked Archimedes with devising a way to discover if the crown was indeed pure gold—without damaging it in any way.

Archimedes stepped into his bath one day, noticed the rise of the water, and the answer occurred to him. He was so flushed with excitement he rushed out into the streets, yelling, 'Eureka! I have it!' not realising he was entirely naked. Without this moment of forgetfulness, his discovery would never have become as famous as it did. Archimedes had recognised silver and gold displace different amounts of water—so he just needed to see whether the crown displaced the same volume as the right-sized lump of gold.

Centuries later, the temple money-changers made use of his discovery to check for fraudulent shekels. The family of the high priest had a sophisticated rort in place. The only way the people could pay the annual Temple tax was using a special shekel not in ordinary circulation. Because the Jews were forbidden to mint their own coins, they imported this special silver shekel from Tyre. Now other production sites across the ancient world offered customised designs, but not Tyre. The engraving on their shekels—the highest sterling available anywhere—was restricted. On one side were the words, 'Tyre, Holy and Inviolable' and on the other was an image of Herakles-Melqart, the patron deity of this formerly Phoenician city. Melqart is another name for Moloch, the fire-god and lord of death. His worship was entirely forbidden to the Jewish people.

So by choosing the quality of the silver over the ban on graven images, the chief priests created an intolerable double bind for the people. They could disobey God by not contributing to the Temple upkeep or they could disobey God by tolerating the image of an idol—the god of death, no

less—inside the Temple and, worse still, trade with that image. They were also forced to pay an extortionate exchange rate to buy the special shekel that had been decreed to be the only legitimate form of payment of the Temple tax.

Now some enterprising individuals had apparently set about making fraudulent copies of these shekels. They plated a thin silver coating onto a base metal, like lead, engraved with the Tyrian emblems. The money-changers checked for such counterfeits using the simple water displacement test used by Archimedes. Which, as you'll recall, he made famous by dashing out naked into the streets of Syracuse.

So it isn't entirely surprising that John matches the money-changers to the linen cloths left behind. Jesus wasn't wearing anything when He left the tomb. On the one hand, this reminds us of Archimedes, on the other it recalls Adam in the Garden of Eden. Jesus has returned to that first estate.

Fortunately, a few days previously a young man lost his fine linen not too far away. Many scholars suspect this young man was John Mark, the writer of the second gospel. In addition, early church tradition identified Mark as the *'rich young ruler'* who asked Jesus what he had to do to inherit eternal life. Both *rich* and *ruler* allow for a significant possibility regarding any lost garments: they might well have been purple. And that would prove ideal in a twofold way: first to link to 'canaa', *purple*, and second in the light of one of Jesus' forthcoming comments to Mary Magdalene.

Why would John be at pains to counterpoint Jesus and Archimedes? Historically, we have no evidence of a theological conflict, but perhaps John's subtle allusions are enough. Both men were, after all, killed by Roman soldiers, despite the fact the Roman leader in charge wanted to save their lives— Jesus died under the prefecture of Pontius Pilate in 33 A.D.

and Archimedes during the Siege of Syracuse in 212 B.C.[218] Reportedly, Archimedes was drawing on the ground when he died, reminding us of John's account of Jesus writing on the ground when the woman caught in adultery was brought before Him.

But what was the conflict for John to have so pointedly pitted One against the other? I think it's likely to have been the position of Creator vs. inventor.

Archimedes is still regarded by many individuals today as the greatest inventor of all time: his genius changed the nature of science as well as warfare. Back in the era when an ordinary bridge-builder, 'pontifex', was considered to have divine powers, Archimedes' screw to move water, his heat ray, his ship grappler, his geometrical discoveries—including a value for π—would all have been stunning. They are remarkable even now. But they engender a curious mindset. For many people, both ancient and modern, the utilisation of the scientific and mathematical secrets of creation and the bending of nature to human will are more impressive feats than the foundation of creation itself. The inventor is thus seen to surpass the Creator.

Not so, John is saying. The inventor merely teases out what the Creator has built into His design. He finishes his gospel with a final swipe at Archimedes—matching the hammer blow to the Pythagoreans in his opening line.

---

218 In the film *Indiana Jones and the Dial of Destiny*, the siege of Syracuse is featured, as is Archimedes and the summoning of time along with the seizing of opportunity at an appointed time. Also in passing are references to Athena (Anat), Dionysius and tombs—and curiously all of these, as we've seen, form part of the matrix of symbols in the background of the second and second-last chapters of John's gospel. I can't bring myself to feel that these elements in the movie are coincidental. The writers, in my view, were picking up the threads of some spiritually significant thoughtline.

> *Now there are also many other things that Jesus did. Were every one of them to be written, I suppose that the world itself could not contain the books that would be written.*
>
> John 21:25^{ESV}

The word for *world* used here is 'kosmos', *universe*. The possible books about Jesus are so uncountable they would overfill the entire cosmos. John thus counters a famous treatise of Archimedes. A Greek king had expressed the notion that the number of grains of sand in the universe was infinite—but Archimedes in 'Psammites', *The Sand Reckoner*, refuted this notion.[219] By implication, everything everywhere was considered countable.

However, John maintains this cannot be applied to Jesus who, so he asserts, is beyond any such reckoning.

In *The Elijah Tapestry*, I've shown how intimately this very last verse of John's gospel is connected to the first verse, *'In the beginning was the Word.'* That, in turn, is also closely tied to the start of Genesis, *'In the beginning God created the heavens and the earth.'*

These famous opening words of the Torah encode multiple mathematical features: many multiples of seven and of 111, three instances of close approximations to the golden ratio, and also one of π.

However, neither God as the author of the Torah, nor even His scribe Moses, was credited with first demonstrating the value of π. Instead it was Archimedes. He famously showed that π is

---

[219] Pythagoras was believed to be the first to use the word 'kosmos' to mean universe, and the second was considered to be Archimedes. Thus John managed to counter two famous ancient philosophers in one go with the final assertion of his gospel.

greater than $^{223}/_{71}$ and less than $^{220}/_{70}$ (or, more commonly, $^{22}/_{7}$, two numbers that both have a sense of 'completeness' in Hebrew).[220] Once again, the discoverer was given precedence over the Creator.

John's subtlety in reasserting the proper position of Jesus is in accord with the Lord's own actions. Jesus never dishonours anyone. He never says that either Noah or Joseph was wrong for dispossessing others, nor does He say anything about Nehemiah or Ezra at the well in Samaria, nor does He mention the defilement both Saul and David brought to the land when He's about to raise Lazarus from the dead. But His actions speak loudly into the silence.[221]

When we are called to heal history in the way Jesus modelled for us, we don't need to justify ourselves or look for vindication. We just need to *do*.

---

220 22 is the number of letters in the Hebrew alphabet, and sometimes is used symbolically to mean the 'complete set of all letters' or 'all words'. Seven is the number associated with the Sabbath, the day when God rested, having completed His work of creation.

221 Ezra and Nehemiah will be featured in the fourth book in this series, and the defilement that Saul brought on the land and that David then perpetuated will be examined during the story of the raising of Lazarus. For previews of these issues, see *Like Wildflowers, Suddenly: Jesus and the Healing of History #01* and *Where His Feet Pass: Jesus and the Healing of History #04*, Armour Books.

7.5 The Weight of Glory

> *The Lord said to Moses, 'When you take a census of the Israelites to count them, each one must pay the Lord a ransom for his life at the time he is counted. Then no plague will come on them when you number them. Each one who crosses over to those already counted is to give a half shekel... This half shekel is an offering to the Lord... The rich are not to give more than a half shekel and the poor are not to give less when you make the offering to the Lord to atone for your lives... It will be a memorial for the Israelites before the Lord, making atonement for your lives.'*
>
> Exodus 30:11–16[NIV]

This commandment is the origin of the Temple tax. It's actually an atonement—a covering, a ransom—for participating in a census. The shekels collected in the first count of the community were later used in the tabernacle. They were melted to make heavy metal bases for the upright poles holding the curtains in place, and for silver hooks at the curtain tops.[222]

The primary meaning of *shekel* is not a currency unit, but *weight*. When Daniel interprets the writing on the wall of Belshazzar's palace, 'Mene, mene, tekel, parsin,' he declares that

---

[222] Exodus 38:25–28

'tekel'—Aramaic for 'shekel'—simply means that the king has been *weighed in the scales* and found wanting.

In the ancient world, weight was associated with honour and glory. That concept isn't entirely absent in today's culture: after all, when we dishonour someone we are said to treat them lightly. Also in our society, the relative 'weight' of things determines their monetary value. Honour, meantime, has become associated with wealth, provision of goods, social status, or contribution to society.

Peter encouraged us to honour everyone without exception,[223] yet we rarely do. We lose sight of the meaning of God's instruction—*'The rich are not to give more than a half shekel and the poor are not to give less when you make the offering to the Lord to atone for your lives.'* We're all valuable in God's sight, but no soul is more precious than another.[224] The rich are no more treasured than the poor.

By the time of Jesus, this atonement offering had morphed into a double bind: if a man didn't pay the tax, he disobeyed God; but if he did pay the tax with its graven image of an idol, he also disobeyed God. The priesthood promoted blasphemy, ensuring that, either way, the worshippers sinned. The choice to prefer the purity of silver content in a coin over any purity of worship—involving the honour of God, the glory of His name, the holiness of His sanctuary, the prayers of His people—brought defilement on the nation.

On the trading floor of the Temple, the money-changers re-enacted the trafficking that occurred in Eden and was the satan's downfall. The exorbitant exchange rates, the rampant injustice, particularly towards the poor, are echoes of God's indictment

---

223 1 Peter 2:17

224 Some Jews see significance in the fact that the gematria (numerical value) of the word, *shekel*, is 430, and so is the gematria of the word, *soul*.

against the guardian cherub who was cast out for the vileness of his trade. The Hebrew word used by Ezekiel implies *trafficking, merchandising, slander, trading in names* or *reputations* or *callings* or *destinies* and *souls*.

Instead of an exchange that atones for the soul, as God originally directed, there was an exchange that sold and enslaved the soul.

It wasn't just injustice that infuriated Jesus, it's the travesty of choosing 'pure' silver and thereby allowing the satan into the Temple itself to perpetuate his depraved entrapment of souls. Jesus, like Elijah, set about removing Baal worship and casting out those minions empowering it.

This problem is still an issue. How often today do we devalue purity of worship in favour of 'purity' of financial giving or hierarchical status or social position or political allegiance or loyalty to those in charge or family associations or doctrinal belief? For what 'silver coin' have we traded our souls? What do we assess, in our own minds, as so important that it trumps honour to God?

A curious link exists between the original silver shekels and the various time shifts in the two pericopes of the second chapter. One item the shekels were used for was curtain hooks. Now, a *hook* in Hebrew is 'vav', and it corresponds to the sixth letter of the Hebrew alphabet. Recall that there are no special digits for numbers in Hebrew. Thus 'vav' also functions as *six*. And that means there were 'vav' stone pots at Cana.

Now the letter 'vav' is not only *hook* or *tent peg* or *six*, it's also used in an unusual grammatical way. When 'vav' is placed in front of a verb it changes the time sense: from past to future or future to past.

I think that, all along, John repeatedly hinted that the miracle of Cana was about changing time.

7.6 Cherubim

So He made a whip out of cords and drove all from the temple courts, both sheep and cattle. He poured out the coins of the money changers and overturned their tables. To those selling doves He said, 'Get these out of here! How dare you turn My Father's house into a marketplace!'

John 2:15–16^{BSB}

But Mary stood outside the tomb weeping. And as she wept, she bent down to look into the tomb, and she saw two angels in white sitting where the body of Jesus had lain, one at the head and the other at the feet.

'Woman, why are you weeping?' they asked.

'Because they have taken my Lord away,' she said, 'and I do not know where they have put Him.'

John 20:11–13^{BSB}

IN THESE CHIASTIC SEGMENTS, JOHN ALLUDES to Eden in two different ways—the first hints at re-enactment and the second at reversal. The prophet Ezekiel was told to take up a lament against the principality behind the maritime empire ruled by Tyre:

> 'You were the seal of perfection, full of wisdom and perfect in beauty.
>
> You were in Eden, the garden of God…
>
> You were anointed as a guardian cherub, for I had ordained you.
>
> You were on the holy mountain of God; you walked among the fiery stones.
>
> From the day you were created you were blameless in your ways—
>
> until wickedness was found in you. By the vastness of your trade,
>
> you were filled with violence, and you sinned.
>
> So I drove you in disgrace from the mountain of God,
>
> and I banished you, O guardian cherub, from among the fiery stones…
>
> By the multitude of your iniquities and the dishonesty of your trading you have profaned your sanctuaries.
>
> Ezekiel 28:12-18[BSB]

The guardian cherub who was cast out of Eden for trading—for trafficking in souls and commodifying destinies, callings, names, identities and reputations—came to be the ruling spirit at Tyre, the capital of the Phoenician empire.

The Phoenicians allegedly invented money as a medium of exchange—substituting iron half-rings that looked like a pair of bull's horns for live cattle, sheep or goats. Coins soon followed—the first of which had an image of the king on it, a tradition still followed in many parts of the world today.

By the time of Jesus, Tyre had long been conquered by Alexander the Great. But, even under the Romans, it still retained its association with money. The mint in Tyre produced the highest quality silver coins available in that era. Their blasphemous currency with an image of Herakles on it had been chosen by the chief priests as the 'Temple shekel'.

Every time the disciples travelled through Scythopolis in the Jordan Valley, seeing the temple of Herakles there—as they had on the way to Cana—they would have been reminded of the idolatrous engraving on the Temple shekel. Perhaps they recognised that the guardian cherub who had been cast out of Eden, and was the power behind the ruler of Tyre in the days of Ezekiel, had set up shop in the courtyard of the temple of Jerusalem. The satan had pushed his way into the earthly counterpart of the heavenly temple. This was the very place where, in the Holy of Holies, heaven touched earth between the outstretched wings of the cherubim on the Ark of the Covenant.

Once Eden had been the 'temple' where heaven touched earth—it was not only a Garden but a Mountain, a place of four fountains, of fiery stones, of face-to-face communion with God. And just as the satan—specifically the principality behind the rise of Tyre—had been cast out of that sanctuary for trading, so now Jesus casts out exactly the same unholy cherub from the Temple in Jerusalem.

His actions were prophetic. The image on the coins was Moloch—the fire-god who demanded the sacrifice of children, particularly firstborn sons. In the Jewish mind Moloch was associated with Death. So, just as Jesus banishes Death from the Temple, He is soon to expel Death from the tomb and from the temple of His body.

And when He does so there are holy cherubim at the slab where His body lay. Now they aren't specifically identified as cherubim but John's description paints them that way. He mentions that one was positioned at the head and one at the foot, just as they would have bowed over the mercy-seat on the Ark of the Covenant. Here, they proclaimed, is the new mercy-seat where heaven touches earth, here is the evidence the atonement has been accepted, here is the place where the once-for-all and all-sufficient sacrifice that provides ransom for mankind and is so superior to the blood of bulls and goats it needs never to be repeated, here is where the remission of sins has been confirmed.

And where is the great High Priest as Mary is conversing with these messengers? Why isn't He still in the immediate vicinity of the tomb? The fact is, He's probably getting appropriately dressed. Because the high priest wore a purple tunic, I suspect the garment John Mark lost several nights previously has to have been purple. If God can arrange the circumstances so neatly and niftily that Jesus was provided with the clothes He needed on resurrection morning, then surely He'd have made certain of the colour as well. Jesus has yet to go to the heavenly Temple to have His appointment ratified as High Priest—not of the line of Aaron, but of the order of Melchizedek—but events are moving towards that endorsement.

Now just as the scene in the Temple is a shadow re-enactment of the expulsion of the satan from Eden, the dialogue in the Garden reverses that of Eden. The cry of Mary's heart is to find the Lord.

In the garden of Eden, God came looking for the representatives of mankind, His 'shomer', *watchmen*, calling, 'Where are you?'

Here the Magdalene, *of the watchtower*, as a representative of mankind comes seeking God and crying, 'Where?'

7.7 Seraphim

So He made a whip out of cords and drove all from the temple courts, both sheep and cattle.

John 2:15^{BSB}

Ezekiel raised a lament over the rulers of Tyre that revealed the satanic power behind their trafficking was inspired by an unholy cherub who had been cast out of Eden. Isaiah raised up a similar song against the king of Babylon, revealing that the profane power backing him was the one who had boasted:

'I'll ascend to heaven, above the stars of God.
I'll erect my throne; I'll sit on the Mount of Assembly
in the far reaches of the north;
I'll ascend above the tops of the clouds;
I'll make myself like the Most High.'

Isaiah 14:13–14^{ISV}

After declaring the unpleasant end of the king inspired by this arrogant spirit, Isaiah immediately turns his attention to the Philistines, who have clearly breathed a sigh of relief when Ahaz—the king who received the prophecy of Immanuel—died.

Don't rejoice, all of you Philistines, that the rod that struck you is broken, because from the snake's root a viper will spring up, and its offspring will be a darting, poisonous serpent.

Isaiah 14:29^{ISV}

Isaiah is saying that the rod Ahaz wielded might now be broken but a viper will spring from the stump. Hardly a comforting image! One of the descendants of Ahaz, a king in the lineage of Jesus, is going to be like a serpent. In fact, the original Hebrew uses two different words to describe this serpent—one is 'saraph', equivalent to the 'seraphim', the fiery, six-winged, flying courtiers of God whom Isaiah observed in his vision of the heavenly Temple crying, 'Holy, holy, holy!' The other is 'nachash', *the bright and burning one* who is skilled in enchantment,[225] and that describes the tempter in the Garden of Eden.

It may seem surprising that some of the oldest commentaries and the Jewish Targums interpreted this verse from Isaiah as a prophecy of the Messiah.[226] In fact, it can seem almost shocking to compare Jesus to a viper, a serpent with a bite of fire and a stinging tail. It takes us aback to even consider that Isaiah could possibly be comparing the Messiah to the sea monster Leviathan— yet 'nachash' is also used, once again by Isaiah, thirteen chapters later, to describe the ferocious, twisting coiler of the deep.[227] It's hard to imagine Jesus being like a seraph, one of the angelic officials in charge of preserving the honour, holiness and glory of the heavenly Temple.

Or is it?

A sting and a lash, a piercing bite that is a reminder to preserve the holiness of the Temple: surely this points to the flick of the

---

225 The word 'nachash' has several meanings, one of which is *enchanter*. It should also be noted regarding the issue of the purity of silver in the Temple shekels that the Hebrew word for *silver* is related to *sorcery*.

226 *The Targum of Isaiah*, edited with a Translation by J. F. Stenning, Oxford at the Clarendon Press, 1949

227 *In that day, the Lord will punish with His sword—His fierce, great and powerful sword—Leviathan the gliding serpent* ['nachash'], *Leviathan the coiling serpent* ['nachash']; *He will slay the monster of the sea.* (Isaiah 27:1[NIV])

whip as Jesus drove the money-changers and merchandisers out of the earthly Temple. Just as Leviathan is a chaos-bringer but also a counterpart of the Levites—whose name he partly shares and who are likewise responsible for preserving the sanctity of the Temple courts—so Jesus brought chaos in order that holiness might be restored to its proper sphere.

If you're still not convinced, bear in mind that Jesus actually compared Himself with a 'nachash'. John links the Temple cleansing to the very next pericope in his gospel through the association of Jesus with a combination of 'nachash' and 'saraph'. When Nicodemus comes to Jesus by night, He tells him:

> *And as Moses lifted up the bronze snake on a pole in the wilderness, so the Son of Man must be lifted up, so that everyone who believes in Him will have eternal life.*
>
> John 3:14–15[NLT]

During the years the Israelites wandered in the desert, they grumbled at one stage and, as a result, they were attacked by fiery serpents, 'nachash'.[228] God then ordered Moses to construct a bronze snake in the image of a 'saraph',[229] and to put it on a pole so that everyone who looked up at it might recover from the poisonous bites and live.[230]

That prophetic action undertaken by Moses looked forward to Jesus on the cross—telling us that those who lift up their eyes, hearts and minds to Him in believing faith will receive the blessing and gift of eternal life.

---

[228] Numbers 21:7

[229] Numbers 21:8

[230] The bronze snake was kept for many centuries and placed in the Jerusalem Temple. It was given the name Nehushtan, from 'nachash', *serpent*, or 'nechosheth', *copper, bronze*, and 'tan', *monster*. Eventually it became an idol. During the time of King Hezekiah, it was destroyed. (2 Kings 18:4)

7.8 Leviathan and Anat

AT THE END OF THE BOOK OF JOB, God devotes the entire finale of His rabbinic-like questioning of His favourite student[231] to Leviathan. If Job happens to be designed in the same chiastic way as John's gospel, we might conclude that the satan who presents himself in the courts of heaven at the beginning of the book is, in fact, Leviathan.

Our tendency, on having transformed 'the satan', a generalised term for *accuser*, into Satan, a personal name, is to decide there

---

231 Most commentators consider that, when God appears, He gives Job a putdown shoving him firmly back into place. My view is different. To me, that kind of interpretation ignores the fact that God's questions reflect many of Job's own comments and those of his friends. The Almighty is saying: 'I heard you, Job. I was listening all the time. I was paying attention. And now, in commendation, I have some tough questions for you to consider. These are the difficult questions I reserve for my favourites.' Rabbinical teaching involves question and answer—not questions that involve an automatic rote response, but questions that encode information designed to make the student think before replying. These are just the sort of questions God puts to Job. For example, Job says, '*He is the Maker of the Bear and Orion, the Pleiades and the constellations of the south*,' (Job 9:9[NIV]) and when God eventually replies, He offers Job insight with His question: '*Can you bind the chains of the Pleiades? Can you loosen Orion's belt?*' (Job 38:31[NIV]) Long before astronomers knew the stars of the Pleiades exerted a gravitational influence on one another, God alluded to it.

is only one enemy of our souls. But that is to ignore the many different adversarial spirits identified in Scripture. So we need to be extremely cautious about simply sliding our thinking across to deduce that 'Satan' is merely another name for Leviathan. The evidence is far more complex than that.

In fact, if we assemble all the different clues about Leviathan dropped on different occasions throughout the Bible, it's difficult to assess his standing in the heavenly realm. God at times shows evident delight in Leviathan's wild strength, displaying almost exuberant joy in His creature's fierce prowess. Yet at other times God declares He will pierce this twisting chaos-dragon. Leviathan is described as a 'nachash' and, because of the repeated parallelism between a 'nachash' and a 'seraph', it's likely Leviathan originally belonged to the angelic class who are the protectors of honour in the royal chambers of the heavenly Temple. Because the gifts and offices of God are irrevocable, Leviathan is still able to function as a protector of honour.

When we enter the courts of God, grumbling and complaining, the seraphim have the right, as they always did, to retaliate against the dishonour we are invoking on the name of God.

God told Job that no one bests Leviathan in a conflict. No one. Yet believers today consider they have the authority to trample Leviathan without coming to harm. This is a misunderstanding of authority—it is a delegated right to uphold the will and the word of God, not to decide the parameters of the law for ourselves. To properly exercise authority, we have to keep within the bounds of God's commands, otherwise we are disobeying and dishonouring Him. Such dishonour opens us to retaliation by those spirits appointed by God to protect His honour—including Leviathan.

Now when we've been on the receiving end of a reprisal attack by Leviathan we can be tempted to look for answers that involve an increase in our own power and authority. Instead of repenting of dishonour and throwing ourselves on the mercy of God, we look for a more powerful prayer, a more anointed minister, a greater level of expertise in approaching the courts of heaven, a new angle, a previously unexplored or unexploited spiritual legal right. In doing so, we may be lured into complicity with Anat.

One of Anat's titles is 'Anat Lotan', in reference to her defeat of the seven-headed monster, Lotan. In Ugaritic mythology, Lotan was the servant of Yamm, *the Sea*—likewise conquered by Anat as she assisted her brother Baal-Hadad overcome the various rivals to his throne. Lotan is the Canaanite name for Leviathan who, according to Genesis was created on the fifth day[232] and whose purpose, so the Psalms tell us, was to cavort in the deep.

> *Here is the sea, vast and wide, teeming with creatures beyond number, living things both great and small.*
> *There the ships pass, and Leviathan, which You formed to frolic there.*
>
> Psalm 104:25–26[BSB]

Romping in the sea is hardly the same as being its servant: here Canaanite lore diverges from the biblical understanding. In fact, Scripture indicates Leviathan is a servant of Yahweh, not of Yamm, *sea*. Furthermore Yahweh Himself demonstrated His mastery over the Sea when He rolled it back so that His people could escape Egypt. He also, according to Asaph, smashed Leviathan at the same time:

---

[232] Most translations say 'great sea *creatures*' were created on the fifth day. One of the few to correctly render 'tannin' as *dragon* or *sea monster* is: 'God created the great sea monsters and every living creature that moves, with which the waters swarmed after their kind, and every winged bird after its kind; and God saw that it was good.' (Genesis 1:21[NASB])

> *You divided the sea by Your strength; You broke the heads of the sea serpents in the waters. You broke the heads of Leviathan in pieces, and gave him as food to the people inhabiting the wilderness.*
>
> Psalm 74:13–14^{NKJV}

Such competing claims between Yahweh and Anat cannot possibly go unanswered. And recall: it's not just the Sea and Leviathan that Anat claims she has vanquished, it's Death too. Having alleged to have ruthlessly smashed, sliced, pummelled and pulverised Death and also to have been instrumental in restoring Baal-Hadad to life, she is by her own admission a challenger for the crown and throne of Yahweh.

There's an intriguing detail about Leviathan early in Job, when he recalls the day of his birth:

> *May it be cursed by those who curse the day—those prepared to rouse Leviathan.*
>
> Job 3:8^{BSB}

It may seem a strange and primitive thought to us that anyone who curses the day of another's birth is ready, willing and able to arouse Leviathan—but I've met several people for whom this is a devastating reality. Their lives turned significant corners when the dishonour spoken over the day of their birth was prayed through—suggesting that 'Day' is an entity in its own right and that our label of 'personification' for what are often deemed abstract concepts needs serious reassessment.

Now, more than one of the Hebrew words in this verse is related to *appoint* and to *time*. The word for *cursed*, 'naqab', is quite different from *curse*, 'arar'. In fact, besides *cursed* and *blaspheme*, 'naqab' can also mean *appoint, designate, pierce*. The word *prepared* or *ready* is 'athud', related to 'attah', *now*, and to 'itti', *timely* or *ready*—all of these derived from 'eth', *appointed time*. As we've seen previously, 'eth' is believed to come from 'anah' with its variant 'anath' or 'anat'.

The implication of Job's lament over the day of his birth seems to be far more than just a grieving comment about skilled enchanters cursing particular days to awaken Leviathan—in the light of God's long and final discourse about Leviathan, it seems almost as if Job has guessed the reason why he has been afflicted by multiple disasters.

There are some really curious overtones in his statement. Leviathan is normally associated with 'yam', *sea*. But here there is a transition to 'yom', *day*, and to words derived from 'eth' and 'anah', *appointed time*.

Call me suspicious if you will, but what I think Job is trying to say here is: as Anat overcame Yamm, *Sea*, so 'anah', *appointed time*, overcomes 'yom', *Day*. Moreover the struggle between *appointed time* and *day* is equivalent to the battle between Anat and the Sea with its servants.

Now you might think this is far too mythological to be credible. In my experience, the only reason many people do not realise how closely their lives conform to a mythic outline is not-so-blissful ignorance. We simply don't know the legendary background behind our own names and thus how our lives are shaping up in accordance with our names. In addition, our culture of scientific rationalism causes us to completely dismiss the possibility we could be living a myth. We decide the whole idea is irrational and it would therefore be a waste of time to even examine the evidence.[233] We actually have to be intentional about choosing to 'enact' the gospel; otherwise we will unconsciously default to enacting a myth—or alternatively a biblical narrative that involves a faith 'hero'. Belief in the gospel must issue out as action that penetrates ever deeper into the core of our being, it should not be confined to a thought system.[234]

If you doubt that this is a significant issue in anyone's life, please consider that Jesus took the so-called 'myths' of the Canaanites seriously—treating them, not as unreal, not as imaginary, not as illusions, but as if the stories were thefts of truth about Himself and His heavenly Father.

Humphrey Carpenter records a dialogue between CS Lewis and JRR Tolkien:

---

233   This is such a huge and misunderstood topic it can only be briefly addressed. Paul Holmer in *CS Lewis: The Shape of His Faith and Thought* says in relation to Lewis' use of myth and symbolism vis-à-vis Jung's archetypes: 'Whether we are all in the grip of unconscious archetypical thoughts and images might be an interesting conjecture. It might even explain how some themes become perennial in world literature and art. But for Lewis this is like an aside but cannot be made anything but a plausible guess. There is, however, another way to claim some of the ground and that is to learn to read the myths and stories.'

Holmer both nails, and also misses, a vital point. Archetypes are far from 'an aside' for Lewis. The image of the faun that recurred in Lewis' mind's eye has its roots in folklore involving his nickname 'Jack'; the Great Lion of Narnia originates in the Welsh name, Lewis, from 'Llew', *lion of the steady hand*, the Celtic lord of light. The most memorable symbols in both Narnia and the *Space Trilogy* revolve around the mythic attachments to the names Jack, Clive, Staples, Lewis and Hamilton (his mother's maiden name and a pseudonym he used for his early poetry).

The struggle to free ourselves from the bondage of name occurs when we live out a myth centred on the source of our names and so are not free to pursue the calling that God has breathed into them. The sovereignty of names and naming was lost by Adam to the satan in the Garden of Eden and is restored to us through name covenants bestowed by God, such as the Abram-Abraham name exchange or the Simon-Cephas one. See *Name Covenant: Invitation to Friendship, Strategies for the Threshold #3*, Armour Books 2018

'But,' said Lewis, 'myths are lies, even though lies breathed through silver.'

'No,' said Tolkien, 'they are not... just as speech is invention about objects and ideas, so myth is invention about truth. We have come from God... and inevitably the myths woven by us, though they contain error, will also reflect a splintered fragment of the true light, the eternal truth that is with God.'[235]

When we look at the names and titles Jesus asserted for Himself and His Father—titles like 'The True Vine' and 'The Light of the World', it's clear He was not simply claiming them but reclaiming them. When He went to places like Sychar and Jericho, He wasn't just healing people, He was healing great historical rifts through His actions. The same is true of the miracle at Cana—it involves an undoing of dispossession.

Jesus is our exemplar in such actions: and as He summoned the appointed time to Himself even as the Day was not appropriate, so we need to consider how we can take hold of appointed times and opportunities in our own lives without sacrificing others in the process. More than simply not sacrificing others—as Joseph did, and as Noah did—we should examine the opportunity and ask God if there is, within it, a possibility of healing history and of blessing others. We are, after all, called to love our enemies and do good to those who hate us.

---

[234] The issue here is that, while various pagan myths, traditions, royal titles and religious liturgies foreshadowed the life and death of Jesus, they also pointed away from Him to different principalities, powers and cosmic rulers—those fallen angelic majesties mentioned by both Peter and Jude. These spiritual entities had sufficient knowledge of God's redemptive plan to usurp the names, honours, and even the work of Jesus in order to deny, defile and undermine His work of salvation.

[235] Humphrey Carpenter, *J.R.R. Tolkien: A Biography*, Houghton Mifflin 1997

Jesus brought forward the appointed time, using it to transform the dispossession that Noah had spoken over Canaan and that Joseph had inflicted on the Egyptians. He called forth the new wine, the symbol of inheritance. So we too can apply the miracle of transformation to restore broken lives in His name and by the power of His atonement.

His disciples remembered that it is written:
'Zeal for Your house will consume Me.'

On account of this, the Jews demanded,
'What sign can You show us to prove Your authority to do these things?'

Jesus answered, 'Destroy this temple,
and in three days I will raise it up again.'

'This temple took forty-six years to build,' the Jews replied,
'and You are going to raise it up in three days?'

But Jesus was speaking about the temple of His body.
After He was raised from the dead,
His disciples remembered that He had said this.
Then they believed the Scripture
and the word that Jesus had spoken.

When she had said this, she turned around and saw Jesus standing there;
but she did not recognise that it was Jesus.

'Woman, why are you weeping?' Jesus asked. 'Whom are you seeking?'

Thinking He was the gardener, she said, 'Sir, if you have carried Him off,
tell me where you have put Him, and I will get Him.'

Jesus said to her, 'Mary.'

She turned and said to Him in Hebrew, 'Rabboni!' (which means Teacher).

'Do not cling to Me,' Jesus said,
'for I have not yet ascended to the Father.
But go and tell My brothers, "I am ascending
to My Father and your Father, to My God and your God."'

Mary Magdalene went and announced to the disciples,
'I have seen the Lord!'
And she told them what He had
said to her.

john 20:11-18 bsb

8.1 Zealous and Jealous

> *His disciples remembered that it is written: 'Zeal for Your house will consume Me.'*
>
> John 2:17[BSB]

> *'...go and tell My brothers, "I am ascending to My Father and your Father, to My God and your God."'*
>
> John 20:17[BSB]

JESUS' FAMILY WAS JEALOUS OF HIM. His brothers were resentful, envious, insecure. John doesn't say so outright but his quote from Psalm 68, when examined in context, is about family dysfunction and estrangement. Moreover, in the scene in the garden, Jesus doesn't tell Mary Magdalene to go to His *disciples*—who, after all, don't need the news since Peter and John have already seen the empty tomb—but to His *brothers*.[236]

Although John doesn't tell us directly that Jesus' family was jealous, I think the coupling of the two pericopes—the cleansing of the Temple and the wedding in Galilee—is meant to imply that they were. His quotation comes from one of David's psalms, where *zeal* is 'qinah' from 'qanah', an obvious wordplay on Cana:

---

236 This can also include *sisters* since Greek 'adelphos' means *from the same womb*.

> *I am a foreigner to my own family,*
> *a stranger to my own mother's children;*
> *for zeal for Your house consumes me,*
> *and the insults of those who insult You fall on me.*
>
> Psalm 68:8–9^{NIV}

There's another psalm of David evoked in the chiastic passage, '*…go and tell My brothers…*' Jesus quoted the first verse of Psalm 22 at His crucifixion, drawing our attention to the intensity of its prophetic vision surrounding His death:

> *My God, My God,*
> *why have You forsaken Me?*
>
> Psalm 22:1^{BSB}

Yet it also prophesies, more subtly, of His resurrection when it says:

> *I will proclaim Your name to My brothers.*
>
> Psalm 22:22^{BSB}

Hebrews 2:12 quotes this verse to indicate believers have entered the family of Jesus so He is not ashamed to call us '*brothers*'. [237] However, surely this applies first to His natural-born kin, then secondly to His born-again kin. Jesus fulfilled this prophecy of David when He gave Mary instructions to tell His brothers just after He said He was ascending to the Father:

> '*Do not touch Me, for I have not yet ascended to My Father.*'
>
> John 20:17^{NET}

This reflects the words of the high priest, dressed in purple on the Day of Atonement: 'Do not touch me, for I have not yet ascended.' This is why it would be so perfectly fitting for the young man who fled naked during Jesus's arrest to have been the 'rich young ruler'

---

[237] Again this is 'adelphos', possibly including *sisters*.

and to have been dressed in purple. As High Priest, Jesus needed a purple ephod.

Because with this proclamation, He swept aside the claims of Annas and Caiaphas, announcing His own elevation to the position. Yet He was not of the line of Aaron, nor even that of Levi. He came from Judah. He could produce evidence to show His right to succeed David as king but not Aaron as high priest. His priesthood could not therefore be Aaronic or even, allowing for exceptional circumstances, Levitical—as was the high priesthood of Samuel.[238] Indeed, as Hebrews 7 testifies, Jesus is a priest after the order of Melchizedek.

In taking up that office, Jesus fulfilled both prophecy and tradition. The prophecy occurs in yet another psalm of David:

> *The Lord has sworn and will not change His mind:*
> *'You are a priest forever, in the order of Melchizedek.'*
>
> Psalm 110:4[NIV]

A traditional and widespread popular belief of the first century was that God would send three messiahs, one of whom would be a priest of the order of Melchizedek.

Now it took a week for a priest to be confirmed in his role. During that time he was to refrain from any possible defilement or ritual impurity. At the beginning of the week, we see Jesus telling Mary not to touch Him but, at its end, He invites Thomas to put his hand into His side. So when He met Mary He was just beginning the process of ordination, He was about to ascend to the Father and present His own blood as the one all-sufficient and atoning

---

238 The opening verse of 1 Samuel gives the impression he comes from the tribe of Ephraim. There is no indication throughout the book he is not an Ephraimite. Only 1 Chronicles 6:33–38, with its list of the musicians who served in the temple, reveals Samuel as the twentieth generation from Levi.

offering that put an end to the need for any further sacrifice—so He needed to remain ceremonially clean.

Once confirmed as a priest by His Father, He could set about healing one of the greatest tragedies in the nation's history—when a jealous priest completely split the brotherhood of tribes in a catastrophic civil war involving unprecedented genocide. Yes, 'unprecedented' is a much-overused word these days, used to describe even a 1% mortality rate. However this conflict resulted in a massacre of 99% of the tribe of Benjamin and began a centuries-long feud between the people of Bethlehem, David's hometown, and the people of Gibeah, Saul's hometown. Long before either of these kings came onto the scene generational hatred existed between their clans.

Yes, it was brothers at each other's throats once again. And rampant jealousy once again.

8.2 Prophet, Priest and King

Through the long history of humanity, brothers have been at one another's throats since the time of Cain and Abel. The jealousy of Jacob for Esau, Judah for Joseph, or between David and his brothers springs to mind. Coupled with jealousy there's often an attitude of despising. Jesus addresses both thought-strongholds in His work of mending the world.

David was involved in one particular incident that required a special touch from Jesus. David was a prophet, as evidenced by his psalms. He was the second king of all Israel. There was also one occasion when he dressed in an ephod and acted as a priest, thus foreshadowing the role of Jesus as the Messiah in the line of Melchizedek.

> *Wearing a linen ephod, David was dancing before the Lord with all his might... As the ark of the Lord was entering the City of David, Michal daughter of Saul watched from a window. And when she saw King David leaping and dancing before the Lord, she despised him in her heart.*
>
> 2 Samuel 6:14–16^{NIV}

Now, because it's David—and because we tend to read with the hero and not with the text—we tend to be oblivious to the darkness in his character and to dismiss Michal's statement:

> '*You acted like a dirty old man, dancing around half-naked in front of your servants' slave-girls.*'
>
> 2 Samuel 6:20^{CEV}

Instead of carefully weighing the legitimacy of this assertion, we exonerate David because of his exuberance in rejoicing before the Lord. It's rarely noticed that he didn't deny Michal's accusation, but doubled down on defending his behaviour with the excuse 'but it was for the Lord!'

Michal was wrong to despise David but she wasn't wrong to point out his semi-nudity was an affront to both God and the people. David, in wearing the ephod, acted as a priest. Consequently there were definite rules to follow. Back in the days of Moses, God had given the priests instructions to use ramps, saying:

> *Do not go up to My altar on steps, or your private parts may be exposed.*
>
> Exodus 20:26^{NIV}

The principle is clear: scrupulous holiness and decency is to be maintained in the vicinity of the Ark of the Covenant. David's nakedness might have been accidental but he didn't apologise, nor repent of it. Instead he excused it and said that, not only would he do it again, he'd go to greater extremes. His last and subtly shameless dig at Michal implied the slave-girls liked their view of his body.

The narrator's final comment on this particular episode is:

> *Michal daughter of Saul had no children to the day of her death.*
>
> 2 Samuel 6:23^{NIV}

It's unclear whether she was barren by the Lord's decree because she dishonoured David, or whether he never forgave her for spoiling one of the most important days of his life and therefore never approached her again. It's a fair chance it was the latter, given the other ways he was active in terminating Saul's bloodline.

Michal is the only woman in Scripture described as passionately loving a man. In this she casts a long shadow forward to Mary Magdalene. The parallels become clearer in the story of Lazarus with its profound echoes of the ancient tragedy involving Michal, her sister Merab and their brother Jonathan. That, however, is for a later book.

On more than one occasion, David failed to keep covenant with Saul and Jonathan. We notice when Saul fails to keep covenant with David, but seem completely oblivious when David reciprocates. Moreover, the story of David acting as a priest is a curious one: after all, Saul's action as a priest in offering a sacrifice when Samuel was late was one reason God deprived Saul's posterity of the kingdom. Saul was motivated by fear of man, but David seems—at least at this point in his life—to not have had enough fear of God.

Yet Jesus is the healer of history. In doing so, history becomes His Story.

He came out of the tomb and was naked—as David was, as Adam was, as Noah was, as perhaps Joseph was—but in the garden He was fittingly covered. Like David, He is a prophet and king, about to be appointed priest—not of the line of Aaron, but of the order of Mechizedek, king of Salem, and like David, king of Jerusalem. But, unlike David, there was not only no shame in Him, but no shamelessness either.

Was Jesus actually wearing an ephod when He met Mary in the garden before He ascended to have His priesthood confirmed that same day? It would certainly have been a mending of the

Davidic kingship, a repair of David's insult to God and of his unforgiveness of his wife.

But how would an ephod even be available?

Let me speculate: if the young man who lost his linen garment was, as tradition states, John Mark, author of Mark's gospel and also the 'rich young ruler' who asked Jesus how to inherit eternal life, then he may have been a member of the high priest's family. That's what *ruler* implies.

So, to round off my conjecture: is there a John or Jonathan in the family of Annas? Indeed, there are two: the older Jonathan was Annas' son and was the high priest immediately after his brother-in-law Caiaphas from 36–37 AD. The younger John was the older Jonathan's nephew and also the grandson of Annas. His father followed his brother Jonathan as high priest from 37–41 AD. History attests that he was Theophilus—the same name and the same honorific, 'Most Excellent', as the addressee of Luke's gospel.

I like to think, despite the fact any evidence is purely circumstantial, that John, the son of Theophilus, was the rich young ruler and also the young man who lost a purple garment—perhaps for some mysterious reason an ephod—in the garden the night Jesus was arrested.

And it was just there, waiting, when the angel rolled back the stone and Jesus emerged from the tomb.

8.3 THE ROAD TO EMMAUS

IN THE THIRD CENTURY BEFORE CHRIST, Hebrew was no longer widely spoken. The Babylonian conquest, and later the victories of Alexander the Great, ensured the dominance of Aramaic and Greek. So a translation of the Hebrew Scriptures into Greek was commissioned. The writers of the gospels and epistles commonly quote from this version, the Septuagint.

In the second century, a minor change of wording was introduced into the Septuagint by Christian scribes. A particular passage in Judges 19 describing a journey past Jerusalem was altered so it precisely matched Luke's depiction of the walk to Emmaus.[239] Carsten Thiede says that, from the earliest times to the present day, scholars have seen the connection between these two stories.

In the Book of Judges, a horrific episode is described involving a Levite, his concubine and his servant who left Bethlehem late one afternoon. They bypassed the fortress of Jebus—later Jerusalem— seeking shelter for the night in the town of Gibeah in the territory of Benjamin. There the citizens demanded that the host who had taken the travellers in for the night send out the Levite so they could have sex with him. Instead, in complete violation of the laws of hospitality and threshold covenant, the concubine was

---

239 Carsten Peter Thiede, *The Emmaus Mystery: Discovering Evidence for the Risen Christ*, Continuum 2005

pushed out into their hands. She was gang-raped, and died at morning light.

The Levite then made a call for war by cutting up her body and sending out a piece to each tribe. They were appalled, but their reactions were mixed. Eleven tribes were eventually pitted against just one, since the people of Benjamin decided to defend the citizens of Gibeah. In the ensuing war, only six hundred men of Benjamin survived. The subsequent decisions made to help them rebuild their tribe were just as harrowing as this lead-up to its destruction.

The parallels between the beginning of this story in Judges and the account of the journey to Emmaus were sufficient for the early church to consider the events were connected. The ending, naturally, is different—it wouldn't be a healing of history otherwise. It's a beautiful coda to an obscene tragedy.

The early church identified the unnamed disciple walking with Cleopas on the Emmaus road as his wife, Mary. She was one of the three Marys who stood at the foot of the cross and witnessed the crucifixion. She was also regarded as Jesus' aunt by marriage, Cleopas being the brother of Joseph the carpenter.

These are significant details because, if they are correct, then Cleopas traced his lineage back to Bethlehem. That's the first parallel. The second is that a man and his wife were travelling together with another person. The third is that the distance past Jerusalem—about eleven kilometres—is the same in both instances. The fourth is the time of day—late afternoon heading into evening. The fifth is that we have details of conversation in both cases, and each time they are between the two men. The sixth is that they seek out lodging as evening falls. The seventh is the broken body—a literal one in the Book of Judges and a symbolic one at Emmaus when Jesus takes the bread and breaks it as He did at the Last Supper, thus causing His disciples—who, if early church tradition is correct, are relatives—to recognise Him.

A simple act of hospitality overturns the trauma of the past, bringing restoration to over a millennium of destruction and grief.

Now, the writer of Judges wasn't altogether keen on revealing the identity of the Levite who started the war. After all, it led to the virtual extermination of an entire tribe, centuries of feuding,[240] and depravity that flowed from one generation to the next. However, he tucked the name in, attempting to moderate the impact of the revelation with some unusual scribal features. Unfortunately those features tend to draw more attention to the Levite's background, not less. By placing some superscripts over the name Moses, the scribe created the word for *forget*.[241] The Levite was the grandson of Moses and he forgot to carry on his grandfather's legacy. His name was Jonathan and he was the ancestor of the apostate priesthood who set up the golden calf in the territory of Dan.

By omitting a lot of context I may have given the impression that Jonathan was an innocent victim. However it's a complex story, nuanced with many far-from-virtuous characters. Jonathan was originally a Levite from Bethlehem who accepted a position as a household priest in the hill country of Ephraim. His annual salary was ten shekels and a shirt. The house he was attached to had some silver idols as well as an ephod. It was no doubt copied from the ephod worn by the high priest Phinehas, the original war messiah, who lived nearby. The idols had been made from 200 of 1100 silver shekels stolen from the mother of Jonathan's employer, Micah. The curse she flung at the thief was so foul that Micah admitted to the crime and gave them back.

---

240 Including the clans of Saul and David.
241 Judges 18:30

All of Micah's ambitions were shattered when his silver idols, graven images, household gods and ephod were stolen by Jonathan who decided to take a higher, more lucrative position promised by the men of Dan.

Moses and Aaron toiled for forty years to weld twelve tribes into a single unity. The dark seed that birthed all the ruin of their hopes was, I believe, Jonathan's jealousy of his zealous cousin Phinehas. The descendants of Moses had fallen into such obscurity there's no record of what happened to his son Gershom while, on the other hand, the descendants of Aaron had steadily risen in prominence because of their service in the Tabernacle.

By the time Jonathan destroyed the league with one devastating stroke, Phinehas had succeeded his father as high priest. But, in fact, Phinehas was already famous for his zeal for God's name and honour—the very thing that consumes Jesus in a later age. In his zeal, Phinehas, the first war messiah, foreshadowed the zeal of Jesus, the last war messiah.

8.4 THE WAR MESSIAH

WE TEND TO THINK JOSHUA WAS in charge of Israel's armies during the time of Moses. However, that was not always the case:

> *Moses sent them to the war, one thousand from every tribe, with Phinehas son of Eleazar the priest, who was in charge of the holy articles and the signal trumpets.*
>
> Numbers 31:6[NET]

The Targums describe Phinehas, the grandson of Aaron, as the priest 'anointed for war'—or the war messiah who led the armies in battle. It's easy to get the wrong impression about Phinehas, his zeal for God and the reasons he would have been appointed as a war leader.

The Israelites were nearing the end of their forty-year desert trek when they camped near the ancient site of Sodom. A plague broke out—the people had broken the covenant by engaging in ritual prostitution with the priestesses of Baal Peor and eating food sacrificed to the idols. God had therefore withdrawn His protection.

Then a prince of Simeon sauntered into camp with one of the priestesses:

> When Phinehas …saw this, he left the assembly, took a spear in his hand and followed the Israelite into the **tent**. He drove the spear into both of them… Then the plague against the Israelites was stopped; but those who died in the plague numbered 24,000.
>
> The Lord said to Moses, 'Phinehas… has turned My anger away from the Israelites. Since he was as zealous for My honour among them as I am, I did not put an end to them in My zeal. Therefore tell him I am making My covenant of peace with him. He and his descendants will have a covenant of a lasting priesthood, because he was zealous for the honour of his God and made atonement for the Israelites.'
>
> Numbers 25:7–13^{NIV}

It would be extremely easy to view this incident as licensing moral vigilantes. It appears God approves violence, especially when it is invoked in the cause of His honour and holiness. But see that word emphasised in bold? *Tent*. Now the usual word for *tent*, 'ohel', is extremely common in Scripture and is mentioned well over three hundred times. This is *not* the usual word. In fact, 'qubbah' is never elsewhere translated as *tent*. It only happens here—*just* here—*just* this once. Normally 'qubbah' is associated with *curse*.

I remain continually astonished that 'qubbah' is rendered *tent* and that translators follow tradition, failing to sense the monumental theological implications of *curse*. It's a stunning foreshadowing of the work of Jesus. Here's a man going into a curse and coming out the other side, not with its defilement clinging to him, but with God's favour—a covenant of peace and an everlasting priesthood.

Atonement is an exchange involving the act *of being one with another,* so Phinehas, in making the decision to enter the curse, was taking the sin of the Israelites on himself. He was risking his life to stop the plague and save others from death; he was making atonement by carrying sin—not just the sin of the prince and the priestess, as well as the Israelites who had worshipped Baal Peor, but his own sin in killing them. He knew the Law and no doubt expected to die.

He foreshadows Jesus who went into the curse to save us from the plague of sin and death. Just as Phinehas understood execution would be the likely consequence of his zealotry, so did Jesus. His cleansing of the Temple prompted the authorities to decide He was too dangerous to live.

And yet Phinehas' action is not just a foreshadowing but also an echo of the past. Atonement is, among other things, a covering. And his atonement evokes the covering by Shem and Japheth of their father Noah as he lay in the tent.

Normally we associate the atonement of Jesus with His death and that, while surely right, is perhaps too restricted an understanding. I suspect John is showing us through these chiastic matchings that the atoning work of Jesus is not limited to His death but is to be found in each and every moment of His life. His healings of history are more than repairs of past national wounds—they are also bridges into atonement.

8.5 The Third Day Reprised

> *On account of this, the Jews demanded, 'What sign can You show us to prove Your authority to do these things?'*
>
> *Jesus answered, 'Destroy this temple, and in three days I will raise it up again.'*
>
> *'This temple took forty-six years to build,' the Jews replied, 'and You are going to raise it up in three days?'*
>
> *But Jesus was speaking about the temple of His body. After He was raised from the dead, His disciples remembered that He had said this. Then they believed the Scripture and the word that Jesus had spoken.*
>
> John 2:18–21[BSB]

John links the adjacent episodes—the Cana wedding and the Temple cleansing—with 'the third day'. By the time he was writing, those words would have been weighted down with an inextricable association to the resurrection. And here, in these words of Jesus, He prophesies towards that very end.

Yet prior to that moment, before the time when Jesus indissolubly linked the 'third day' to a revelation of His glory at the resurrection, the phrase would have evoked the revelation of God's glory at Mount Sinai. Of course there were other associations: the three days Jonah spent in the belly of the fish,[242] the raising of Hezekiah

---

[242] Jonah 1:17

from his deathbed on the third day,[243] the prophecy of Hosea that God will revive His people on the second day, bind our wounds and raise us up on the third,[244] the journey of Abraham to Mount Moriah with the intention of sacrificing Isaac,[245] the fast of Esther before risking her life to approach the king[246] and the third day coinciding with Pharaoh's birthday. Many of these foreshadow the resurrection of Jesus.

However, the *pre-eminent* association involving the third day was God's descent to Mount Sinai in a revelation of majestic power.

> *'Be prepared for the third day,' [Moses] said to the people. 'Do not draw near to a woman.'*
>
> *On the third day, when morning came, there was thunder and lightning. A thick cloud was upon the mountain, and a very loud blast of the ram's horn went out, so that all the people in the camp trembled... Mount Sinai was completely enveloped in smoke, because the Lord had descended on it in fire.*
>
> Exodus 19:15–18[BSB]

The giving of the Law at Sinai was understood as a marriage covenant between the nation of Israel and God. John highlights this connection between the 'third day' and a marriage covenant along with a revelation of glory in his recounting of the wedding at Cana. He starts that pericope with 'on the third day', goes on to describe the events of the wedding and finishes up with:

> *He thus revealed His glory, and His disciples believed in Him.*
>
> John 2:11[BSB]

---

243   2 Kings 20:5
244   Hosea 6:2
245   Genesis 22:4
246   Esther 5:1

John then set in place a similar set of connection points in the chiasmus—this time between the marriage covenant at Sinai and the resurrection.

> *'Woman, why are you weeping?' Jesus asked. 'Whom are you seeking?'*
>
> *Thinking He was the gardener, she said, 'Sir, if you have carried Him off, tell me where you have put Him, and I will get Him.'*
>
> *Jesus said to her, 'Mary.'*
>
> *She turned and said to Him in Hebrew, 'Rabboni!' (which means Teacher).*
>
> *'Do not cling to Me,' Jesus said, 'for I have not yet ascended to the Father.'*
>
> John 20:15–17[BSB]

The weeping, the seeking, and the garden are forefronted here. But in the background are the mountain of spices, the friends who've come and gone, the guards who've disappeared, the sense of just missing the One searched for, the half-light of dawn, the emergence of the strong leader: all elements featured in the Songs of Songs. The dialogue between Jesus and Mary harks back to the nuptial conversation there.

Furthermore, the Magdalene represents believing humanity as the Bride of the Second Adam. She does this according to the three divisions of the world in contemporary Jewish mindset: first Jews, second Samaritans, and third Gentiles. Ethnically, she's Jewish; her name has Samaritan overtones; and the essence of 'Where is the Lord?' points to the Gentiles.

Magdalene means *of the watchtower*—precisely what *Samaritan* means. The name 'Samaria' originally came from a landowner, Shemer, *watcher* or *watchtower*.

As regards the Gentiles, the Magdalene's search outside a tomb at the end of winter, repeatedly asking about the Lord's whereabouts evokes the Canaanite ritual involving Baal's return from the underworld.

Jesus cast seven demons out of Mary Magdalene. John hints she was the woman caught in adultery who was dragged in front of Jesus for His judgment. Whether that's true or not, she's definitely not the most virtuous of humanity's possible representatives. Yet God chose her as His primary witness to the resurrection. He chose her to receive an angelic visitation, just like Mary, the mother of Jesus. He chose her as His messenger to Jesus' natural family. He chose her as the 'apostle to the apostles'. He chose her to represent the Bride, the Second Eve. He chose her to usher in the reversal of Eden. He chose her to testify, through her own personal redemption as to what it would be like if the Jezebels of this world were delivered. And perhaps the Athaliahs too.

Despite all this, Jesus told her not to touch Him, not to cling to Him, not to keep hold of Him. In part, this was because He was yet to be ratified as High Priest. But there's also another aspect to be borne in mind. It's rare for there to be only one motivation.[247] Remember that Moses had said as the people reached Mount Sinai:

> *'Be prepared for the third day... Do not draw near to a woman.'*
>
> Exodus 19:15[BSB]

When God descended on the third day to the mountaintop, He called Moses to ascend to Him for the reading of His betrothal contract, the Ten Commandments. Jesus, about to ascend to the Father, was keeping the rule of preparation for the 'third day': *do not draw near a woman.*

He did not, after all, come to do away with the Law, but to fulfil it.

---

247 Another, although fainter, echo here of 'Do not touch me' once again takes us back to Joseph's story—to the episode with Potiphar's wife.

8.6 Forty-six Years

> *'This temple took forty-six years to build,'* the Jews replied, *'and You are going to raise it up in three days?'*
>
> John 2:20[BSB]

IT TOOK, ACCORDING TO THE CRITICS of Jesus, 46 years to build the Temple. Actually it took closer to 500 years but let's not quibble. The second Temple, rebuilt after the return of the exiles from Babylon, was an anaemic shadow of its former self until Herod the Great began an impressive expansion and lavish refurbishment. Since Jerusalem wasn't adequately supplied with pools or springs, his magnificent renovation involved aqueducts sluicing water all the way from Bethlehem to wash away the blood of sacrifice.

Herod's building spree entailed 46 years of works. They began in 20 BC and therefore ended in 26 or 27 AD. This, as we've seen, was very possibly the Year of Jubilee—perfect timing for an extravagant celebration[248]—and also very likely the inauguration of Jesus' ministry. If that's so, then another three-and-a-half years had gone by until Jesus was chastised for suggesting He can rebuild the Temple in three days.

What is the significance of the 46-year time interval? Is there any other in Scripture?

From the time the spies returned from their survey of the Promised Land to the time when the conquest of Canaan was effectively over, and the distribution of tribal land was finally underway, was 46 years.[249] This was the inheritance that God had pledged to Abraham. The people of Israel could have taken up possession decades previously however ten of the twelve spies sent in to reconnoitre the land had become so discouraged by the sight of the giants at Hebron that they had failed to trust God and had then convinced the entire assembly to do likewise.

Again, we find subtle links between the two pericopes in the second chapter. Assuming it is correct that the baptism of Jesus occurred on the first day of the month of Elul—the beginning of the traditional season of Teshuvah, *repentance, coming back,*

---

248 It may have been finished in time for the Year of Jubilee. With extra crowds in Jerusalem anticipating the proclamation of Jubilee, it would have been an ideal moment to celebrate the magnificent project's completion, particularly since the first Temple was said to have been officially consecrated during Sukkot. A politically astute leader like Caiaphas might well have used this opportunity as a distraction to bypass the potentially disruptive proclamation of Jubilee.

Two thoughts, if this were so: first, the satan had taken Jesus to the Temple's highest point on Yom Kippur. There Jesus should have been able to hear the announcement of the Jubilee. Perhaps He witnessed a clever distraction instead. Second, if the year of Jubilee was not announced when it should have been, then Jesus apparently gave the authorities every chance to rectify their mistake. He waited until almost the last possible moment before announcing it Himself. On the 51st Sabbath of the year, the reading portion *Nitzavim* in synagogues throughout the world is from Isaiah 61. The first nine verses are now excluded from Jewish reading portions because of their inextricable associations with the words of Jesus when He opened the scroll at the synagogue in his hometown, Nazareth. The excised words speak of setting captives free and the year of the Lord's favour. They are clearly about Jubilee—thus suggesting Jesus made a proclamation that Caiaphas had avoided.

249 The Israelites did not drive out the Canaanites completely, although they did clear out the central hill country with the exception of the Gibeonite stronghold. I conclude it was 46 years because Caleb, who seems to have made the first request for land, mentioned he wanted Hebron and that, even after 45 years, he was confident of taking it and eliminating the giants.

returning home—then the wedding at Cana would have been 46 days later. In both pericopes, there are faint echoes of inheritance, dispossession, re-possession.

When Jesus spoke of destroying the temple, referring to His body, He used an unusual word, normally referring to the annulling, dissolving or cancelling of a legal agreement. Elsewhere 'luó' is translated *loosen*, as in Jesus' famous charge to the church in Matthew 16:19 that whatever we loose on earth shall be loosed in heaven. It's as if He's saying, 'You can tear up My scroll of life, but You will not be able to dispossess Me for more than three days.'

The Promised Land can be considered a Body. The names of some towns correspond to various sense organs of the body: Jericho, *fragrant*, to the nose; Ai, to the eye; Shimron-Meron, *watcher-flapper*, again to the eye but also to waving arms; Hazor, *trumpet sound*, to the ear; Debir, *bread* or *word*, to taste or the mouth. The Israelites renew their covenant with God at Shechem, *shoulder*. All these references to parts of the body indicate that the conquest of the Promised Land is a symbol of the conquest of self.

Yet it's more than that, too. As the people left the wilderness for a new inheritance, a new 'body', so Jesus puts in a claim for His inheritance when He is confronted by those who disbelieve His statement about rebuilding the temple in three days. Just as that temple was His body, so too our bodies are now temples of the Holy Spirit. And we engage in the conquest of the territory of our body by subduing and eliminating the pockets of iniquity, idolatry and unbelief within ourselves.

John 2:23–25 BSB

While He was in Jerusalem at the Passover Feast, many people saw the signs He was doing and believed in His name. But Jesus did not entrust Himself to them, for He knew them all. He did not need any testimony about man, for He knew what was in a man.

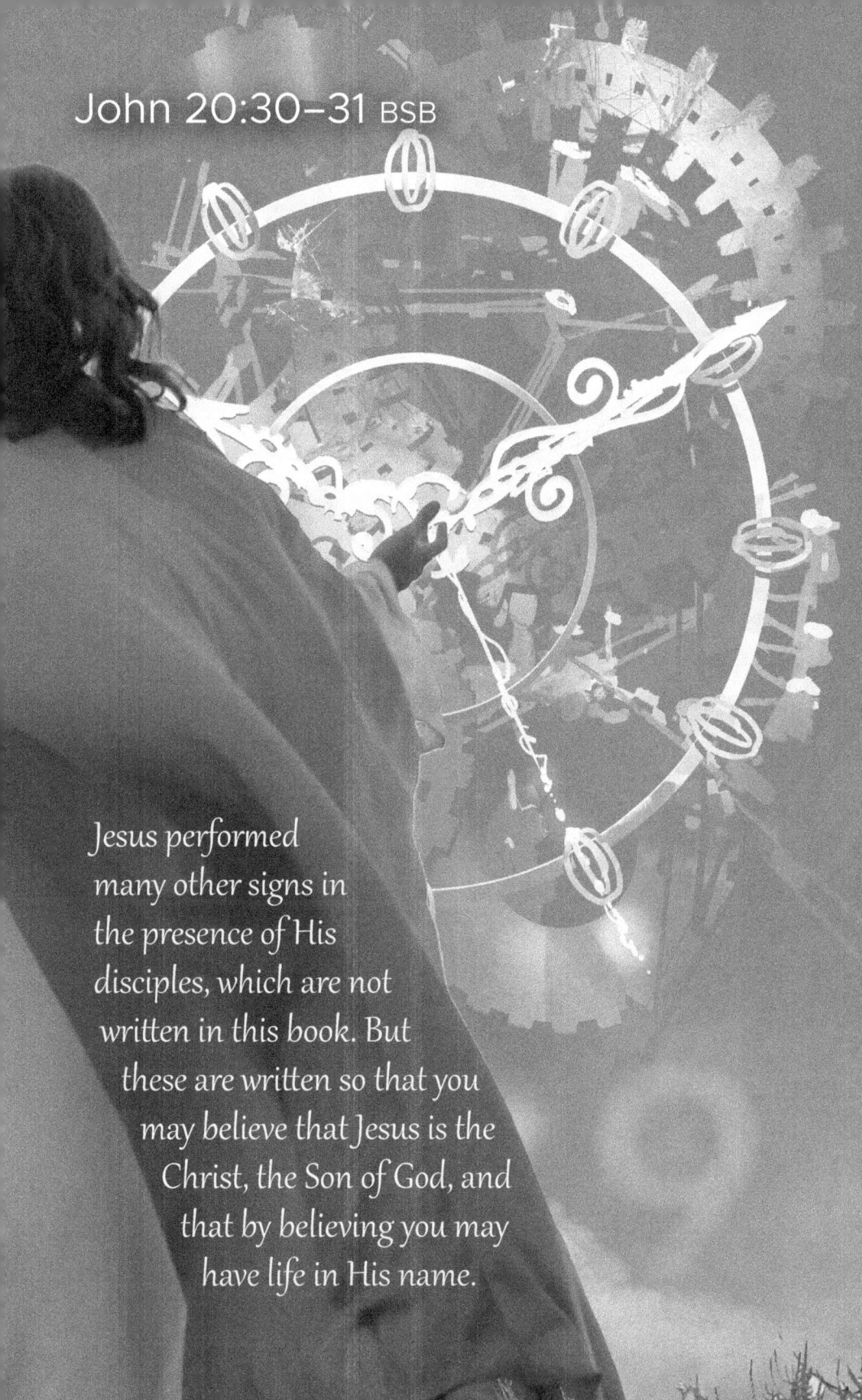

John 20:30–31 BSB

Jesus performed many other signs in the presence of His disciples, which are not written in this book. But these are written so that you may believe that Jesus is the Christ, the Son of God, and that by believing you may have life in His name.

9.1 Signs and Epiphany

> *These are written so that you may believe that Jesus is the Christ, the Son of God, and that by believing you may have life in His name.*
>
> John 20:31^{BSB}

THIS VERSE SEEMS LIKE SUCH A natural conclusion to the gospel many scholars believe John's account originally ended here. Hence the chapter describing the encounter of the disciples with Jesus during a lakeside breakfast was added later. If you've read *The Elijah Tapestry*, I hope you can safely dismiss that possibility. The first and last chapters are so tightly matched—far more so than the second and second-last chapters—they can only have been conceived at the same time.

John makes clear that his witness is to inspire others to believe. The word 'epiphany' has come to be associated in Christian thinking with the coming of the magi to worship the child Jesus, yet its true meaning is simply *to reveal, to make what is hidden visible*. John uses this idea when he says Jesus *'manifested His glory'*:

> *This, the first of His signs, Jesus did at Cana in Galilee, and manifested His glory. And His disciples believed in Him.*
>
> John 2:11^{ESV}

The second of these two chiastic sections about signs and belief occurs after the story about Thomas and his doubts. In *The Elijah Tapestry*, I showed how that matches Nathanael and his doubts and how, together, their stories form a commentary on the healing by Jesus of massive wounds in Israelite history: first, the devastation caused by the unbelief of the spies who scouted out the Promised Land and, second, the hurt and harm emanating from the rift between the twins, Jacob and Esau.

That jealousy over inheritance and birthright, that sense of missing out, that resentment of the younger for the older—not just in brothers or sisters, but across generations—flows from the first chapter to the second and forms yet another link with it.

The brothers of Jesus probably perceived they were contending with Him for any inheritance that Joseph left. In their thinking, Jesus was not Joseph's natural son, so He had no claim on the estate. They may also have experienced shame because of small-town gossip about their father and mother, shame exacerbated when Jesus started saying and doing things offensive to the authorities.

> *Many people saw the signs He was doing and believed in His name. But Jesus did not entrust Himself to them, for He knew them all. He did not need any testimony about man, for He knew what was in a man.*
>
> John 2:23–25[BSB]

Jesus knows how fickle our belief is. It's easy to imagine that, if we'd been at the foot of the Cross, we'd have been amongst those weeping, but we might equally be amongst those jeering. We can't know until the test finally arrives what we'll choose.

Jesus reassured His brothers and sisters He was not going to take from them, but give to them. His message to them in that first public miracle, with all its symbolism of restored inheritance, was simply: *jealousy is unnecessary. I'm not here to disinherit you, I'm here to return the inheritance of all who have lost it. I'm here to restore what was lost by Adam, by Canaan, by Esau. I'm here to grant a new birthright to those dispossessed by Noah, by Jacob, by Joseph, by Ahab. I'm here to prove these claims by supernatural signs.*

In John's last chapter, he narrates the passing of Elijah's mantle to Simon Peter: the mantle that carried with it the unfinished task of preaching to the Gentiles about Yahweh and welcoming them into the Kingdom of God.

In the second-last chapter, we see the passing of Joseph's mantle: the mantle that carried with it the unfinished task of restoring a family despite resentment, trafficking and abandonment, and reinstating their inheritance among the nations. That mantle was passed to Mary Magdalene as she was instructed to go and tell His brothers and sisters that He was ascending to His Father and their Father, to His God and their God.[250]

She's the one who represents the new Eve, so it's fitting she receive a royal 'ketonet', a spiritual covering of exquisite elegance. She was given a message for all nations: *Jesus is alive!* And she's the appropriate messenger-angel-apostle because she represents the Samaritans and thus the land where Joseph is buried; she also represents the Gentiles when she enacts and reclaims the liturgy that named Jezebel, originally from Phoenicia. She's also, in her encounter in the garden, a participant and a witness to the redemption of the bloodline of Jezebel and Ahab—rulers who, like Joseph, dispossessed others.

---

250 John 20:18 says she told His *disciples*. However, if the early church was correct in identifying the disciples at Emmaus as Jesus' uncle and aunt, then Luke 24:22–24 tells us the women informed disciples who included His near-relatives.

The Magdalene's words become part of the healing of history. She's the one who represents the Friends and the Bridemaids from the *Song of Songs*; moreover, she also represents the Bride. She's the one who, in diligently searching and seeking and asking for Jesus even after others had given up and returned home, brings about the shakedown of Anat that Joseph of Egypt should have pursued.

Joseph's many-coloured, grace-woven dreamcoat she inherited was like the Elijah mantle given to Peter—it did not, of course, have physical form but was passed on in the spirit. It's also a mantle like that of the kinsman-redeemer of ancient Israel which, wrapped around all believers, is a covering that brings outcasts into the fold, the dispossessed into their inheritance, the abandoned into an embrace of love.

9.2 Time and Takedown

The complex interweaving of the two pericopes in the second chapter of John's gospel combine with trailing threads from the first chapter and gracefully loop across to the second-last and last chapters. It's so dense and rich a pattern it's difficult to pick out the main thrust of John's messaging.

However, what stands out for me is threefold:

- the multi-faceted healing of historical breaches
- the relentless takedown of the principalities of the nations
- the inauguration of a new era.

Given the background of dispossession in so many cases, I suspect John's message here is: *if the past is locked by trauma, then so is the future. If we truly believe in Jesus, He can release the future so that our calling can come to us. He summoned the future when He turned water into wine, and that is what He is willing to do for us.*

CS Lewis expressed the longing well: 'Our hope finally to emerge if not altogether from time... at any rate from the tyranny, the unilinear poverty, of time, to ride it not to be ridden by it, and so to cure that always aching wound.'[251]

---

251   CS Lewis, *Reflections on the Psalms*, Harcourt Brace 1958

In His takedown of various divinities—in particular, Canaanite and Greek deities, and most especially those violent rulers who claim the lordship of time, Kronos, Kairos and Anat—Jesus restores what was meant to be. He has won for us a return of rightful inheritance; He has championed our cause; He has called us up to receive the birthright we were always meant to receive.

At the turn of the age when the world transitioned past the Flood, Noah planted a vineyard and made new wine. To herald the turn of the age when Jesus came, His first miracle was the transformation of water into new wine. As we've seen, the Hebrew word for *new wine* is related to *inheritance*.

It is no coincidence that the announcement of Jubilee should have been just over a week before the first sign of His glory, the epiphany of His messiahship, the revelation of His Sonship within the Godhead—and, for a waiting world, that Jubilee was meant to be precursor to the return of our lost inheritance.

9.3 Almost Final Thoughts

Why was John so subtle?

His clues about the passing of Elijah's mantle are quite straightforward, once the chiasmus is examined closely. His clues about the passing of Joseph's mantle are, at least to my mind, almost impenetrably obscure. Only the chiasmus, only the unnecessary mention of 'Joseph of Arimathea', clued me into realising John was deliberately, not coincidentally, referencing Joseph of Egypt when Jesus' mother quoted Pharaoh.

So what, I wondered, had Joseph done wrong? What had I missed? Because whenever Jesus heals history, He's mending some unaddressed past tragedy. What harm or hurt or wound had Joseph been responsible for, that remained unresolved after nearly two millennia?

I was astonished to discover how often I'd read right over Joseph's dispossession of the Egyptians. Like Elijah failing to fulfil the mandate of God to change the governments of Samaria and Aram by not anointing two army commanders, Joseph had failed in his exercise of governmental authority. He hadn't given the Egyptians any way to redeem their land once the famine was over.

Prophets like Elijah, rulers like Joseph, patriarchs like Abraham have such dazzling haloes it's easy to be blinded to their flaws.

In general, we're worse than blinded—we rationalise their faults, invert them into virtues, then defend those flaws theologically.

How many believers are so invested in a faith hero as a role model they can't bear to face the dark side of that hero's character?

So one reason for John's subtlety is gentleness. He knows we'll resist the exposure of the clay feet of Scripture's most revered superstars.

John wanted Mary Magdalene acknowledged for her rightful role. It seems likely, by the time he was writing, that she had—ironically—been dispossessed of her status, stripped of recognition as the primary witness to the resurrection as well as the representative of the Bride of Christ. Just as Jesus had despoiled Baal-Hadad by taking his story, so the stories featuring her were being excised from the gospels.

The end of Mark's gospel is highly disputed. Our earliest manuscript copies lack his last twelve verses. Some copies of John's gospel do not include the scene with the woman caught in adultery. Common to both missing passages is God's grace to less-than-virtuous women. Mark's gospel in its short form stops just before Mary Magdalene's name is mentioned.

Ivan Panin pointed out that these are the only two passages of any substantial length in the four gospels that are disputed. He has further noted, at least in the case of Mark's gospel that, while our earliest *copies* lack the last twelve verses, *even* earlier writings refer to them. He suggested that some copyist, like Uzzah who reached out his hand to steady the Ark of the Covenant, felt the need to 'right' the testimony of the apostles when it came to the place of women.

But what was the motivating factor? Was it because these women were immoral? Was it because they were women? How deep were the inroads into the church of Pythagorean-Gnosticism with its view of the feminine as 'evil'? Was this the reason for the removal of these two stories?

Why did Paul so pointedly strip the women out of his list of the witnesses of the Resurrection?

> *Christ died for our sins according to the Scriptures… He was buried… He was raised on the third day according to the Scriptures, and… He appeared to Cephas, and then to the Twelve. After that, He appeared to more than five hundred of the brothers and sisters at the same time, most of whom are still living, though some have fallen asleep. Then He appeared to James, then to all the apostles, and last of all he appeared to me also, as to one abnormally born.*
>
> 1 Corinthians 15:3–8^{NIV}

Paul gives the impression his list is comprehensive, when it has serious gaps.[252]

So did John attempt to ensure that Mary was honoured as Jesus wanted her to be? His approach was profoundly sensitive and subtle. He paired two women with sullied reputations—Mary, the mother of Jesus,[253] and Mary the Magdalene—and, by doing so, he indicated that God's favour was as much upon the latter as the former. Still, if this was the purpose behind his extremely judicious

---

252 This is not to imply that Paul is necessarily responsible for these omissions. This list may simply be what was reported to him.

253 By the time John was writing, Gnosticism was rising and with it came the thought that Jesus was the natural son of Mary and Joseph and that His divinity had not come upon Him until His baptism in the Jordan. He had therefore had been conceived during his parents' betrothal period before they were officially married. The mother of Jesus was thus seen as a fallen woman. Furthermore, the opponents of Christianity sometimes said that she had been raped by a Roman soldier. Consequently her reputation was far from immaculate in many quarters.

clues, then he didn't entirely succeed. His story of the woman caught in adultery was often consigned to the trash anyway. Still, the story of the woman who anointed Jesus managed to make it through. Although the incident is related in all four gospels, only John identifies the 'sinful woman' by name: Mary.

Is this simple misogyny—a clear-cut hatred of women that infiltrated the church with a combination of Hebrew disdain, Gnostic philosophy and Platonic-Pythagorean religious sentiment? Or is it deeper?

Elijah apparently thought God was wrong to choose wild Jehu and brutal Hazael as kings, so he never anointed them. Neither did Elisha, though he eventually commissioned Jonah to anoint Jehu. However, that was decades after God had told Elijah to do so. Just as Elijah thought God was wrong and so declined to fulfil the assignment he was given, so too some early believers apparently thought Jesus was wrong to choose Mary Magdalene as the primary witness of the resurrection, as the representative of His Bride, and as His messenger of restored inheritance and thus as His architect of government.

Just as Elijah said, 'Not *them!*', some Christians said, 'Not *her!*' So they removed some episodes, unnaming her, and hiding her identity.

Yet the passing of Joseph's mantle to a woman was hardly unprecedented. Joseph's granddaughter Sheerah had carried on his construction work by becoming the first Hebrew to build a city in what was to become the Promised Land. Her unusual design symbolised covenant—and throughout Israelite history God regularly intervened in battle with stupendous miracles at that place.

Nor was Sheerah the only woman to inherit Joseph's mantle. Its most memorable female carrier was Deborah. She accomplished what he apparently failed to do—fiercely and fearlessly oppose Anat and make it clear that Yahweh's claims are supreme over hers. It's no coincidence that the major battle in which Deborah was involved happened near Cana.

So this passing of the mantle to a woman was not some innovation by Jesus. Still John had to attempt a very fine balancing act in reintroducing the Magdalene while also trying to ensure her controversial role wasn't erased once again. I suspect the very things Jesus had battled against had returned in all their ugliness—dispossession, jealousy and arrogance; for, after all, it is arrogant to think we know better than the Lord.

John's gospel tries to tell us that no one is left out, no one is left behind, no one need covet another's calling. The many-coloured mantle is meant to be shared, to pass from hand to hand, to bring with it sufficient grace and favour for the entire world. We don't need to jostle one another aside for our rightful slice of the pie of inheritance. We don't need to fear there won't be enough to go around. Our God is the one who multiplied loaves and fishes, after all.

And multiplying the pie of inheritance is, I suspect, a whole lot simpler than turning water into wine.

9.4 Final Thoughts

The symbols of inheritance in the first chapter of John's gospel—the untied sandal, the man sitting under the fig tree, the angels ascending and descending that evoke the God of Bethel—intensify, in the second chapter, with the grace-gift of new wine. But now, there's a new inheritance God wants to gift to His children: resurrection. New life. Life not just in the spirit but life in a raised and perfected body.

In the first chapter, John claims to have seen God's glory revealed in Jesus. In the second chapter, he starts to unpack that epiphany, describing the first of the signs that caused the followers of Jesus to believe in Him.

Also in the second chapter, John introduces the theme that dominates the third and third-last chapters of his gospel—the divine Bridegroom and the wedding of the Lamb.

Truly, he's preparing us to understand the lustral waters of new birth.

Other Books by Anne Hamilton

STRATEGIES FOR THE THRESHOLD series

Dealing with Python: Spirit of Constriction (with Arpana Dev Sangamithra)
Dealing with Ziz: Spirit of Forgetting
Name Covenant: Invitation to Friendship
Hidden in the Cleft: True and False Refuge
Dealing with Leviathan: Spirit of Retaliation
Dealing with Resheph: Spirit of Trouble (with Irenie Senior)
Dealing with Azazel: Spirit of Rejection
Dealing with Belial: Spirit of Abuse and Armies (with Janice Speirs)
Dealing with Kronos: Spirit of Time and Abuse (with Janice Speirs)
Dealing with Lilith: Spirit of Dispossession

DEVOTIONAL THEOLOGY series

God's Poetry: The Identity & Destiny Encoded in Your Name
God's Panoply: The Armour of God & the Kiss of Heaven
God's Pageantry: The Threshold Guardians & the Covenant Defender
God's Pottery: The Sea of Names & the Pierced Inheritance
God's Priority: World-Mending & Generational Testing
More Precious than Pearls (with Natalie Tensen)
As Resplendent as Rubies (with Natalie Tensen)
As Exceptional as Sapphires (with Donna Ho)
Spiritual Legal Rights (with Janice Sergison)
Core Values: Love (with Rebekah Robinson)
Core Values: Joy (with Rebekah Robinson)
Core Values: Peace (with Rebekah Robinson)

JESUS AND THE HEALING OF HISTORY series

Like Wildflowers, Suddenly
Bent World, Bright Wings
Silk Shadows, Rings of Gold
Where His Feet Pass
The Singing Silence
In the Meshes of the Net
Interpreted by Love

Grace Drops with Anne podcast: https://gracedropswithanne.com

This series begins in Volume 1:

ISBN 978-1-925380-53-8

The Elijah Tapestry is an unusual treatment of John's gospel. It focuses on the poetic patterning characterising the first and last chapters.

The primary purpose of this study is devotional, yet it is not content to paddle in the shallows. Rather it seeks to take the reader down to pearl-divers' depth into a lustrous world that has rarely been explored. It aims to bring to the surface and into our awareness the numerical-literary style that typifies John's mode of thinking and writing so we can better decipher his message of truth and beauty, and understand its ongoing relevance for us today.

This series continues in Volume 3:

ISBN 978-1-925380-67-5

In the first two volumes of this series, *Mystery, Majesty and Mathematics in John's Gospel*, the passing of Elijah's mantle and Joseph's mantle was investigated. The third volume continues to explore the surprising chiastic parallels at the front and back of John's gospel and brings to light the passing of a third mantle—that of Moses—to yet another disciple. A deep theme of John's writing, that the followers of Jesus are called to complete the unfinished work of the those who have walked in the faith before us and to do so in unexpected ways, is brought to the fore.

From the Strategies for the Threshold series:

ISBN 978-1-925380-74-3

The Summoning of Time has, in many ways, only scratched the surface of the significance of the Canaanite goddess Anat in Israelite history, particularly in reference to Deborah and Mary the Magdalene. It has not addressed the relationship between Anat and the legendary vampire spirit Lilith nor examined their modus operandi and how to counter their attacks. For more information on this topic regarding their tactical ploys and how to heal from the wounds they inflict, see *Dealing with Lilith: Spirit of Dispossession: Strategies for the Threshold #10*.

www.ingramcontent.com/pod-product-compliance
Lightning Source LLC
Chambersburg PA
CBHW070504120526
44590CB00013B/747